Israel

There can be few countries that have inspired the amount of political coverage and controversy as Israel. For some, Israel has been an inspirational example of statebuilding, achieving in just half a century a level of political and ecomonic development well beyond the grasp of other newly independent states. For others, it is a far less admirable example of a colonial outpost, constructed at the expense of a dispossessed indigenous population and maintaining an aggressive posture within its regional environment. Either way, the spectrum of opinion is tinged with ideological and emotive considerations that have left little room for truly objective analysis.

This book, however, is an impartial analysis, introducing contemporary Israel through the main debates, whilst simultaneously providing the essential information needed to contextualise these discourses. The book focuses on the central issues of Israeli democracy and identity: both unique but ultimately flawed constructions.

Israel's early political culture took little account of ethnic diversity in its first efforts to build a state; for as long as Israel believed itself to be vulnerable to the hostility of its neighbours, the contradictions and dilemmas of identity could be subsumed within a greater need for national unity. But as it grew in economic and strategic strength, fundamental questions began to surface in the public political arena, in the form of protest groups and violence. Indeed, even the notion of a Jewish identity is subject to constant challenges: is it religious, ethnic or national; private, public, personal or political?

This book provides an invaluable analysis of the current and past state of Israel for anyone interested in the Middle East.

Clive Jones is Senior Lecturer at the Institute for Politics and International Studies, University of Leeds. He is the author of *Soviet Jewish Aliyah, 1989–1992*, and co-editor of *International Security in a Global Age*.
Emma C Murphy is Lecturer in Middle East Politics at the University of Durham. She is the author of *Economic and Political Change in Tunisia* and co-editor of *Economic and Political Liberalization in the Middle East* and *European Expertise on the Middle East and North Africa*.

The contemporary Middle East
Edited by Professor Anoushiravan Ehteshami
Institute for Middle Eastern and Islamic Studies, University of Durham

For well over a century now the Middle East and North Africa countries have formed a central plank of the international system. **The Contemporary Middle East Series** provides the first systematic attempt at studying the key actors of this dynamic, complex, and strategically important region. Using an innovative common format – which in each case study provides an easily digestible analysis of the origins of the state, its contemporary politics, economics and international relations – prominent Middle East experts have been brought together to write definitive studies of the MENA region's key countries.

Jordan
A Hashemite legacy
Beverley Milton-Edwards and Peter Hinchcliffe

Syria
Revolution from above
Raymond Hinnebusch

Israel
Challenges to identity, democracy and the state
Clive Jones and Emma C Murphy

Israel

Challenges to identity, democracy and the state

Clive Jones and Emma C Murphy

London and New York

First published 2002 by Routledge
11 New Fetter Lane, London EC4P 4EE

Simultaneously published in the USA and Canada
by Routledge
29 West 35th Street, New York, NY 10001

Routledge is an imprint of the Taylor & Francis Group

© 2002 Clive Jones and Emma C Murphy

Typeset in Times by Keyword Typesetting Services Ltd
Printed and bound in Great Britain by MPG Books Ltd, Bodmin

British Library Cataloguing in Publication Data
A catalogue record for this book is available from the British Library

Library of Congress Cataloging in Publication Data
A catalogue record for this book has been requested

ISBN 0-415-27087-1 (hbk)
ISBN 0-415-27088-X (pbk)

I have stated many times that Zionism is not a first name, but a surname, a family name, and this family is divided, feuding over the question of a 'master plan' for the enterprise: How shall we live here? Shall we aspire to rebuild the kingdom of David and Solomon? Shall we construct a Marxist paradise here? A Western society, a social-democratic welfare state? Or shall we create a model of the petite bourgeoisie diluted with a little *Yiddishkeit*? Within the Zionist family there are some members who would be happy to be rid of me, and there are some whose familiar relation to me causes me discomfort. But the pluralism is a fact. It is imperative that we come to terms with it, even with clenched teeth, and not get caught up in excommunications and ostracisms and banishments beyond the Pale.

Amos Oz, *In the Land of Israel*

Contents

Tables

Chronology

The modern history of Palestine and Israel

Palestine

1517		Ottoman conquest and rule begins.
1831		Egyptian conquest of Palestine.
1834		First Palestinian revolt against Egyptian occupation.
1840		Ottomans regain control of Palestine.
1882–1903		First *aliyah* of Jewish immigration into Palestine.
1884		Dreyfus trial in France.
1896		Theodor Herzl publishes his pamphlet, *Der Judenstaat*.
1897		First World Zionist Congress is held in Basle, Switzerland.
1904–1914		Second *aliyah* of Jewish immigration into Palestine.
1914	November	Ottoman Empire enters WWI on side of Germany.
1915	October	Sir Henry McMahon promises independence to the Arabs.
1916	May	The Sykes–Picot Agreement determines the post-war division of Arab lands between France and Great Britain.
1917	November	The Balfour Declaration promises British support for a Jewish national home in Palestine.
1917	December	The British army captures Jerusalem.
1919–1923		Third *aliyah* of Jewish immigration into Palestine.
1920	April	The San Remo Conference awards Britain the Mandate over Palestine.
1922		British Mandate formalised by League of Nations.
1924–1931		Fourth *aliyah* of Jewish immigration into Palestine.
1929		Zionist claims to the Wailing Wall lead to Muslim riots in which 133 Jews and 166 Arabs are killed.

1935		The Revisionist Zionist movement, led by Vladimir Zeev Jabotinsky, secedes from the World Zionist Organisation.
1936		The first *intifada*, or Palestinian uprising, begins. It is directed against British rule in Palestine and lasts for three years. Palestinian resistance is ultimately fiercely crushed and the leadership exiled.
1939		The British White Paper limits Jewish land transfers and immigration into Palestine.
1939	September	WWII begins.
1942	May	The Baltimore Conference establishes Jewish American support for the Zionist enterprise.
1945	May	War ends in Europe.
1947		Great Britain turns the Palestine issue over to the United Nations. The UN Special Committee on Palestine is established to examine the problem, ultimately recommending partition.
	November	The UN General Assembly approves partition.
1948	April	The Zionist forces takes the offensive to secure Jewish positions.
		A massacre at the Arab village of Deir Yasin by Irgun fighters encourages Arab refugees to leave Palestine.
1948	May	British Mandate is terminated.
		The independence of the State of Israel is proclaimed and a provisional government formed. Arab armies invade.

Israel

1949		The Transition Law (or Small Constitution) is passed.
		Elections to the First Knesset.
		David Ben-Gurion becomes the first prime minister.
		Chaim Weizmann is elected as the first president.
	January–July	Israel and the Arab states reach armistice agreements.
1950		The Law of Return is passed, confirming the right of every Jew to settle in Israel.
1951		Elections to the Second Knesset.
1952		Chaim Weizmann dies and Yitzhak Ben-Zvi is elected as president.

		The New Economic Policy (NEP) is introduced by the new government.
1953		David Ben-Gurion resigns as prime minister.
1954		Moshe Sharett becomes prime minister.
1955		Elections to the Third Knesset.
		David Ben-Gurion becomes prime minister.
1956	July	The Egyptian president, Gamal Abdul Nasser, nationalises the Suez Canal.
	October	Israel attacks Egyptian forces in Suez Canal zone, supported by British and French troops.
1957		Israel evacuates the Sinai Peninsula. The UN Emergency Force is established.
1958		The Knesset passes the Basic Law on the Knesset.
1959	November	Elections to the Fourth Knesset.
1960		Adolf Eichmann kidnapped from Argentina and tried in Israel. After being found guilty, he is executed in 1962.
		The Knesset passes the Basic Law on The Lands of Israel.
1961	August	Elections to the Fifth Knesset.
1963		Yizhak Ben-Zvi dies and Zalman Shazar is elected as president.
		David Ben-Gurion resigns as prime minister.
		Levi Eshkol becomes prime minister.
1964		The Knesset passes the Basic Law on the President.
1965	November	Elections to the Sixth Knesset.
1966		Military rule over the Arab population of Israel is lifted.
1967	June	Israel attacks Egypt, resulting in the Six-Day War, which Israel wins resoundingly. Israeli forces occupy the West Bank, Gaza Strip, East Jerusalem and Golan Heights.
1968		The Knesset passes the Basic Law on The Government.
1969		The War of Attrition begins along Israel's border with Egypt.
	February	Levi Eshkol dies.
	March	Golda Meir becomes prime minister.
	October	Elections to the Seventh Knesset.
1970		The War of Attrition is ended by cease-fire.
		The Black Panther movement of disillusioned Oriental Jews emerges.
1973	April	Ephraim Katzir is elected president.

	October	Egyptian and Syrian troops attack Israeli positions in Sinai and the Golan Heights. After 19 days of war, a cease-fire is agreed.
	November	The Agranat Commission is established to enquire into the failures of the 1973 war.
	December	Elections to the Eighth Knesset. David Ben-Gurion dies.
1974	April	Golda Meir resigns as prime minister. Yitzhak Rabin becomes prime minister.
1975		The Knesset passes the Basic Law on The State Economy.
1976		The government is wracked by financial and political scandals, some of which centre on the prime minister himself.
	March	Israeli Arabs declare an annual Land Day to demonstrate against discriminatory land practices.
	May	The Koenig Report, commissioned by the Ministry of the Interior, rejects the possibility of Arab integration into the state. The Knesset passes the Basic Law on The Army.
1977	April	Yitzhak Rabin resigns and Shimon Peres takes over as prime minister.
	May	Elections to the Ninth Knesset result in the first non-Labour-led coalition, an event that became known as 'the earthquake'. Menachem Begin becomes prime minister.
	November	Anwar al-Sadat, president of Egypt, visits Jerusalem and addresses the Knesset.
1978	March	Israel launches Operation Litani against the PLO in Lebanon.
	April	Yitzhak Navon is elected president.
1979	March	Israel signs a peace treaty with Egypt, the so-called Camp David Accord.
1980		The Knesset passes the Basic Law on Jerusalem: The Capital of Israel, extending Israeli sovereignty over East Jerusalem.
1981	June	Elections to the Tenth Knesset. Israel annexes the Golan Heights.
1982	April	Israel completes withdrawal from Sinai.
	June	Israel launches Operation Peace for Galilee to destroy the PLO in Lebanon.
	September	Massacres at Sabra and Chatilla refugee camps lead to the establishment of the Kahan Commission, which lays partial responsibility on

		Israel. Defence Minister, Ariel Sharon, is ultimately forced to resign.
1983	March	Chaim Herzog is elected as president.
	August	Menachem Begin resigns.
	September	Yitzhak Shamir becomes prime minister.
1983		A banking sector crisis throws the economy into chaos. Hyperinflation becomes the most pressing issue for the government.
1984		The Knesset passes the Basic Law on The Judiciary.
	July	Elections to the Eleventh Knesset. The controversial ultra-nationalist Rabbi Meir Kahane is elected to the Knesset.
	September	A government of National Unity is formed. Shimon Peres becomes prime minister.
	December	Ethiopian Jews are airlifted to Israel in Operation Moses.
1985		The Emergency Stabilisation Programme is introduced.
1986		Under the terms of the National Unity Government, Yitzhak Shamir becomes prime minister.
1987	December	A new Palestinian *intifada* begins in the West Bank, Gaza Strip and East Jerusalem.
1988		The Knesset passes the Basic Law on The State Comptroller.
	November	Elections to the Twelfth Knesset. Another Government of National Unity is formed. Yitzhak Shamir remains as prime minister.
1989–1992		*Aliyah* of Soviet Jews begins.
1990		The Government of National Unity falls apart, Yitzhak Shamir forms a new coalition of right-wing parties.
1991	January	Israel comes under attack from Iraqi Scud missiles.
	October	Israel attends the international peace conference in Madrid, sponsored by the USA and USSR.
1992		The Knesset passes the Basic Laws on Freedom of Occupation and Human Dignity and Freedom.
	March	A Knesset law is passed establishing the direct election of the prime minister in the Fourteenth Knesset elections. Menachem Begin dies.
	May	Multilateral negotiations with the Arab states and a Palestinian delegation begin.

	June	Elections to the Thirteenth Knesset, with Labour winning the largest number of votes for the first time since 1977.
		Yitzhak Rabin becomes prime minister.
	October	The USA grants $10 million in loan guarantees to Israel to help settle the new immigrants from the former Soviet Union.
1993	May	Ezer Weizman is elected president.
	September	Israel and the PLO sign a Declaration of Principles on Palestinian Self-Rule.
1994	April	Israel and the PLO sign an agreement on economic relations.
	May	Israel and the PLO sign accord in Cairo detailing arrangements for Palestinian self-rule.
	October	Israel and Jordan sign a full peace treaty.
1994–1995		A series of Islamist suicide bombs in Israeli population centres.
1995	September	Israel and the Palestinian National Authority sign an Interim Agreement on the West Bank and Gaza Strip.
	November	Yitzhak Rabin is assassinated by a Jewish religious nationalist.
		Shimon Peres becomes prime minister.
1996	April	Israel launches Operation Grapes of Wrath against *Hizb'allah* bases in south Lebanon.
	May	Elections to the Fourteenth Knesset, and the first direct prime-ministerial elections.
		Benyamin Netanyahu becomes prime minister.
1997	January	Israel and the Palestinian National Authority conclude agreement on the withdrawal of Israeli forces from Hebron.
	April	Police recommend that Netanyahu be charged with fraud and breach of trust.
1998	May	Israel celebrates its fiftieth anniversary.
	October	In response to failures to make progress in the peace talks, US President Clinton invites Netanyahu and Arafat to the Wye Plantation for intensive talks, resulting in a Memorandum aiming to conclude final status talks by May 1999.
1999	March	Shas party leader, Aryeh Der'i, a close friend of Netanyahu, is found guilty of bribery, fraud and breach of trust by the Jerusalem District Court.
	May	Elections to the Fifteenth Knesset.

		Ehud Barak becomes prime minister and appoints an Israeli Arab to a ministerial post for the first time.
	July	Ehud Barak announces his intention to withdraw all troops from Lebanon.
2000	June	Israel completes unilateral withdrawal from Lebanon.
		Moshe Katsav is elected president.
	September	Ehud Barak announces his Civil Revolution to roll back the power of religious groups over society. The plan ultimately falls apart as he turns to the same groups for support during the new Palestinian uprising that begins later in the month.
	September/ October	A visit by Ariel Sharon to al-Harem ash-Sheriff/ Temple Mount sparks riots in Israel by Arab communities. Jewish gangs attack Arab shops and communities, and police shootings leave 13 Arabs dead.
		A new Palestinian *intifada* begins in the Occupied Territories.
2001	February	Elections to the Sixteenth Knesset.
		Ariel Sharon becomes prime minister.

Preface

There can be few countries that have inspired the quantity of political coverage that is available regarding modern Israel. For some, Israel has been an inspirational example of state-building, achieving in just half century a level of political and economic development well beyond the grasp of other newly-independent states. For others, it is a far less admirable example of a colonial outpost, constructed at the expense of a dispossessed indigenous population and maintaining an aggressive posture within its regional environment. Either way, the spectrum of writing is tinged at every point with ideological and emotive considerations that have left little room for truly objective analysis. Therein lay the challenge that faced the authors of this volume as we determined how we could complete an original introductory text without resorting to a simple survey of events and institutions.

Rather than either repeating descriptive material found in abundance elsewhere, or advancing any particular critical position, we have tried here to introduce the reader to the main contemporary debates while simultaneously providing the essential information needed to contextualise the discourses. Inevitably, the result has been to focus on the central issues of Israeli democracy and identity. Both may be considered as unique but ultimately flawed constructions. Early efforts at state-building emphasised the notion of consensus while suppressing the tensions that arose from the multiplicity of identities to be found within the new state. The prevailing political culture took little account of ethnic diversity among Jewish citizens or of divisions between religious and secular aspirations. Equally, the desire to create democratic political structures was compromised by the need to accommodate a sizeable non-Jewish population within what was to be a distinctly Jewish state.

For as long as Israel believed itself to be vulnerable to the hostility of its neighbours, the contradictions and dilemmas of identity could be subsumed within a greater need for national unity in the face of adversity. As Israel gained strategic and economic strength, however, and as its polity matured beyond the rhetoric and idealism of the early years, fundamental questions began to surface in the public political arena. The rise of protest groups, the political power exercised by small, special-interest political parties, an

increase in the use of political violence – all are symptomatic of the fragmentation of the consensus on what it means to be a Jewish state. Indeed,
the notion of a Jewish identity itself is subject to constant challenges. Is it
religious, ethnic or national? Is it a private or a public identity, personal or
political?

The significant advances made towards regional peace in the 1990s and
the consolidation of Israel's position within the Middle East both served to
remove any remaining inhibitions to raising such potentially divisive questions, and provided a new impetus for their resolution. In practical terms,
the 'ingathering of the exiles', the *raison d'être* of the Jewish state, was all
but over. The last great wave of immigrants had arrived from the former
Soviet Union over the previous decade and the remaining diaspora communities are unlikely to relocate to Israel. The time appeared ripe, therefore, for
Israelis to determine a new destination in their collective political life. Israeli
intellectual debates on the origins and development of the state reflected this
apparent reality. Controversial scholarship that questioned and even
revoked conventional Zionist orthodoxy moved from the peripheries of
Israeli academia to the mainstream of public debate.

By the summer of 2000, however, the peace process had sunk into dismal
decline. In September 2000, a visit by Likud Knesset member Ariel Sharon
to al-Harem ash-Sharif, or Temple Mount, in Jerusalem, sparked a wave of
protests among Palestinians of the West Bank and Gaza. Sharon has long
been regarded as the main culprit in the massacres of Palestinian refugees in
the Sabra and Chatilla camps in Beirut in 1982, and his declarations while
visiting the site, that no part of Jerusalem would ever be relinquished from
Jewish hands, were considered to be particularly insensitive and provocative. The protests spread to the Palestinian communities of Israel itself, an
almost unprecedented phenomenon, with Israeli Arabs asserting their
national solidarity with their brethren across the borders. In the newspapers
and on the streets, Israeli Jews began castigating their fellow citizens for
what was viewed as treachery and sabotage of the state. During two days
over the festival of *Yom Kippur*, the Jewish Day of Atonement, mobs ran
through Arab towns in the Galilee region, throwing stones at Arab shops
and shouting anti-Arab slogans. The Israeli police responded to the Arab
demonstrations and strikes with bullets, leaving 13 Arab citizens of Israel
dead by the end of October.

In an effort to repair some of the inter-communal damage, the government made hasty efforts to consult with Arab members of the Knesset,
establishing a Judicial Commission of Enquiry into the chain of events
and promising to begin the immediate implementation of a five-year plan
designed to raise the Arab sector to a standard and quality of life not too
dissimilar to that enjoyed by Jewish citizens. It was publicly acknowledged
that institutional discrimination had obstructed assimilation and created a
legitimate sense of grievance. It was suggested that Sharon's visit had merely
exacerbated deeply-held beliefs that the more the religious Jewish identity of

the state was stressed, the more the non-Jewish population would become politically and economically marginalised.

Less sympathetic interpretations of the Arab riots came from the Israeli right-wing, for whom the violence was ample evidence that the Arab community has in recent years become politically Islamised and as such can never be assimilated into a democratic, essentially Zionist entity. Either way, as the newspaper *Ma'ariv* put it, Israel was left 'burning, bleeding and in pain, and it will not be the same state that it was, even after the last Jewish and Arab victims are laid to rest'. The traumatic impact of these events resounded not only in the Israeli national psyche, but on the very real political stage. As the new *intifada* raged on in the Occupied Territories, the Labour-led coalition government of Ehud Barak was close to collapse. Tensions grew within Israel as *Hamas* car bombs and *Hizb'allah* raids ensured that the conflict persisted on Israeli soil. As Barak's mandate to pursue peace all but dissolved, he threw down the gauntlet to the opposition by declaring his intention to resign and to call fresh elections. The elections in early February resulted in a landslide victory for Ariel Sharon, yet it would be a mistake to think that his victory came from widespread belief that he offered any new and radical solution to Israel's security dilemmas. Rather than reflecting any national consensus on Israeli norms or strategies, the elections indicated the strength of the divides within Israeli society. Nine out of ten Israeli Arabs had voted for Barak in the 1999 election. In 2001, they largely boycotted the elections, leading to a dramatic loss of Labour votes and demonstrating the scale of Arab loss of faith in both the rhetoric and substance of Israeli citizenship. The ultra-Orthodox, in contrast, turned out in larger than usual numbers to vote for Sharon, their rabbis having commanded them to do so in reaction to Barak's efforts the previous year to institute a 'civil revolution' that would reverse the encroachments of religious life upon the public sphere. Sharon had not so much won the election as Barak had lost it, evidence if it were needed that personality politics in Israel is a growing trend in so far as those individual politicians can appeal to numerous, and often contradictory, interests. The particular problem lies in the fact that those various interests are located across a range of apparently irreconcilable identities.

It remains to be seen whether the plethora of competing identities that have sprouted within the modern Israeli state can be reconciled within the existing political structures; it seems a doubtful prospect. It may well be that, in some distant future, normalisation of Israel's international relations will be matched by a normalisation of its internal dynamics. The *Jewish* state may ultimately have to be exchanged for a truly democratic Israel in which individuals derive no special status from their religious or ethnic affiliation. Alternatively, for those unwilling to abandon the covenantal and exclusivist mission of the Zionist dream, the modern state may have to choose its Jewish identity over democracy. Religious zealots will meanwhile be equally keen to hone the definition of that identity to one which rejects secular political constructions and returns the state to an ideal drawn from a largely imagined theocratic past. The future of any such political development may appear to be hostage to Israel's relations with its Palestinian neighbours, since the call to arms in the face of insecurity will always deflect Israeli attention from the trauma of getting its own house in order. In the long term, however, it is questionable whether the current political formation can be sustained as demography eats away at its viability. Both the Arab and ultra-Orthodox populations of Israel are growing relative to other communities. Thus the ethnic and religious–secular fault-lines that run through Israel, and the challenges that they present to democratic intentions and structures, may not be indefinitely contained.

This book, therefore, while examining the historical record of Israeli political, economic and international affairs, orients the reader towards the future. If the first half-century of Israel's existence has been one of passionate enterprise, ideological and military conflict, and political experimentation, the next is likely to be no less full of controversy, excitement and surprise.

As with most endeavours of this kind, the authors find themselves indebted to a number of people for their support and assistance. Clive Jones would like to thank Caroline Kennedy-Pipe, Ritchie Ovendale and James Piscatori for their academic advice over the years, and Guy Abrahams, Fiona Butler, Tamara Duffey, Malena Rembe and Neil Winn for just being there. Also thanks to Rolf and Birgitte Rembe for their hospitality in Stockholm, where much of this was written. Emma Murphy owes similar debts to her colleagues at the Centre for Middle Eastern and Islamic Studies and, most especially, to Anoush, who never ceases to encourage. Ardeshir was a distraction but gets full marks for inspiration. Needless to say, the authors are alone responsible for the contents of the book.

Glossary

Agaf Modi'in   Israeli Military Intelligence, and more commonly known by its Hebrew acronym of *Aman*.

Aliyah (pl. Aliyot)   Term translated literally as 'ascent' and used to describe any Jewish migration to Israel.

Arba Imahud   The Four Mothers Movement. Formed in 1997, this movement campaigned successfully for the withdrawal of Israeli troops from south Lebanon.

Eretz Yisrael   The Land of Israel. A term originally of spiritual significance, it has increasingly been used to describe Jewish sovereignty over the West Bank and Gaza Strip.

Gush Emunim   Bloc of the Faithful. Settler movement founded in the wake of Israel's slow disengagement from Egyptian forces in the Sinai peninsula in 1974. It aimed to forestall any government concessions in the West Bank and Gaza Strip by expanding existing settlements and establishing new ones.

Haganah   Defence. The main military arm of the pre-state *yishuv* and closely affiliated with Socialist Zionism.

Halacha   Religious law derived from the interpretation of sacred Judaic texts.

Ha Mossad LeModi'in U'Letafkidim Meyuhadim   Institute for Intelligence and Special Duties. The foreign intelligence agency of Israel, more commonly known as *Mossad* or 'The Institute'.

Haredi (pl. Haredim)   Generic term used to describe a member of the Ultra-Orthodox community.

Haskalah   A nineteenth-century movement of enlightenment that tried to combine some elements of Jewish tradition with modern secular thought.

Histadrut   The General Federation of Labour. Formed in 1920, it remains Israel's largest single labour union, although the political power it enjoyed has been significantly reduced.

Intifada (Arabic)   The Palestinian uprising in the Occupied Territories of the West Bank and Gaza which began in December 1987 and finally petered out following the signing of the Oslo Accords in 1993. The term has retrospectively been applied to the Palestinian uprising against the British in 1936–39 and to the resurgence of active resistance to occupation that began in September 2000.

Irgun Zvai Leumi National Military Organisation. A pre-state guerrilla organisation and the military wing of the Revisionist Zionist movement. Led by Menachem Begin, it employed terrorist methods to drive the British out of Palestine. It was forced to amalgamate in controversial circumstances with the *Haganah* (see above) in 1948 to form the Israel Defence Forces.

Kibbutz (pl. Kibbutzim) Collective agricultural settlements where, traditionally, no private wealth existed.

Knesset Assembly. The single-chamber legislature or parliament of Israel.

Lohame Herut Israel Fighters for the Freedom of Israel. Also known by its Hebrew acronynm *Lehi*. An extreme-Zionist terror organisation. It was banned and disbanded in 1948. Its one-time leader, Yitzhak Shamir, later went on to become Prime Minister of Israel.

Ma'abarot Transit camps used to accommodate new immigrants in the 1950s.

Mahapach Term used to refer to the electoral upheavals of 1977, when Ben Gurion's labourist élites were replaced for the first time by the right-wing Likud party as the main grouping in coalition government.

Mamlachtiyut A definition of statism indigenous to Israel. First espoused by David Ben-Gurion, it placed the demands of nation-building above individual or party interests. This concept dominated the political development of Israel from 1948 through to 1967.

Medinat Yisrael The State of Israel.

Meshiach Messiah.

Mizrachi (pl. Mizrachim) Term derived from the Hebrew for 'East' and used to describe those Jews who came to Israel from Iraq in particular, though it is used to describe the ethnic origin of Jews from all Arab states.

Moshav (pl. Moshavim) Collective farm settlement, but one which combines both co-operative and private farming.

Oleh (pl. Olim) Term used to describe a new immigrant to Israel.

Palmach (Plugot Machaz) Strike Companies. Permanently mobilised Jewish strike forces established by the *Haganah* in 1941.

Sabra Term used to refer to Israelis born in, and thus native to, Israel.

Sephardi (pl. Sephardim) Term used to describe those Jews who came to Israel from North Africa, and in particular Morocco. It is a term which, like *Mizrachim*, can be used to describe Jews whose ethnic origins are to be found in the states of the Middle East and North Africa.

Shabak General Security Service. Also known as *Shin Bet*. It is Israel's internal security service, responsible for counter-espionage and counter-terrorism.

Shabbat   Sabbath. Jewish holy day, the seventh day of the week, characterised by the absence of work and observance of social and prayer rituals.

Shalom Achshav   Peace Now. The main peace movement in Israel, formed in 1978.

Tseirim   Young Ones. Term applied to Ben-Gurion's political protégés, who were ardent supporters of his doctrine of *Mamlachtiyut* (see above).

Yesha   Council of Jewish Settlements in Judea and Samaria. An umbrella organisation that represents the interests of all settlers in the West Bank and Gaza Strip. It lobbies hard through right-wing political parties for continued Jewish settlement throughout the Occupied Territories. It has in the past been closely associated with *Gush Emunim* (see above).

Yeshiva (pl. Yeshivot)   Religious seminaries or colleges that cater for Talmudic study among pious Jews.

Yishuv   Settlement. It can be used to describe any individual Jewish settlement in either Israel or the Occupied Territories, but is also used as a generic term to describe the Jewish community in Palestine between 1917 and 1948.

Zva le'Haganah Israel   The Israel Defence Forces (IDF). Known by its Hebew acronym, *Tzahal.*

LEBANON

SYRIA

*Mediterranean
Sea*

GOLAN
HEIGHTS

Haifa

*Sea of
Galilee*

Irbid

Hamerkaz

WEST BANK

Tel Aviv

Amman

Jerusalem

Dead Sea

GAZA STRIP

JORDAN

I S R A E L

0   kilometres   50

1   The weight of history

Introduction

In 1998, the state of Israel celebrated its fiftieth anniversary. The first five decades of statehood had witnessed the wholesale transformation of the population, political system, economy, social structures and culture of the former British imperial outpost. But even as the official festivities proclaimed what has in many respects been a remarkable success story, academics, journalists and political analysts were reflecting more critically on Israeli achievements. At the start of the new millennium, Israel is a state torn in numerous directions, not only by religious, ethnic and national affiliations, but also by the varying interpretations of its own history which have been utilised in accounting for its failure to produce an ideal, homogenised, modern society. This chapter examines the various narratives that have explained the creation and consolidation of the state of Israel, drawing from them a number of contradictory portraits of the state itself. The emergence since the mid-1980s of a revisionist school of historiography that has challenged both the orthodox Zionist version of events, and to some extent also the conventional leftist critique, has opened the way for non-partisan critical analysis of many of the claims of either side. Tracing the historiographical debates provides illumination on the fundamental questions posed about the nature of the Israeli entity: is it a maturing pioneering social democracy or an outmoded offspring of European colonialism characterised by internal racial, ethnic and socio-economic discrimination? Should it been seen as the rightful home and sanctuary of the Jewish peoples, bringing together a nation with a collective identity and a common destiny; or is it better understood as a product of historical circumstance, based on an artificially constructed and subjective notion of identity, and lacking in true national cohesion?

The origins of the state of Israel

Tracing the origins of the state of Israel is a controversial task in itself as one quickly becomes embroiled in claims and counter-claims regarding the historical Jewish attachment to the biblical land of Israel and its relevance to the process of modern state creation. Accounts generally fall into two categories: those that view the contemporary Jewish state as the latest stage of a continuous Jewish presence in the area which has lasted since Abraham – the first of the patriarchs of Judaism – migrated to the Promised Land around the second millennium BC; and those that begin the story with the rise of ultimately competing Jewish and Arab nationalisms in the nineteenth century.

The first of these versions, which is common to texts sympathetic to the Zionist enterprise,[1] traces Jewish roots to the land back to the biblical narrative; the exodus of Moses from Egypt, the trek through the desert to the Promised Land, the Israelite conquests under Joshua and the Judges, and the kingdoms of Saul, David and Solomon. After Solomon's death the kingdom was divided and a Babylonian invasion saw the Jewish population largely exiled and its temple in Jerusalem destroyed. Subsequent occupations by Persians, Greeks, Syrians and Romans saw the Jews returning to the land and their temple rebuilt, although the institutions of the kingdom were never re-established. A failed revolt in 66 AD resulted in the re-conquest of Jerusalem, with the temple being destroyed for a second time, but matters were to get worse still for the Jews. Following another revolt, led by Simon Bar Kochba in 132–5 AD, Jerusalem was destroyed entirely and the great majority of the Jewish population was either killed, enslaved or exiled. The scattering of the Jews around first the Middle East and North Africa, and later to Europe and beyond, became known as the *diaspora*. A small Jewish population did survive throughout succeeding generations and still more conquests of the land by European Crusaders, Arabs, Turks and finally the British. Thus by the time Jewish refugees began to arrive, fleeing the pogroms in Russia in the late nineteenth century, there had been a continuous Jewish presence in Palestine for over three thousand years.

In beginning a history of modern Israel by returning to these ancient roots, the narrative becomes embedded in three implicit but questionable assumptions. Firstly, the narrative adopts justifications derived from religious assertions; that the Land of Israel was given to the Chosen People – the Jews – by God himself as part of his covenant with them.[2] Their moral claim to the land therefore precedes and supersedes any material claim by another people. Secondly, the establishment of the modern Jewish state becomes a part of a greater process of redemption of the land by the Jewish people, their reclaiming it from usurpers. Thirdly, the modern history becomes the most recent chapter of a greater story of Jewish suffering and struggle. Attempts to deprive them of their biblical rights to the land in the contemporary era are equated with their persecution and the denial of their rights during the last three millennia. The narrative becomes partisan, distinguishing between Jewish and subsequent conquests of the land, and between Jewish and other occupations on the basis of contested intangible moral and religious claims.[3] The non-Jewish population prior to the modern era is mentioned only in the context of their roots in alien conquering forces and their harsh treatment of the Jews. They are attributed with no rights and no affinity to the land. The stage is set, therefore, for a righteous re-conquest by Jews.

The linking of the modern state of Israel with its ancient counterpart has had very direct implications for the ideology and mythology of the contemporary state. Many of the symbols and institutions of the modern state have been drawn from the earlier epoch. The flag (a star of David between two blue lines) has been interpreted as representing both the Jewish claim to the land between the Nile or Mediterranean and the Euphrates rivers and the traditional pattern of a Jewish prayer shawl; the national assembly, the *Knesset*, takes its name from the *Knesset Hagedola* – the supreme legislative assembly of earlier times. The currency comprises *shekels* and *agorats*, as it did in biblical times, and *Shabbat*, the religious day of rest, has been adopted as the start of the national weekend. Thus the line of continuity between Jewish sovereignty past and present has been deliberately reinforced and given tangible form.

This approach has inevitably had its limitations. Today's state is essentially a secular phenomenon, ruled neither by priests nor by a Godly-inspired king. Its population includes a significant non-Jewish population and even the Jews themselves are not united by a common interpretation of their faith or their identity. Just as problematic is the fact that the modern nation state cannot operate within an international system on the basis of a divine mandate which peoples of other religions do not recognise. Finally, the account is not itself unquestioned. Prominent Arab scholars like Henry Cattan have argued that the biblical narratives have themselves been proven inaccurate, and that the Arab population of Palestine is descended from the *Canaanite* and *Philistine* peoples who occupied the biblical lands previous to, or simultaneously with, the Hebrew *Israelites*.[4] Others have gone further, arguing that the narrative has been deliberately distorted by the neglect of the ancient history of Palestine as anything other than the location for the Hebrew experience. Keith Whitelam, for example, has suggested that Palestinian history has been 'ignored and silenced by biblical studies because its object of interest has been an ancient Israel conceived and presented as the taproot of Western civilisation'.[5] The disciplines of history, archaeology and theology have been absent from studies of ancient Palestine, with the field being left to biblical scholars who have 'constructed' their understanding of ancient Israel via uncritical examination of the religious texts into an image not unlike the modern nation state which is fundamentally divorced from the reality.

The second starting point for historical accounts is the nineteenth century, when objective conditions coincided with the emergence of philosophical and ideological trends in favour of the global creation of nation states.

At the time, Palestine was under Ottoman rule (1516–1918). It did not exist as an autonomous geographical unit but was a part of the larger *vilayet* of Syria, being divided itself into a number of administrative *sanjaks*. The land and its predominantly Arab population were poor, having long been neglected by their Ottoman rulers and been subject to corrupt and disorderly local administration. Land reforms, imposed from Constantinople with the objective of raising revenues and conscripts for the army, effectively privatised previously collectively owned lands. In order to avoid taxes and the loss of their sons, villagers registered the land in the names of notable rural families. Thus they became sharecroppers, engaged in producing cash rather than subsistence crops and quickly falling into debt and abject poverty as they were forced to buy what they had previously grown for themselves.

Meanwhile, elsewhere life was proving equally hard for the Jews of the *diaspora*. The bulk of the world's Jewish population (around 75 per cent) lived in Eastern and Southern Europe, around 14 per cent lived in Western and Central Europe, and 3 per cent in the United States. Small communities also existed in the Arab countries of Yemen, Egypt, Morocco, Tunisia and Iraq and the remainder were scattered elsewhere around the world. The disparate communities suffered varying degrees of persecution, never fully integrating into host societies. It is now commonly accepted that conditions in Arab and Muslim lands were relatively good, since as 'people of the book' they held a higher status than non-believers or polytheists. Even so they were not considered to be legal or moral equals and were subjected to discriminatory taxes, legal and social codes. In Western Europe, the combination of western European enlightenment and a desire to mobilise the resources of minority populations had led to the emancipation of the Jews in many countries. While they had moved out of the ghettos, however, and in many cases had cast off their religious and cultural traditions in order to seek assimilation into European life, *de facto* – if not *de jure* – discrimination remained rife. Despite improvements in their economic, political and legal status, Jews were effectively barred from high society, were overly concentrated in certain professions (such as banking and teaching) and were considered to have collective degenerate characteristics that made their company undesirable (not least due to Christian considerations that they were collectively responsible for the death of Christ). The choice for both the individual and the community was illustrated in 1807 when Napoleon Bonaparte gave assurances that the *sanhedrin* (the Jewish Council that has issued and enforced laws in ancient times) could be reconstituted in France on condition that it promised a halt to rabbinical jurisdiction in Jewish civil and judicial matters. Only by turning their backs on public aspects of their religious and cultural identity, would Jews be able to fully enjoy the rights of citizenship. French Jews would thereby no longer belong to a Jewish nation held together by religious affiliation, but rather to the French nation-state. By implication, secularisation, rationalism and assimilation were positive human features while cultural pluralism, adherence to religious dogma and exclusivist ethnic identities were negative. Unfortunately for the Jews, even when they tried to cast off the latter in favour of the former, the host societies remained suspicious of Jewish motives and jealous of their own privileges. Consequently, threats to the economic or political welfare of the nation-state were immediately met with accusations of a Jewish fifth column and adherence to an alternative loyalty.

However difficult this was for Jews in Western Europe, they enjoyed a pleasant and bourgeois life in comparison to the Jews of Eastern Europe and Russia. The Tsarist Empire subjected its Jewish population to severe oppression and great poverty. Jewish populations had been forcibly confined to the western and southwestern peripheries of the empire – what became known as the *pale of settlement* – and were forbidden either to own land or live outside city or town confines. They were restricted to certain professions and their surpluses were ruthlessly taxed. Their sons were prime targets for conscription into the army and those who were left became victims of numerous merciless efforts at forced conversion, assimilation and cultural annihilation. They were forced to live a life distinct and separate from others, turning in upon their own culture and traditions to sustain themselves.

The end of the nineteenth century saw a combination of events which served to mobilise Jews in both Eastern and Western Europe, although the mode and purpose of those mobilisations was to differ dramatically. In Russia, Tsar Alexander II (1855–1881) initiated a reformist movement, which appeared to bode well for the Jewish minority. Jews were allowed to reside in the Russian interior, to participate in local government, to attend universities and to practise new professions. They responded with an enlightenment of their own, the *Haskalah*, the proponents of which encouraged their fellow Jews to participate fully in Russian life, to engage in constructive discourse with the gentiles, and to preserve their 'Jewishness' for their home lives. Their burgeoning hopes were to be abruptly and tragically crushed. In 1881 the Tsar was assassinated and his son, Alexander III, ascended to the throne. The new Tsar, committed to a policy that based his rule on national homogeneity and resurgent *Slavophilism*, turned against the empire's minorities. The Jews, who by now numbered over five million, were given special attention. They were accused of being revolutionaries and a series of fiercely restrictive measures were imposed upon them, which became known as the May Laws. The Tsar appeased the Russian peasantry by allowing them to hound the Jews off the land and back into the city ghettos. They were once more banned from most educational institutions and expelled from their employment, dramatically denying them their means of subsistence. Matters became worse still as the government sanctioned a series of pogroms in 1881–82 and again in 1903–05. Millions were massacred or fled as refugees to the western peripheries of the empire and beyond. Their numbers swelled the already impoverished and politically deprived Jewish communities in Austria, Poland and Romania, while those that were left in Russia were subjected to abject poverty, continuing humiliation and the attempted eradication of their religious and cultural life.

Western Europe was to prove no more impervious to emergent nationalism than had been Russia. In Germany, Austria and France, the tide of nationalism was sweeping through intellectual and popular circles alike, leaving in its wake resurgent anti-Semitism that led disillusioned assimilationist Jews to re-think their attitudes towards Europe and their own positions within it. The processes of change wrought by industrialisation reshuffled the existing socio-economic order, creating an insecurity that served only to reinforce embedded stereotypes of Jews. They became the scapegoats for all social evils as politicians and ideologues sought to leave their mark.[6]

The common suffering of European Jews, East and West, prompted two responses. The first, born of desperation, was the emigration of Russian and Eastern European Jews to the United States, Western Europe and Palestine. For the majority of these refugees, their destination was chosen for practical purposes. However, for some of those emigrating to Palestine the reasoning was more complex and reflected the second response to persecution – the development of a nationalism of their own based on their Jewish identity. There was not a single understanding of this identity, however. Since Judaism is first and foremost a religion, its translation into the essentially secular conceptual framework of nationalism led to numerous, often contradictory, variations on a theme. The earliest suggestions for the transfer of Jews to, and the settlement of, Palestine sprouted from religious understandings of the obligation to return, something which had previously been more a spiritual notion than a plan of action. Rabbi Judah Alkalai and Rabbi Zvi Hirsch Kalischer wrote in mid-nineteenth-century Central Europe of the need for an immediate return to Zion in order to fulfil messianic prophecies for the redemption of the Jews. By the end of the century, anti-Semitism and persecution had also turned both secular assimilationists and the advocates of the *Haskalah* into ardent Jewish nationalists in search of a home of their own. Writers such as Moses Hess, author of *Rome and Jerusalem*, Moshe Lilienblum, the Russian essayist, Perez Smolenskin, the editor of the Hebrew monthly *HaShachar* (the Dawn), Leo Pinsker, author of *Selbstemanzipation* (Auto-emancipation) – all called for mass emigration to and settlement of Palestine. For some this was a quest for spiritual or cultural emancipation; for others it was a specifically political enterprise. Perhaps the best known writer, and the man who has become known as the father of political Zionism, was Theodor Herzl. As a journalist, Herzl witnessed the trial of a French Jewish army captain, Dreyfus, in which the defendant was made a scapegoat for the crimes of others on the basis of his Jewish identity. His subsequent pamphlet, *Der Judenstaat* (1896), argued that anti-Semitism was a medieval anachronism that was nonetheless failing to die out. The suffering of the Jews would ultimately lead them to establish their own state, removing the causes of friction between Jews and the

Gentile states. He advocated international diplomacy to win the support of the European states for a Jewish-governed national home, preferably in Palestine, where the Jews could build a progressive, aristocratic republic characterised by universal equality before the law, the culture of secular bourgeois Europe and a modern scientific economy. Unlike the writings coming from Eastern Europe and Russia, this tract was unconcerned with first inspiring a cultural renaissance among Jews – although he was fiercely critical of the combined effects on the Jewish mentality of ghetto life and the philanthropy of wealthy Jews. For him, this was a pragmatic political mission based on the belief that all Jews were one people and that their self-government would relieve them from persecution.

Herzl's ideas provoked controversy among his fellow Jews; cultural Zionists like Asher Ginzberg (also known as Ahad Ha'am) argued that Herzl's understanding of the Jewish nation included little that was actually Jewish – the Hebrew language, culture, literature and education were either ignored or condemned as irrelevancies that had helped to hold Jews back from their national potential. Ginzberg also thought that international diplomacy was a secondary consideration, arguing for settlement to begin immediately. Jewish survival was above all a cultural task, not a political mission. Spiritual Zionists like Martin Buber also countered Herzl's proposals with calls for a spiritual renaissance that would stress the mystical and humanist aspects of Jewish life. Herzl was, above all, a man of his time. He had fused together a combination of secularism, nationalism, liberalism and Western European bourgeois values to construct his solution to the Jewish question. Moreover, in his view any indigenous population of the territories to be settled were to have no say in the programme; the suggestion that they be 'spirited across the border' reflected the prevailing colonial mentality that considered any land outside European borders to be 'empty' and available for settlement, their populations being barbarous and uncivilised.

For left-wing Jewish ideologues this presented a major dilemma. Labour Zionists, so called because they believed the basic precondition for Jewish redemption was a return to productive labouring on the land (long denied them by Tsarist policies), were themselves divided. Nachman Syrkin, for example, claimed that 'Socialism will solve the Jewish problem only in the remote future', that class struggle would help only the Jewish middle class and therefore a Jewish state was the immediate decisive response to Jewish suffering.[7] Some regarded historical determinism and their own commitments to modernisation as sufficient justification for the displacement of Palestinian Arabs. Others, like A. D. Gordon, believed in co-operation and co-existence. Ber Borochov, who led efforts to integrate Zionism with Marxism, argued that Jews must first win the national struggle against ethnic oppression before they could engage in the universal class war. Yet however they defined their cause and its solution, the turn-of-the-century Zionists were drawing up blueprints for a Jewish entity, the consequence of which was to be the dispossession of the Palestinian people. Thus, accounts of the Zionist enterprise which begin with these early ideological formulations tend to view modern Israel as a colonial entity arising out of secular European notions of national identity and beliefs in the right of superior peoples to settle the lands of, and dominate over, indigenous non-European peoples.

Historical evidence points to the fact that Zionism, as we know it, was born within the framework of imperialist thoughts and designs of the early decades of nineteenth-century Europe and enthusiastically embraced by some Jewish intellectuals and activists who were influenced by the prevalent chauvinist and racist ideas of the latter part of the century.[8]

Not surprisingly, this view of events has assumed political dimensions, not least since it raises questions concerning the legitimacy of the modern state of Israel. Initially the domain of Arab and radical European critics of Israel, it has, nonetheless, come to inform a school of contemporary Israeli sociology that counters the orthodox Israeli account of the early settlement of Palestine. While the *colonialism* perspective emphasises aspects of land acquisition, immigration, settlement, political domination and economic exploitation of Palestine's resources, the orthodox version paints a picture of courageous pioneering, the taming of previously neglected and unproductive lands, economic development and modernisation, and the introduction of political and social norms that equate with a civilising mission. It is not our intention here to assert the validity of either perspective, but a cursory survey of the issues involved offers some insights into the nature of the state that was to emerge.

Colonisation under the Mandate

There can be little argument that European colonialism played a part in Israel's history. The end of World War I saw the establishment of a British Mandatory government in Palestine. With a typically colonial disregard for the native inhabitants of Ottoman Palestine, the British had set about trying to win allies to their cause during the war by making a series of contradictory promises regarding the post-war status of Arab lands. To the Sherif Hussein of Mecca there had been a series of letters indicating that the British considered territories at the eastern end of the Mediterranean to be Arab. Although the actual delimitations of any such territory were never specified in the correspondence, with consequent disagreement over which lands were those intended for inclusion in the original (Arabic) text, the purpose of the promise was to encourage Hussein to mobilise his Arab armies of Arabia to revolt against Ottoman rulers allied to Germany. With devastating cynicism, however, the British had simultaneously been conducting secret negotiations with the French, to whom they promised a post-war carving-up of the Middle East into spheres of influence (with Palestine falling into the British allocation of territory).[9] In a third document, they muddied the waters still further by publicly stating that the British government 'viewed with favour' the establishment in Palestine of a Jewish national home. The Balfour Declaration, named after the Foreign Secretary in whose name this open letter was written to the head of the British Zionist Organisation, acknowledged only the civil and religious rights of the non-Jewish population of Palestine, but made no reference to their political or national rights. In the end, Britain successfully lobbied the newly created League of Nations to be awarded a mandate in 1922 to govern Palestine itself. The contradictions of war-time policy were continued in the terms of the mandate, which included both the notion of ultimate independence for the inhabitants of mandated territories, and the responsibility for Britain to facilitate Jewish immigration into Palestine with the purpose of enabling the Jews to construct a national home therein.

For the next 25 years, Britain was to struggle to reconcile the need for orderly administration of its new acquisition with the destabilising impact of Zionist immigration and colonisation. Jewish relocation to Palestine was nothing new. At the beginning of the eighteenth century there had been only around 6,000 Jewish inhabitants in Palestine (out of a total population of around 400,000), mostly residing in the towns of Safed, Hebron, Tiberias and Jerusalem. Romantic Christian *proto*-Zionism and Jewish philanthropy financed a small trickle of Jewish emigration from Europe to Palestine during the first half of that century, encouraged by a capitulatory arrangement between Britain and the Ottoman Empire that included a clause protective of Jewish interests, and arriving for predominantly religious reasons. They were joined in the 1880s by a wave of settlers who were fleeing from the persecution and pogroms in Russia. Between 1882 and 1903 some 25,000 such immigrants arrived, often with idealistic or nationalist aspirations and dedicated to establishing new communities and societies that could facilitate further emigration from Russia.[10] These were to become known as the first *aliyah* – or wave of immigrants – and, despite the agricultural ambitions of the more ideologically driven, the vast majority settled in towns where they either opened small businesses or remained dependent on charitable donations from philanthropists such as Baron Edmond de Rothschild. A second *aliyah* of 30,000 Jews was to arrive between 1904 and 1914. By this time Herzl had transformed his vision into a movement, convening the first World Zionist Congress in Basle in 1897. A World Zionist Organisation was established to lobby international support for a Jewish state in Palestine, with a Jewish Colonial Trust being set up to raise funds for emigration to and settlement in the land. The movement spread rapidly, Zionist associations sprouted up around the world and individual doctrinal organisations developed within them. Further upheavals in Russia, combined with appeals from the Zionist community in Palestine itself (the *yishuv*) for new members, inspired a second wave of more politically mature immigrants who began the co-ordinated organisation of Jewish political and social institutions in Palestine. The Russian Revolution in 1917 and the subsequent purging of Russian Zionists as counter-revolutionaries after their brief honeymoon with the new regime, inspired a third wave (1919–23), also of predominantly Russian and Eastern European Jews. A fourth (1924–28) arrived from Poland, but it was events in Western Europe, and principally the rise to power of a violently anti-Jewish regime in Germany, which was to mobilise the largest *aliyah* so far. Between 1929 and 1939 some 250,000 Jews arrived in Palestine, bringing with them capital and skills on an unprecedented scale and facilitating the real development of the Jewish capitalist economy.

The Arabs, not surprisingly, were largely hostile to the Zionist colonisation efforts, and to the British rule that deprived them of their own independence. Yet they were ill equipped to resist either. The population was for the most part impoverished and illiterate. The notable families resided in the cities, away from the rural population, and were more tuned in to their previous Ottoman overlords than to the new British officials. Moreover, they were deeply divided among themselves and utilised connections with the British to improve their positions relative to one another, quickly losing any bargaining power that they might have held by joining ranks. Even as they complained about British sales of state-owned land to the Jewish immigrants, they would sell land themselves, pushing the price up well beyond the means of prospective Arab purchasers and resulting in the forced eviction of Palestinian tenants. The Zionist settlers for the most part rejected the idea of employing any but 'Hebrew' labour and thousands of already indebted Palestinians were pushed off the land to cities like Jaffa, living in burgeoning shanty towns as they sought work in the port or small industrial concerns. British policies did facilitate some improvements in the education, health, sanitation and transport infrastructure available to the Palestinians, but the introduction of new, more efficient taxation systems and economic policies that inadvertently encouraged the Zionist cash-crops at the expense of traditional Arab agriculture, only served to widen the gap between Jews and Arabs.

Literature on this period of Palestine's history interprets events in a number of ways. Some writers have been keen to propagate the 'dual economy' or 'dual society' thesis – that the Jewish and Arab populations lived apart, their lives barely touching one another other than in the military or political realms.[11] Until recently, this was the official view of Israeli history, emphasising the progressive and utopian aspects of Zionist settlement and denying any directly negative impact of Jewish settlement upon the indigenous population. As Michael Shalev has pointed out, this narrative places enormous weight on ideology and leadership as sources of social transformation, leaving little room for economic conflicts and constraints. It conceives of ethnic tensions as reflecting cultural divisions rather than distributive struggles and views the national conflict between Arabs and Jews as a challenge to Israeli society from beyond its walls, rather than as an endogenous dynamic deeply implicated in the very constitution of that society.[12]

Proponents of this history cite a number of reasons for rejecting the colonial paradigm. Jewish employers, especially the collective settlements, preferred to rely exclusively on 'Hebrew' labour and were thus rejecting the possibility of exploiting the Arab population. Land for settlement was purchased (often at grossly inflated prices) rather than expropriated. The Zionist enterprise introduced new technology into farming and reclaimed uncultivated lands, 'turning the desert green'. The *yishuv* was largely self-reliant, benefiting proportionately less from British expenditures since the community provided its own schools, health facilities and even defence. In the extreme versions of this view, the Arabs become villains rather than victims, being portrayed as culturally derelict, economically foolish and politically vindictive. Arthur Koestler, for example, states that:

> The fundamental fact about the Jewish colonization of Palestine is that it was carried out neither by force nor by the threat of force, but, contrary to popular belief, with active Arab connivance. . . . The Arabs sold voluntarily, and had the fullest possible protection against acting rashly or being taken advantage of. If, despite all warnings and restrictions, they persisted in selling, they did it with open eyes.[13]

Koestler blames any Arab loss in the transaction on an élite *effendi* class. He also claims that visitors to Palestine during the mandate era would notice 'the apparent jumps in the progress of reclaiming the waste land which had lain fallow and deserted during the centuries of Turkish misrule, and in the rise of the living standard of the population'.[14] In his view, the Zionist agricultural achievements provided the moral basis to their claim to the lands.

Advocates of the colonial paradigm dispute the validity of these claims, arguing that even Herzl understood that Jewish settlement in Palestine could not continue indefinitely unless Jewish political control was assured. As he said: 'An infiltration is bound to end badly. It continues until the inevitable moment when the native population feels itself threatened, and forces the Government to stop a further influx of Jews. Immigration is consequently futile unless based on an assured supremacy.'[15]

They argue that, although the Zionists actually held less than 7 per cent of the land of Mandate Palestine in 1947, the fact that they were subsequently able to seize control of the best part of the territory indicated both the strategic nature of the purchases which they did make, and the advantages which they were able to draw from the mandate in order to secure their military strength relative to the Arabs. Just because they considered themselves to be the true inheritors of the land, their activities were nonetheless similar to, and in the spirit of, the prevailing European colonial mentality. As such, they viewed themselves as the bearers of a civilising mission. Again, in Herzl's words: 'It is more and more to the interest of the civilised nations and of civilisation in general that a cultural station be established on the shortest road to Asia. Palestine is this station and we Jews are the bearers of culture who are ready to give our property and our lives to bring about its creation.'[16]

The links with Europe were not just cultural but also practical, with Britain utilising the Zionist endeavour to advance its own strategic interests in the Middle East. Chaim Weizmann, on behalf of the Zionists, offered Jewish allegiance in return for political support for British interests, acknowledging in the *Jewish Chronicle* of 13 August 1937 that: 'The transfer [of power] could only be carried out by the British Government and not by the Jews'. At a later point, and following the 1939 MacDonald White Paper that sought to appease Arab fears and the potential for an Arab rebellion on the eve of war in Europe, the Zionists transferred this allegiance to the United States. The American Zionist Emergency Council sought US patronage, culminating in the 1942 Biltmore Programme and early American recognition of the new state of Israel in 1948. Thus the Zionist colonisation of Palestine and the subsequent creation of a Jewish state were dependent upon and coincided with both the imperialist philosophies and interests of the Great Powers.

As with other colonial endeavours, territoriality and an attachment to the land were crucial. Borochov himself had said: 'territorialism must be the central concept of the structure, whose whole and synthetic form is Zionism, the conquest and colonisation of a territory'.[17] The implication of indefinite immigration has always been a correlational requirement of land for settlement. As Moshe Dayan said in 1968:

> It is absolutely essential, in my opinion, to understand that Degania [an old *kibbutz* in the Jordan valley] is not an end, that Nakhal Oz [a new kibbutz facing the Gaza Strip] is not an end, and that three million Jews are not an end. Each new generation will add its own share. . . . For one hundred years the Jewish people have been undergoing a process of colonisation to enlarge the borders here – let there be not a Jew to claim that this process is over.[18]

According to the colonialist paradigm, the exploitation of land resources can be equated with the exploitation of indigenous labour resources – indeed there is some evidence that Arab labour was after all employed by Hebrew enterprises in some instances. Neither the desire to break free of the metropolitan centre, nor the efforts to expel rather than exploit the native population, are evidence of non-colonial intentions; they are after all little different from the white settler intentions in North America or Australia. The comparison has led to a body of literature that considers Israel to be a colonial-settler state, a concept most effectively developed by Arghiri Emmanuel.[19] Such states are characterised by the attempt to achieve independence from the mother-country, the inheritance by settlers of the original colonial administrative infrastructure, their expropriation of the land, the expulsion or often violent political subordination of the native population, the conferment of intrinsic symbolic value on the land itself, ongoing settler immigration matched by continued emigration of the indigenous population, and finally a culture and system of institutionalised discrimination which reinforces the settler 'right to rule' over the colonised peoples.

The best-known assertion that Israel is such a colonial-settler state is to be found in Maxime Rodinson's *Israel: A Colonial Settler State*.[20] Rodinson concludes that the process of the creation of the Israeli state was part of the 'great European-American movement in the nineteenth and twentieth centuries whose aim was to settle new inhabitants among other people or to dominate them economically and politically'. Other writers[21] have used the concept to argue that Israel developed along a similar trajectory to Apartheid South Africa, with the Zionism–Apartheid analogy becoming a highly controversial part of international diplomacy in the 1970s and 1980s. Such analysis has been based on consideration of imposed ethnic segregation within Israel, the political and economic subordination of Israeli Arabs to their Jewish counterparts, the racist ideological and legal justifications for such segregation and subordination, and the regional imperialistic tendencies of the two states. A final variation on the colonial theme was offered by Elia Zureik,[22] who assessed the specific nature of the relationship between the coloniser (Israeli Jews) and the colonised (Israeli Arabs). His research traced the relationship back to the Mandate era and asserted three fundamental features of the relationship. Firstly, the Jewish *yishuv* and later the Israeli entity had imposed a Jewish capitalist economy on an Arab traditional peasant economy. Secondly, the settlers had come to dominate urban or metropolitan areas while the Arabs were relegated to the rural 'hinterland'. Finally, the settlers had developed a justificatory ideology that dehumanised the native population and allowed the colonial peoples to subordinate them to their own hegemonic purposes. He concluded that today's Arabs exist as an internal colony within the Israeli state; they are dependent on it yet discriminated against and disempowered by it.

The colonial paradigm was predominant among radical and Arab opponents of Israel during the second half of the twentieth century, but was fiercely disputed by Israeli scholars who were eager to project a democratic and progressive image of the Israeli state. This would hardly have been possible if they had accepted its birth as being little more than a stage in a colonialist enterprise. In recent years, however, some such scholars have come to acknowledge the value of the paradigm as a methodological tool rather than a political statement. For sociologists like Avishai Ehrlich and Shlomo Swirski, the traditional Israeli dual society narrative has treated the Arab population as external to the history of the *yishuv*, when in fact that history can only be properly understood in terms of relations with the Arabs.[23] Acknowledging this has led others to re-examine the nature of the contemporary state by comparing *yishuv* settlement of Palestine with Israeli settlement of lands occupied after the 1967 war.[24]

The colonial paradigm is an example of what Zachary Lockman has called *relational history*, the consideration of the histories of specific ethno-national groups with regard to their relations with one another and within the context of larger processes affecting all. The Arabs, Jews and British in mandate Palestine all impacted upon one another, even as they were all subject to the dynamics of the Ottoman legal and social legacies, capitalist development, and international diplomatic manoeuvrings. His own work is part of this growing trend within Israeli academic circles which has broken away from concentration on the historical specificity of the Zionist enterprise. It remains a largely marginalised trend as yet, but offers great potential for bridging the gap between Israeli and Palestinian narratives and for divesting historical accounts of their more mythological and partisan components.

The battle for Palestine, 1948

The greatest 'battlefield' for the revisionist historiographers has, however, been over the interpretation of events leading up to the end of the British mandate and the actual creation of the Israeli state.

> The focus of the historiographical revisionism in Israel [as mentioned] has been the 1948 war. This is not surprising. This formative year epitomizes for the Israelis the most miraculous point in their national history, while for the Palestinians 1948 is the most tragic and cata-strophic year in their history. Most of the Israeli foundational myths revolve around the war and its consequences. Challenging these myths is more than just a historical debate, it also casts doubt on some of the principal moral assumptions and perceptions dominating the Israeli national agenda.[25]

In the build-up to war in Europe, the British had altered their stance in Palestine towards appeasing Palestinian opinion as part of an effort to prevent insurgency against British rule at such a critical time. The 1939 White Paper restricted Jewish immigration into Palestine just as events within Europe were creating a wave of Jewish refugees. The war itself pro-vided a temporary hiatus in Jewish–British–Arab tensions, with the *yishuv* aligning itself with Britain against the Axis powers. Some Palestinian lea-ders, such as Hajj Amin al-Husseini, did make overtures towards securing German guarantees for their own independence, but it was only after the conclusion of the war that overt hostilities broke out within Palestine itself. Jewish terrorist groups, such as the *Lehi* (Fighters for the Freedom of Israel – also known as the Stern Gang), openly took up arms against the British[26] and even the *yishuv* leadership worked hard to circumvent British efforts to

control Jewish immigration and settlement. The war had led to the displacement of up to 250,000 European Jews, many of whom were unwilling to
return to their countries of origin. The stupefying horrors of the holocaust[27]
had for many proved to be the final proof of the impossibility of assimilation or the eradication of European anti-Semitism. Thus the demand for
entry into Palestine was greater than ever.

The British, however, were in no position to facilitate *yishuv* demands.
Weakened by the war and conscious of the need to retain Arab goodwill in
the post-war environment, they retained the limitations on Jewish immigration to the extent of imposing a physical naval blockade. The contradictions
of pre-war British policy were now coming back to haunt them. As conditions threatened to deteriorate into chaos, the British decided to wash their
hands of Palestine entirely, handing the problem over to the United Nations
and announcing their own unilateral withdrawal, scheduled for May 1948.
A United Nations proposal for partition of Palestine into a Jewish and an
Arab state in 1947 met with Arab rejection. The Zionist leaders accepted it
in principle but reserved the right to designate the borders themselves, intent
upon taking advantage of international recognition for their right to a state
but without being confined by any imposed notion of borders for that state.
While the plan for partition was still being debated, both Arab and *yishuv*
forces began pre-emptive manoeuvring for territorial advantage.

What happened next has been the subject of ferocious debate ever since.
Palestinian historiographies have recounted how the Zionist settlers, who
were better trained and equipped than the Arab forces, conquered the best
part of Palestine, driving out the Palestinian inhabitants according to a
systematic programme (the infamous Plan Dalet[28]). Betrayed by King
Abdullah of Jordan, who collaborated with the Zionist leadership in
order to advance his own Hashemite claims to the West Bank, and with
the disunited Arab armies unable to take on the challenge of Zionist military
supremacy, the local Palestinian population were subjected to threats, violent attacks and even massacres (the most notable example being that at
Deir Yassin) by the Zionist forces. Understandably they fled, expecting to
return once the war had been resolved one way or another.

The orthodox Zionist version of this period paints an entirely different
picture. For them, the war was brought on by Arab refusal to accept the
eminently sensible option of partition. When the Mandate expired and the
Jews proclaimed their own state, seven Arab armies swept in, intent on
annihilating the Jewish presence in Palestine. The tiny new Jewish state
bravely resisted the onslaught, fighting heroically and ultimately successfully
against great odds. The flight of Palestinian inhabitants was instigated by
calls from Arab leaders to clear the battlefield, despite Zionist pleas for them
to stay. Arab casualties were unwelcome but were ultimately the inevitable
result of a conflict that the Jewish community had never sought. Jewish
casualties, on the other hand, were the result of barbarous atrocities on
the part of the Arab forces.

The degree of variation between these two contradictory narratives can be accounted for by two explanations. The Palestinian version, which sees itself as giving voice to the victims of a new pogrom, has relied heavily on oral accounts since supporting documentation has been scarce. Where it does exist, in official Arab archives, it is frequently inaccessible for political reasons.[29] Palestinian refugees and Arab soldiers alike have been motivated by the need to explain why the loss of Palestine and the exile of a large part of its population was not the result of their own failures and weaknesses. Sympathetic leftist historians have been equally keen to locate the Palestinian accounts within a broader critique of Zionism and Israeli colonialism. Without extensive hard documentary evidence to support their arguments, however, their voices were until recently largely drowned out by the prevailing orthodox Israeli narrative.

The Zionist account has also relied almost entirely on versions put forward by politicians, soldiers and sympathetic journalists and chroniclers. Not surprisingly, and as evidence of the truth of the cliché that history is written by the victors, they were concerned to portray their own actions in as positive and moral a light as possible. Their version of history was to become the official 'national' version and the narrative was consequently sanitised to make it both domestically acceptable and suitable for propagation abroad. For example, when Yitzhak Rabin first published his memoirs in 1979, the official censor removed a passage that recounted how Arabs were forcibly evicted from Lod and Ramle in 1948 in line with the direct wishes of David Ben-Gurion himself. The orthodox Zionist account thus also became more dependent upon political imperatives than unquestionable documentary evidence.

In the 1980s, however, a third narrative began to emerge that was based on archival material newly released under Israel's 30-year rule. The authors of this body of work,[30] collectively known as Israel's 'new' or 'revisionist' historians, have used official documents drawn from the Zionist establishment of the 1940s to challenge the orthodox Zionist narrative on a number of points. Avi Shlaim has summarised the main points of contention as follows: British policy at the end of the Palestine Mandate, the Arab–Israeli military balance in 1948, the origins of the Palestinian refugee problem, the nature of the Israeli–Jordanian relations during the war, Arab war aims, and the reasons for the continuing political deadlock after the guns fell silent. With the fundamental myths of the orthodox narrative coming under attack, the way was open for other areas of Israeli historiography to be re-examined. Prevailing views on the political, economic and social conditions in pre-Mandate Palestine, the impact of Zionist colonisation on Mandate Palestine, the policy-making role of David Ben-Gurion, and Israel Defence Force compliance with the notion of the 'purity of arms' have all been subjected to critical re-examination in recent years and found wanting.

Reactions to the new historiography have been mixed, ranging from the acrimonious, vitriolic and abusive attacks of 'old guard' academics such as

Shabtai Teveth[31] and Efraim Karsh,[32] to a more measured acceptance that a mythological 'national' history is no longer required and that the time is ripe for mature reflection on the origins of the state. For example, in 1998, on the fiftieth anniversary of the establishment of the state, the Israel Broadcasting Company produced a controversial series of programmes under the title *Tkuma* (or rebirth) that gave voice to many of the arguments and conclusions of the new historians. The following year the Ministry of Education introduced new school textbooks that also referred to previously taboo issues such as the existence of a particular Palestinian people and their forced expulsion and in some cases massacre by militarily superior Zionist forces.[33]

Acceptance of a somewhat tarnished history, in which the prime driving force has been political necessity rather than moral assertion, strips Israel of much of its uniqueness for the historian. However, it does pave the way for some kind of reconciliation of the contrasting national narratives. It also opens the door to less polemical efforts to understand the nature and form of the state itself, as it developed after independence was declared in 1948.

The creation of the state

The declaration of the State of Israel took place at four in the afternoon on Friday 14 May 1948, some eight hours before the British were scheduled to leave Palestine. As the mandate formally came to an end, Arab armies from Egypt, Syria, Jordan, Iraq and Lebanon moved against the Israeli armed forces, and what had for six months previously been a chaotic but essentially internal struggle between British, Jewish and Palestinian communities, was transformed into all-out war between nation-states. Almost a year later, it was clear that the Israeli forces were victorious and that most of Palestine was lost to the Arabs. Israel now controlled 77 per cent of Mandate Palestine (as opposed to the 56 per cent allotted to it by the UN Partition Plan). Some 360 Arab villages and fourteen Arab towns within the new Israeli state had been destroyed and 85 per cent of the Palestinian population of those areas had fled or been expelled. There were now 726,000 Palestinian refugees living either in neighbouring Arab states or in those parts of Palestine still in Arab hands (Gaza and the West Bank), for whom Israel disclaimed any responsibility and refused the right of return. During the war, the Israeli leadership, under David Ben-Gurion's charismatic guidance, had determined that it would be foolhardy to leave pockets of Arab resistance behind its own front lines. Once the war had been concluded, the priority was to establish a state of and for Jews.

There can be little doubt about the tremendous personal influence of Ben-Gurion in those early years. Although he was portrayed at the time as representing the national consensus over the form and direction that the new state should adopt, today's historians recognise the significant extent to which he personally shaped and drove the construction of the state itself. He summed up his vision for Israel thus:

> We had come into existence as a state not merely to give freedom and independence to the 650,000 Jews who were its citizens on May 14, 1948, but also and above all to create a sovereign Homeland for all Jews waiting outside. It was our immediate responsibility to see that the Homeland should be organised in accordance with modern democratic principles and that the entry of the newcomers into the land that was theirs as much as ours should at least have the basis and promise of reasonable social and economic conditions.[34]

This mission necessitated a number of simultaneous processes. Firstly the institutional infrastructure of the state and of government had to be established. Political Zionism was infused with liberal ideals of political pluralism but also with the legacy of Jewish communal life in the European *diaspora*. Self-regulation of Jewish communities can be traced back to tenth-century Europe and included the establishment of educational and social institutions comprising officials from the *kehilot* (Jewish councils) elected through common suffrage. Such a consensual approach to maintaining the social cohesion of Jews as viable communities throughout Europe, essential under the amorphous threat of racial and political persecution from existing state structures, came eventually to influence the broad strategy of the early Zionist movement. As Alan Dowty has noted, this tradition of voluntarism contained several drawbacks with regard to the development of democracy as the organisational basis of any future Jewish entity.

> One was the long habit of secrecy, of concealment and closing off from the outside. A second was the absence of civic habits of an ingrained deference to legitimate public authority, and the development of any attitude of expediency towards the law along with a contentious and even unruly style of politics. But perhaps the most glaring weakness of Jewish politics was the fact that, being rooted in a strong sense of community, it offered little guidance in including those who were not members of this community.[35]

The tension between these two features of twentieth-century Jewish political life was not readily apparent in the early years of state consolidation. Instead Herzl's initial vision of Zionism, based on the communal affinity of symbols, history and iconography of Judaism, manifested itself in an electoral system based on proportional representation to elected Zionist bodies. This produced a strong executive but a relatively weak legislature. The legacy of this approach is still to be seen in Israeli politics, where once the inevitable horsetrading involved in the formation of a coalition government has been completed, the legislature, or *Knesset*, remains circumscribed from any real input into the decision-making process.

The second task was to facilitate massive Jewish immigration. In the eighteen months following independence alone, some 340,000 Jews arrived in Israel. The 1950 Law of Return established the right of any Jew to make *aliyah*, or to immigrate to Israel and assume citizenship. But while the principle was ideological, the immediate needs of the state for large-scale immigration were economic and military – to provide a population for the development and defence of the new state. After the displaced persons' camps in Europe had been emptied, the Israeli government turned to the Arab world, facilitating the removal of whole communities to Israel as their own governments turned against them. Airlifts from Yemen and Iraq, Libyans, Syrians, Tunisians, Algerians, Moroccans, and Egyptians, joined Turkish and Iranian Jews such that by 1953 Israel was the home of 13 per cent of world Jewry. By 1956 the population had tripled, to over 1.6 million, imposing enormous strains on the economy.

Thirdly, the borders had to be secured and the defence machinery consolidated to protect the infant state. Again this was a costly drain on the country's resources. Ben-Gurion's faith in military supremacy led Israel to embark on a massive spending spree as it sought the best in technology and arms for its defence forces. The army itself was consolidated and regularised, and policies of disproportionate retaliation and pre-emptive capacity were implemented in the belief that only when the Arabs realised the disadvantages of a permanent state of war would they finally acknowledge Israel's rightful place in the community of nations.

Finally, economic and social development had to proceed apace in order to attract and support the immigration programme. Scarce natural resources meant dependence on imported capital, on *diaspora* revenues, foreign loans and even war reparations. The demands of defence, immigrant absorption and rapid infrastructural development led the state to take a heavy planning hand, managing both consumption and supply through a range of regulatory austerity measures. Despite price controls and rationing, the rapid economic growth creation suppressed inflationary pressures and in 1952 a New Economic Policy was introduced which aimed to balance the budget. The demand for high living standards to attract (and keep) immigrants, however, prevented the market from reasserting itself as the state sought to subsidise employment and consumption. While this was generally in accordance with the ideological preferences of the Labour leadership, it was motivated by primarily political considerations.

The enormity of the tasks outlined above was not unlike that facing a revolutionary government, and Ben-Gurion rose to the challenge with a new doctrine for national management – *mamlachtiyut* – or 'statism'. In essence, the concept suggested that in this new stage of Jewish history, the role of individuals and voluntary organisations in determining the fate of the Jews (as had been the case during the *yishuv* years) would be taken over by the impersonal state and the bureaucracy. Thus he would be able to 'transform a voluntary, idea-oriented, social movement into a tool capable of forging reality'.[36] *Mamlachtiyut* had various dimensions. As well as the operative aspects which saw the state apparatus assuming dominance over the political system, concentrating political power and subordinating particularistic interests to those of the nation-state as a whole, there were symbolic and cultural aspects which located the state at the centre of the emerging Israeli identity. The processes of state-building and nation-building were fused such that individuals associated their own fates with that of the collective as represented by the state.[37] For Ben-Gurion this would allow the new nation-state to develop internal cohesion, a task which was profoundly difficult given the disparate national and ideological origins of its Jewish citizens. It would also serve to mobilise the resources of the new state for the purposes of supporting continued immigration that required imposing significant economic hardship on the population.

In his implementation of the doctrine, Ben-Gurion was in theory leaving behind his own Labour-Zionist roots in an effort to create a political system in which national interest predominated over the interests of religious or ideological sub-cultures. In reality, the establishment of state institutions drew heavily on the Zionist organisations set up during the Mandate years, most of which were dominated by Labour-Zionist personnel and influences. The *yishuv*'s People's Council became, upon independence, the Provisional State Council of Israel and the People's Administration was empowered to act as the provisional government. Thus the *Vaad Leumi* and the Jewish Agency were restructured into an initial thirteen ministries which survived the subsequent national elections. Ben-Gurion's own labourist *Mapai* party was to dominate government coalitions for thirty years, and institutions such as the *Histadrut* (Labour Federation) featured heavily in the economy as a whole. Nonetheless, Ben-Gurion was always prepared to sacrifice his socialist ambitions to his vision of the construction of a new Jewish political culture appropriate for statehood. This was illustrated by a number of his key decisions in the early years, one of the best examples being his refusal to countenance a formal written constitution.

The first elected *Knesset* (parliament) devoted a large part of its first year in office to the question of whether Israel should have an organic written constitution, with the arguments centring on whether such a document was a requisite for democracy. The constitutionalists argued that only a written constitution would protect fundamental freedoms and that without it the direction of the state would be determined by majority voting rather than by principle. Those opposed to the idea, led by Ben-Gurion, argued instead for the evolution of a constitution through the passing of *fundamental laws*.

> He felt that the country should not be bound by a document, a 'holy writ', so long as it awaited millions and millions of newcomers who should have a voice in determining their future. In addition, he thought

that under wartime conditions it would be impossible to deal justly with the Arab citizens of Israel. Also, a written constitution would have to either declare separation of 'synagogue' from state, thus snatching power from the religious authorities who maintained the Jewish heritage throughout the long years of the Diaspora, or decree Judaism to be the state religion, which would give the rabbinic authorities and their adherents a privileged position, implying disadvantages for secularists, nonconformists, and non-Jews.[38]

In other words, pragmatism and the need to avoid principled but divisive courses of action motivated him and his statist followers to resist moves that might force the new state to confront potentially controversial aspects of Jewish and Israeli identity. A compromise was ultimately reached whereby *fundamental laws* would collectively become the constitution but the problems of defining Jewish identity, and the relationship between religion and the state, have persisted and continued to haunt Israeli politics and society ever since.

A second arena in which the state was to assume supremacy over particularist interests was that of defence. Towards the end of May 1948, two orders were issued by the Provisional Government concerning the armed forces of the new state. The first authorised conscription in times of emergency, and prohibited the existence of armed entities other than a newly formed Israel Defence Force. The second announced that the *Haganah* (the main armed Jewish underground defence force) would now form the basis of the new national armed forces. Other paramilitary groups, such as the *Palmach,* the *Irgun* and the *Lehi,* were to be banned and their members should join the regular forces or, in some instances, come under their command. Ben-Gurion was determined that the various political factions should not run what he termed their own 'private armies' that might ultimately turn against one another on ideological grounds. His orders thus referred as much to groups of the left as to the right. A further Defence Education Bill (1949) established that the army was to play a crucial role in the educational processes of nation building and unification, beyond its more orthodox defence obligations. The Army would teach young conscripts the language, topography and history of the country as part of their military training. It would inspire them with egalitarian and pioneering values, moulding the young immigrants into a cohesive body with a common identity, personified in their allegiance to the state itself.

Education was another realm in which Ben-Gurion had to fight to achieve national coherence over particularist diversity. During the mandate era, a number of educational 'trends' had developed within the *yishuv.* Rejecting the educational system provided by the mandate authorities as being qualitatively poor and culturally inappropriate, the various Jewish political communities each sought to establish their own provision in line with their ideological persuasions and ambitions. The religious establishment expanded the *yeshiva* system of orthodox religious education (the so-called *Agudah* trend). A less rigorous approach was taken by the *Mizrahi* trend, whose schools supplemented the basic curriculum with long hours of religious teaching and segregated the genders in an effort to create a more religiously observant society. The Labour movement established schools that were more concerned with social experimentation, inculcating in the children the values and ideals of pioneering socialism. Finally, the *General* trend, which was numerically the largest, stressed a secular but still culturally *hebraic* curriculum. After independence, educational authority passed to a newly formed Ministry of Education, whose administration and structures acknowledged the existence of, and maintained, the trends. The system was not immune to crisis, not least as the various trends competed for students from among the new immigrant communities.[39] With the *Mapai* party dominating government coalitions, and with its personnel filling the ranks of the institutions that facilitated absorption, the Labour movement had the most immediate access to new immigrants and was able to foster a sense of reliance upon and loyalty towards itself that resulted in rapid growth in demand for its own schools.

Ben-Gurion recognised that this post-independence success of the Labour schools was endangering the co-operative relationship which he had built between his own party and those of the religious and centre-right camps in the name of national consensus. He therefore sacrificed the Labour school system by endorsing the view of the centre-right that a single secular educational system should be created, although appeasing the religious parties by agreeing that parents could choose an alternative religious education for their children. The 1953 State Education Law effectively ended the 'trends' system, introducing a single national curriculum, limiting the amount of additional ideological material that could be imparted to students, and forbidding political parties or organisations in playing a role in educational institutions. For Ben-Gurion education, like the army, belonged to all of the nation, not simply one class. Socialist ambitions were to be deferred until the state was able to stand above all class interests, rather than to be the servant of one.

Ben-Gurion's statism was characterised by two additional dimensions: the selective adoption of traditional Jewish symbols and rituals and a messianic depiction of statehood as the realisation of the renewal, restoration and redemption of Jewish life. Both required the endorsement of the religious establishment but were nonetheless fundamentally secular missions. New immigrant communities would be offered a recognisable cultural environment even as their own divergent collective personalities were stripped away. In effect, *mamlachtiyut* was a mammoth undertaking aiming not only to provide strong executive and administrative organisation of the new state, but also to construct an essentially new identity that would form the basis for national unity and cohesion during a period of massive socio-economic transformation. By constantly referring back to a glorious biblical past during which the Jews were one people, attached to the land of Israel by divine covenant, and by denouncing the intervening generations of exile as a diversion from the true destiny of the Jewish nation, Ben-Gurion hoped to eradicate cultural differentiation and create a new, consensual, political culture centred on the state.

The imposition of this political religion[40] defied democratic intentions and, contrary to the preferred depiction of the early years as exhibiting widespread consensus on the values and aims of the state, led to bitter resentment on the part of Ben-Gurion's political opponents, as well as those religious and new immigrant communities who were made to feel alien in what they had believed would be their own state.

For the so-called 'Oriental' immigrants, those arriving in Israel after its independence from Arab, African or Asian lands, the process of immigrant absorption, which in theory aimed to provide for both their socio-economic and politico-cultural needs, has been likened in retrospect to communal destruction. In the infamous *ma'abarot* (transit camps), they were humiliated by sanitation, medical and security procedures. They were forced to adopt new Hebrew names, to abandon their own languages in favour of Hebrew, in some cases to undergo adult circumcisions, and to forgo media access to their own cultural heritage. As Ben-Gurion himself said: 'the aim of the Government is to inculcate the Yemeni immigrant with Israeli values to the point where he forgets where he came from. . .'.[41] The Oriental community quickly became convinced that racial integration in fact meant the economic, political and cultural domination of European (*Ashkenazi*) Jews over Oriental (*Sephardi* and *Mizrahi*) Jews. From the transit camps, they were herded as cheap, uneducated labour into development towns, the poverty and deprivation of which soon led to their being likened to the ghettos of the Jewish past. Institutional and social discriminatory practices prevented their upward mobility and led to the deliberate abuse of their human rights, perhaps the most scandalous incident of which was the abduction of Yemeni children and their adoption by citizens of European origin without the consent of their natural parents.[42] The political parties, which were dominated until the 1970s by *Ashkenazi* apparatchiks who had gained their positions during the *yishuv* years, excluded the Oriental Jews from full representation, leading to unrepresentative government despite a growing Oriental majority. In sum, the Israeli identity was to be a fundamentally European identity regardless of the cultural or national origins of citizens, exhibiting a crucial flaw in the new democracy and one that still bears resonance today.

It was not only at the level of the common people that the democratic credentials of *mamlachtiyut* were questioned. Ben-Gurion's personal sponsorship of a group of young *Mapai* activists, who became collectively known as the *Tseirim* (younger generation), and their installation in positions of political power over the heads of older *Mapai* veterans, provoked great resentment within the party. The *Tseirim* were the children of Ben-

Gurion's philosophy, viewing the party more as a necessary tool at the disposal of the state than an ideological vehicle for determining the direction that the state should take. They claimed above all to be *bitsuistim* (doers): Shimon Peres, one of the foremost of the *Tseirim*, said that their task as the new generation was 'not to know what we want to be, but what we want to do',[43] a position which seemed to leave little room for the socialist aspirations of his party elders. The controversial promotion of the *Tseirim* was at the heart of party angst over the 'Lavon Affair', a political scandal arising from ill-fated and ill-advised Israeli covert activity in Egypt. The Israeli agents concerned were caught, tried and sentenced, and – in the absence of evidence as to exactly who had ordered the operation – the then Defence Minister, Pinhas Lavon, was forced to resign. Lavon took up a new position as head of the *Histadrut*, even as he continued to assert that his demise had been engineered by the *Tseirim* (in particular Shimon Peres and Moshe Dayan). The scandal continued to rumble on, with Lavon and the *Tseirim* coming to blows again over the role of the *Histadrut*. Ben-Gurion and his young helpers sought to nationalise many of the functions of the *Histadrut*, while Lavon argued that the *Histadrut* and the state should be partners since the *Histadrut* represented the majority of workers and the role of the state was to represent them, not rule over them. The argument became more vociferous and more personal as Dayan and Peres moved into the *Knesset* on the party list under Ben-Gurion's patronage. Old-guard veterans like Golda Meir, Levi Eshkol and Pinhas Sapir were alarmed at the growing influence of these young men who had no Labourist credentials and were able to act independently of the party base. Thus they sided with Lavon when he demanded exoneration for his part in the Egyptian fiasco from Ben-Gurion. Ben-Gurion refused, arguing that it was not his place to make such a declaration and furthermore refused to accept a Cabinet Committee report that asserted Lavon's innocence. That Ben-Gurion privately thought Lavon guilty was not the point; he was more concerned that the Cabinet had taken upon itself a task which rightfully fell to a Court of Law, thus asserting the rights of the political establishment over the due processes of the state. His response was to hand in his own resignation, and to cripple his party by dividing it and establishing his own *Tseirim*-led *Rafi* party.

The Lavon Affair suggested the extent to which Ben-Gurion and his chosen heirs had moved away from the ideals of, and commitments to, the party on whose ticket they had claimed their political power. This was viewed as evidence of the subordination of democratic politics and the notion of the state as the manifestation of electoral choice to the all-powerful state itself, the helm of which was firmly under the control of Ben-Gurion and his personal protégés. The man himself would have fiercely denied that he considered his own role to be so critical. Moshe Dayan recounts how, following Ben-Gurion's resignation, the Central Committee of the *Mapai* Party drafted a resolution that, without him, *Mapai* would refuse to form a new government. Dayan refused to support the resolution, arguing that:

'Ninety-nine percent of my pro-Ben-Gurionism is not pro the person of Ben-Gurion, but for the identification of Ben-Gurion with the state. The state takes precedence over all, even over Ben-Gurion.' When Ben-Gurion learned of his words four years later, he was reportedly delighted, saying: 'He is a wise fellow. How could the others say that without Ben-Gurion we shall not form a government? Ben-Gurion is only flesh and blood. It is not the man who is important – he passes from the scene. It is his path that is important – and that goes on.'[44]

In sum, *mamlachtiyut* provided the driving force behind institutional and administrative arrangements for the new state in terms of defining the dominant role of the state. It required and facilitated the mobilisation of national resources to support massive immigration and develop the national economy. It proved, however, to have within it the seeds of its own destruction. In order to create a society worthy of democracy, it led to direct confrontation between the state and the institutional framework of democracy, i.e. the primacy of elected and representative government over the bureaucracy. The actual and philosophical processes of immigrant absorption created a two-tiered Jewish society imbued with festering ethnic resentments. Expedient political compromises intended to unify the people around a common identity papered over fundamental contradictions between the multiple visions of what the Jewish state should look like. As Lavon argued, the state and statism were in danger of becoming ends in themselves, entirely replacing voluntaristic activity with state compulsion and eroding the efficacy of democratic institutions.

The problems associated with reconciling the creation of a national identity around which the population could homogenise, with democracy, found expression particularly in the treatment of the non-Jewish population. Despite the Zionist leadership's efforts to precipitate an evacuation of the country's Arab population during the military campaign, the conclusion of the war saw 156,000 Arabs remaining in the new state. The democratic values that were supposed to act as the norms for the new state required that they be afforded citizenship, with equal rights as the Jewish population. Yet two problems arose, one practical and the other essentially philosophical but with practical dimensions. Security considerations led political leaders to assume that the Arab minority represented an internal threat. Thus their status and conditions had to be circumscribed to prevent them from subverting the state. For the immediate term, military rule was imposed over areas with Arab majority populations (officially in 1950 although it came into effect in 1948). Arabs could be arrested, detained, prevented from moving freely, and otherwise effectively controlled without recourse to legal protection. A vast amount of Arab-owned land was either declared 'closed' or was expropriated by the state, for redistribution among the Jewish population as part of the 'inalienable Jewish patrimony'. Freedom of speech, protest and political organisation were curtailed, and the Arab population was actively prevented from communicating with other Arab political forces outside the state. Formal and informal discrimination was actively practised in government policies towards education, expenditure, employment and economic development, with priority always going towards developing the Jewish infrastructure and Jewish opportunities, even at the cost of provision for the Arab population. The dilemma was how to preserve democratic meaning in the institutions and policies of a state which was intended to be Jewish but which included a significant non-Jewish population. In the end, Israel has in practical terms become what has been described as an 'ethno-democracy' – a political entity that observes full democratic practices for the ethnic majority of the population but only partial democracy for the rest.

The question of how to deal with the Arabs naturally arose with regard to foreign as well as domestic policy. Here too, Ben-Gurion's preferred strategies met with challenges from within the ranks of his own, as well as other, political parties. He believed that the Arabs would never accept a negotiated peace and that peace had to be forced on them via Israeli military superiority and a pro-active, pre-emptive defence policy. His opponents, led principally by Moshe Sharett – another of the state's founding fathers – argued instead for concentrated diplomatic efforts and a rejection of what he believed to be military adventurism that could only antagonise the Arab states further. In the early years of statehood it was Ben-Gurion's line that ultimately won out, with the virtues of direct action over diplomacy having apparently been proved in the manner of the establishment of the state itself. The differences between Ben-Gurion and Sharett revolved around, but were by no means confined to, this issue. Sharett was in many ways the principal defender of the *Mapai* party, of its internal democracy and of its commitments to socialism and social democracy, all of which he believed were threatened by Ben-Gurion's charismatic but nonetheless often dogmatic approach. The two leaders clashed frequently and with increasing intensity but, until the Lavon Affair ripped the party apart in the 1950s, the impact of their arguments upon national politics was contained within what was effectively an 'élite cartel'.[45] The leadership of the *Mapai* party, under Ben-Gurion's direction, maintained the illusion of ideological and political consensus as far as possible, limiting disagreements to an inner circle of veteran *yishuv* party activists in order to prevent disunity and fragmentation at the grass-roots level. Recent research, however, has led to the unravelling of this portrayal and an understanding of how, once Sharett had been removed from the scene through ill-health, official and unofficial historiographers alike perpetuated the mythology by all but erasing Sharett from accounts of the period. Despite have played a major role in pre-state politics and having been Israel's second Prime Minister, he has been allocated a relatively minor role in official histories, frequently being portrayed as a weak figure whose miscalculations and foreign policy moderacy directly encouraged Egyptian belligerency and Palestinian *fedayeen* raids. In reality, however, Sharett was largely responsible for the crystallisation of a moderate as opposed to the hawkish line within the *Mapai* party. He fought to reconcile Israel with the *diaspora*, whom Ben-Gurion despised for both their failure to immigrate to Israel and for what he said was their cultural and political poverty. He advocated policies that would appease rather than aggravate the international community. He opposed the expulsion of Arab citizens, sought compensation for them for lost lands, and was prepared to consider a Palestinian entity in the West Bank – all positions that were anathema to Ben-Gurion and the *Tseirim*. This was not simply a clash of political personalities or policies – it represented a more fundamental struggle for the soul of the state. But while the party élite, contrary to the popular history, were bitterly divided over these issues, the prevailing political practices ensured that the disputes were shrouded in secrecy, were confined to senior party structures, and were not allowed to disrupt the processes of nation or state-building.

Ben-Gurion's legacy has been an enduring one. The projection of a national consensus, the domination of the state over other political actors, and the hegemony exercised over decision-making by a largely *Ashkanazim* élite remain features of Israeli politics today. However, the fabric of Israeli society has evolved beyond the confines of the pioneering state, and the cracks in the edifice created by Ben-Gurion are not only beginning to show but to determine increasingly the political landscape of the Jewish state.

Notes

1 See, for example, Bernard Reich and Gershon Kieval, *Israel: Land of Tradition and Conflict* (Boulder, Co: Westview, 1993).

2 'And I have also established my covenant with them, to give them the land of Canaan, the land of their pilgrimage, wherein they were strangers' (Exod. 6:4).

3 An excellent example of this may be found in Martin Gilbert, *The Dent Atlas of the Arab-Israeli Conflict: The Complete History of the Struggle and Efforts to Resolve It* (London: Orion Publishing, 1993 edn). The book begins with a map of the Jews of Palestine Before the Arab Conquest 1000 BC–636 AD. The legend on the first states: 'For more than one thousand six hundred years the Jews formed the main settled population of Palestine. Although often conquered – by Assyrians, Babylonians, Persians, Greeks, Egyptians and Romans – they remained until the Roman conquest the predominant people of the land, with long periods of independence.' The following two maps are dedicated to describing the subsequent extent of the Jewish presence until 1914, and their persecution by invading Christian and Muslim armies. No mention is made of the settlement and indigenisation of non-Jewish populations and Arabs are only mentioned in the context of their violent resistance to Jewish settlement in the nineteenth and twentieth centuries.

4 Henry Cattan, *The Palestine Question* (London: Croom Helm, 1988). One of the strongest advocates of this line is the controversial French writer, Roger Garaudy, who has argued that 'Far from being the first "occupiers" of Palestine, the Hebrews were but one component among many others in the mixture of peoples in the "fertile crescent". They have no grounds for claiming

an exceptional place in this long history. Political Zionism engages in a systematic manipulation and misrepresentation of the facts when, in Israeli schoolbooks as in propaganda for the outside world, it retains as significant for the history of Palestine only those few moments when the Hebrews played a certain role.' Roger Garaudy, *The Case of Israel* (London: Shorouk International, 1983), pp. 35–6.

5 Keith Whitelam, *The Invention of Ancient Israel* (London: Routledge, 1997), p. 1. Also Michael Rice, *False Inheritance* (London: KPI, 1994), pp. 109–26.

6 See, for example, the writings and speeches of Eugen Dühring in Germany, Karl Lüger in Austria or Edouard Drumont in France.

7 Nachman Syrkin, *Die Judenfrage und der Sozialistische Judenstaat*. See *Essays in Socialist Zionism* (New York, 1935).

8 A.W. Kayyali, *Zionism, Imperialism and Racism* (London: Croom Helm, 1979), p. 9.

9 The Sykes–Picot Agreement of 1916.

10 For example, *Chovevei Zion* (Lovers of Zion), a Russian Zionist group established in the 1970s, led by Leon Pinsker and dedicated to settling the Land of Israel, or the *Bilu* (a biblical acrostic for 'House of Jacob – Let Us Go'). This was established in 1882 in Kharkov by middle-class university students, many of whom subsequently abandoned their studies to depart for the Land of Israel and establish a progressive model agricultural colony. The remainder stayed in Russia, recruiting new *Bilu* members for emigration.

11 See, for example, S.N. Eisenstadt, *Israeli Society* (New York: Basic Books, 1967), or Dan Horowitz and Moshe Lissak's *Origins of the Israeli Polity: Palestine Under the Mandate* (Chicago: University of Chicago Press, 1978).

12 Michael Shalev, *Labour and the Political Economy in Israel* (Oxford: OUP, 1992), pp. 13–14.

13 Arthur Koestler, *Promise and Fulfilment* (London: Papermac, 1983 edn), pp. 24–5.

14 Ibid., p. 27.

15 Theodor Herzl, *The Jewish State: An Attempt at a Modern Solution* (London: Rita Searl, 1946).

16 Theodor Herzl in his address to the First Zionist Congress in A. W. Kayyali, op. cit.

17 Quoted in Kodsey and Lobel, *The Arab World and Israel* (London: Monthly Review Press, 1970), p. 119.

18 Quoted in Alan Taylor, *The Zionist Mind: The Origins and Development of Zionist Thought* (Beirut: Institute for Palestine Studies, 1974).

19 Arghiri Emmanuel, 'White Settler-Colonialism and the Myth of Investment Imperialism', *New Left Review*, No. 73 (May–June 1973). Also in Hamza Alavi and Theodor Shanin (eds), *Sociology of Developing Societies* (London: Macmillan, 1985), pp. 88–108.

20 Maxime Rodinson, *Israel: A Colonial Settler State* (New York: Monad, 1973).

21 Samih Farsoun, 'Settler Colonialism and Herrenvolk Democracy' in R. Stevens and A. Elmissiri (eds), *Israel and South Africa: The Progression of a Relationship* (New York: North American Inc, 1977). Uri Davis, *Israel: An Apartheid State* (London: Zed Books, 1987). CAABU, *Israel and South Africa: Zionism and Apartheid* (London, CAABU, 1986). R. Locke and A. Stewart, *Bantustan Gaza* (London: Zed Books, 1985). R. Stevens, 'Israel and South Africa: A Comparative Study in Racism and Settler Colonialism' in A. W. Kayyali (ed), *Zionism, Imperialism and Racism* (London: Croom Helm, 1979). G. Jabbour, *Settler Colonialism in Southern Africa and the Middle East* (Khartoum: Khartoum University Press, 1970). Baruch Kimmerling, *Zionism and Territory* (Berkeley, California: University of California, 1983).

22 Elia Zureik, *The Palestinian in Israel: A Study in Internal Colonialism* (London: Routledge & Kegan Paul, 1979).

23 A. Ehrlich, 'Israel: Conflict, War and Social Change' in C. Creichton and M. Shaw (eds), *The Sociology of War and Peace* (New York: Sheridan, 1987). Shlomo Swirski, 'Comments on the Historical Sociology of the Yishuv Period', *Notebooks for Research and Critique* 2 (1979).

24 See, for example, Gershon Shafir, 'Zionism and Colonialism: A Comparative Aproach' in Ilan Pappé, *The Israel/Palestine Question: Rewriting Histories* (London: Routledge, 1999), pp. 81–96.

25 Ilan Pappé, 'Introduction' in Ilan Pappé, ibid., p. 5.

26 There had in fact been a subversive campaign against the British by the Stern Gang throughout the Second World War.

27 The holocaust has itself been the subject of a body of revisionist historiography, the credibility of which is highly contested. While orthodox historians have claimed that as many as six million Jews were deliberately exterminated in the concentration camps, so-called 'holocaust deniers' have questioned the figures, the intentions and the methods of annihilation. The overwhelming body of evidence supports the orthodox claims that Jewish civilian fatalities resulting from a deliberate policy of extermination numbered several millions.

28 See particularly the various works of Walid Khalidi in this regard. Also David Hirst, *The Gun and the Olive Branch* (London: Faber and Faber, 1977).

29 This point is made in Avi Shlaim, 'The Debate about 1948' in Ilan Pappé, op. cit., pp. 171–92.

30 The principal 'revisionist historiographers' concerned were Simha Flapan (*The Birth of Israel: Myths and Realities*), Benny Morris (*The Birth of the Palestinian Refugee Problem, 1947–49*), Ilan Pappé (*Britain and the Arab-Israeli Conflict, 1948–51*), Avi Shlaim (*Collusion Across the Jordan: King Abdullah, the Zionist Movement and the Partition of Palestine*).

31 Shabtai Teveth, 'The New Historians', *Ha'aretz*, 7, 14, 21 April and 19 May 1989.

32 Efraim Karsh, *Fabricating Israeli History* (London: Frank Cass, 1997).

33 Ethan Bronner, 'New Grade School Texts for History Replace Myths with Facts', *The New York Times*, 14 August 1999.

34 David Ben-Gurion, *Israel: Years of Challenge* (London: Anthony Blond Ltd, 1964), p. 53.

35 Alan Dowty, 'Israel's First Fifty Years', *Current History*, Vol. 97, No. 615 (January 1998), pp. 26–7.

36 Israel Kolatt, 'Ben-Gurion: Image and Reality' in Ronald W. Zweig (ed), *David Ben-Gurion: Politics and Leadership* (London, 1991), p. 19.

37 Eliezer Don-Yehiya, 'Political Religion in a New State: Ben-Gurion's *Mamlachtiut*' in S. Ilan Troen and Noah Lucas, *Israel: The First Decade of Independence* (New York: Suny, 1995).

38 Israel T. Naamani, *Israel: A Profile* (London: Pall Mall Press, 1972), p. 84.

39 In 1949 and 1950, for example, disturbances broke out when the government was accused by the religious parties of coercing new Yemeni immigrants into secular schools.

40 A term used and justified by Eliezer Don-Yehiya, 'Political Religion in a New State: Ben-Gurion's *Mamlachtiut*' in S. Ilan Troen and Noah Lucas, op. cit.

41 Knesset Minutes, Vol. 8, 1102, 14 February 1951. Quoted in G.N. Giladi, *Discord in Zion* (London: Scorpion Publishing, 1990), p. 197.

42 559 such children 'disappeared' in the early 1950s and it was only in the 1990s that full details of their abduction were released by the authorities.

43 Quoted in 'Peres: Living in a Dangerous Era', *Jerusalem Post*, 30 August 1960, p. 1.

44 Moshe Dayan, *Story of My Life: Moshe Dayan* (London: Sphere Books, 1976), pp. 287–8.
45 Gabriel Sheffer, 'Sharett's "Line", Struggles and Legacy', in S. Ilan Troen and Noah Lucas (eds) op. cit., pp. 143–69.

2 Political structures and social processes

Introduction

The development of Israel's democratic structures and institutions has been shaped by the coterminous demands of ensuring the external security of the Jewish State while cohering disparate elements of the Jewish people into a collective whole under the aegis of competing Zionist ideologies. The main cleavages that now define the political landscape in Israel – communal divisions between *Ashkenazi* Jews and those of an Oriental *Mizrachi* background, religious dissonance between the *Haredim* (Ultra-Orthodox Jews) and the main body of secular Israelis, the continued marginalisation of Israel's Arab minority – stem in no small part from ongoing debates within Israeli society over the very nature of Zionism itself and how an Israeli identity is therefore to be defined. Moreover, the very idea of a state being both Jewish and democratic is seen by some to be a contradiction in terms, the apparent ethno-religious basis of what it means to be an Israeli being antithetical to the idea of nationality and citizenship grounded in territorial affinity and cultural pluralism. In this regard, the term 'ethnocracy' is seen by some as providing a more accurate template in any assessment of state–society relations in Israel.[1]

These observations notwithstanding, Israel, with a present population of 6.3 million, does possess a vibrant democratic tradition whose origins pre-date both British rule over Mandate Palestine in the inter-war period and the founding of the State in May 1948. Universal adult suffrage, freely contested elections, the independence of the judiciary and press, freedom of assembly and association, have, at least within Israel's pre-1967 borders, come to define the political system. Moreover, since the 1970s, the gradual demise of 'statism' as the main organising principle of the economic and social structures in Israel has allowed civil society to flourish, with associations and groups allied to a myriad of causes and persuasions now defining Israel's political and social landscape.[2]

However turbulent the domestic discourse of Israeli politics, the external animus surrounding the existence of a Jewish State in a predominantly Arab and Muslim Middle East has inevitably shaped Israel's democratic tradition.

Avner Yaniv has observed that democracy and national security are perceived often as polar opposites. Democracy, a political value that emphasises the rights of the individual, sits uneasily with the state-centric demands of national security.[3] That they have managed to coexist in Israel, particularly in the period 1949 to 1967, has been due in no small measure to the efficacy of the political tradition inherited from the *yishuv*, the pre-state Jewish community in Palestine. Moreover, the immediate strategic threat Israel faced in a hostile Arab world held in abeyance ideological debates over territory to be claimed as part of a Jewish sovereign state. It is ironic that Israel's military victory in the June 1967 war, while removing the existential threat to Israel, witnessed a revival of these divisive debates. Israel's domination of the physical and political space in the West Bank and Gaza Strip has not only appeared incongruent with democratic values, but exposed deep rifts in a society adapting to rapid social, economic, and political change. Israel's very collective identity – its Jewishness – has now become a contested issue.

Israel's political system: the legislature and executive

The main contours of Israel's political system have – with the exception of direct elections for the office of Prime Minister – remained relatively constant since the foundation of the state. Israel's 'Declaration of Independence' of 14 May 1948 openly embraced 'full social and political equality for all its citizens, without distinction of religion, race, or sex; will guarantee freedom of religion, conscience, education and culture', although the demands of internal political cohesion denied the introduction of a written constitution enshrining such lofty ideals.[4] What has emerged is a series of what have been termed 'fundamental' or 'Basic Laws' which over time are meant to evolve into a fully fledged state constitution. Thus, basic laws, such as the Law of Return passed by the *Knesset* in 1950, defined an incremental approach to codifying and regulating political and social relations within the newborn state. The Law of Return remains central to the external identity of Israel as a Jewish State, conferring as it does the right of Israeli citizenship upon all Jews who make *aliyah* (emigrate) to the State of Israel. While the political structures and electoral procedures came to be enshrined in a series of basic laws, defining the *internal* character of the Jewish state and, in particular, the exact balance to be struck between religious and secular identities, remained in suspended animation.

Direct elections to a *Knesset* comprising a single chamber legislature of some 120 members are held every four years, with the leader of the party or bloc securing the most votes being asked by the state President – for the most part a non-political post – to form a viable government. The electoral system continues to be one based upon a pure system of proportional representation with the whole of the electorate treated as one single constituency. Until 1992, parties or blocs required only 1 per cent of the popular vote for a

Knesset member to be elected. This low threshold has allowed for a proliferation of parties to compete in any election, parties who have often been
representative of only a narrow slice of the electorate and whose party
platform was directed more towards a parochial rather than a national
agenda. This has been the case, though not exclusively so, with religious
parties representing the *Haredim*.[5] Even with the raising of the threshold to
1.5 per cent of the popular vote to gain a single *Knesset* seat in 1992 the
demographic increase of the *Haredim* in relation to the more static population growth among secular Israelis has allowed religious parties political
leverage incongruent with the actual size of their support base, particularly
when bargaining for positions within a coalition cabinet. Accordingly, the
portfolios of education, religious affairs, and the interior ministry came to
be prized cabinet positions among religious parties, since they allowed the
propagation and inculcation of their particular values throughout Israeli
society.[6]

Such concessions are deemed essential by the dominant party or political
grouping aiming to forge a viable government. Indeed, since the foundation
of the state, no single party or party bloc has ever been able to form a
government independent of the support of smaller parties. All governments
have been based upon coalition, a position that often leads to friction in
cabinet where policy objectives of the Prime Minister and his or her party
can conflict with the agenda of a coalition partner. Thus, for example, the
decision by former Prime Minister Yitzhak Shamir, under intense pressure
from Washington, for Israel to participate in the Madrid peace talks of
October 1991, led directly to the resignation of two junior coalition partners,
Tehiya (Revival) and *Moledet* (Motherland) who, on ideological grounds
alone, opposed any form of territorial compromise with the Arabs. The
result was the fall of the Shamir coalition government and the subsequent
election of a Labour-led coalition government under Yitzhak Rabin in May
1992.

As laudable as proportional representation claims to be in reflecting the
diverse nature of political opinion in Israel, once a coalition cabinet is
formed, real power remains the gift of the executive. The *Knesset* is reduced
to little more than a talking shop with the opposition parties unable to wield
much influence over the scope and pace of legislation. As Yossi Beilin noted,
'The *Knesset* at most can voice an opinion through its members, but has no
power of decision.'[7] The exact powers that can be placed at the disposal of a
Prime Minister have never been enshrined in law. Rather, a Basic Law
merely defines the position of Prime Minister as 'head of government',
with little reference to the type or scope of relationships that such an office
should have with Cabinet colleagues. In practice, the exercise of power and
influence is heavily dependent upon the matrix of personal relationships that
a prime minister establishes and develops with immediate colleagues. As
such, the position of prime minister has been described as being that of
'first among equals', a position of influence that has allowed strong prime

ministers to set the government agenda and instruct cabinet colleagues to adopt specific positions, particularly on issues surrounding foreign policy or national security that they might otherwise oppose.[8]

From the mid-1980s onwards, however, the increasingly fragmentary nature of Israel's political scene resulted in a series of unstable coalition governments that reached a crisis in March 1990. In attempting to form a viable government both the Labour Alignment on the centre left and the *Likud* bloc on the right became hostage to what Ehud Sprinzak and Larry Diamond called the 'political blackmail and extortion by small extremist parties', as well as 'open political bribery', in their attempts to attract enough support in the *Knesset* to form a government.[9] This crisis of governance, let alone government, propelled the passing of a bill through the *Knesset* on 18 March 1992 that allowed for the direct election of a prime minister independent of the more partisan vote for individual political parties. The new electoral law, known as *The Basic Law: The Government*, actually represented a much diluted proposal for electoral reform, a proposal that had originally included provision for the adoption of a written secular constitution. Resistance from religious factions within the *Knesset*, whose very power rested upon maintenance of the *status quo*, meant that reform remained limited to the empowerment of the executive branch of government. The system, adopted and applied for the first time in the May 1996 general election, allowed for individual votes to be cast by the electorate for Prime Minister and for the party or bloc of their choice. This electoral reform, a conflation of both parliamentary and presidential systems of government, was based on the belief that by enjoying a majority mandate delivered by the electorate, a prime minister elect would be 'free from the extortionist demands of small parties and individual MKs (Knesset Members) when forming his cabinet'.[10] The first beneficiary for the direct election of Prime Minister was Binyamin Netanyahu, who defeated his rival Shimon Peres by less than 1 per cent of votes cast in the national elections of May 1996.

It is perhaps premature to pass judgement on whether the direct election to the office of prime minister has, in fact, resulted in more stable government coalitions founded upon broad popular consent. The fact that a prime minister is now elected by a majority vote has not necessarily circumvented the often bitter process of cohering a stable government. Moreover, the experience of both the 1996 and 1999 elections suggests that the presidential-parliamentary system is leading towards a more factionalised *Knesset* as voters can now vote for a particular candidate for prime minister while casting their votes for an entirely different party. As the experiences of 1996 and 1999 suggest, the true beneficiaries of this dual system of voting have been the religious parties and those parties representing particular constituencies such as recent immigrants or *olim* from the former Soviet Union. The growing influence of such parties has come at the expense of the two main political alignments that, in one guise or another, dominated

Israeli politics from the founding of the state through to the late 1980s: the Labour alignment and the *Likud* bloc.

Political parties and the politics of ethnicity

The genealogy of Israel's party system can be traced back to the foundation of the British mandate in Palestine in 1922. Under British tutelage, two distinct political blocs emerged within the *yishuv* that shaped the contours of Israel's political map. These blocs can broadly be categorised as Labour Zionists and Revisionist or nationalist Zionists, with a small number of religious parties, most notably the *Mafdal* or National Religious Party (NRP), located in between. More recently, the emergence of single issue parties identified with a clear ethnic base have come to erode the broad base of electoral support that the main political parties within these blocs could previously command.

It should be stated that the boundaries between these blocs have never been immutable. The history of Israeli politics has been littered with examples of factions within each party or bloc splitting away from their parent bloc, either to cross ideological, political or religious lines or to align themselves with the opposition party or government of the day. Such was the fate of the Democratic Party for Change (DMC), formed by Yigal Yadin, a former general and archaeologist, on the eve of the 1977 *Knesset* elections. Yadin placed electoral reform at the centre of the DMC's political manifesto. Coming at a time of growing public disenchantment with a ruling Labour alignment struggling to cope with high inflation, a series of corruption scandals, and bitter infighting among the party hierarchy, the DMC did enough to win 12 *Knesset* seats. Moreover, Yadin captured enough disaffected votes from the Labour alignment to enable the election for the first time in Israel's history of a *Likud*-led coalition government under Menachem Begin. While becoming part of Begin's coalition government, Yadin was unable to further his party goal of electoral reform. Indeed, in a cabinet dominated by the charismatic Begin, Yadin proved weak and ineffectual. This resulted in the DMC splitting into a number of factions, a process that led Yadin to dissolve the party prior to the 1981 elections.[11]

Socialist Zionism

From the formal establishment of the British Mandate in Palestine in 1922 through to the 1977 general election, politics in both the pre-state *yishuv* and in Israel came to be dominated by parties associated with what has been termed Socialist or Labour Zionism. Socialist Zionism, or more precisely its ethos, came to dominate the four main pillars upon which Israel as a state came to be founded: the *kibbutzim*, the *Haganah* from which the Israel Defence Forces (IDF) emerged in 1948, the Jewish Agency, and the *Histadrut*. Nonetheless, Socialist Zionism did not develop into a single homogeneous party. Rather, it comprised a mosaic of several centre-left and Marxist parties that came to be dominated by *Mapai*, a democratic socialist party led by David Ben-Gurion. In 1968, it merged with *Achdut Ha'Avoda* (Unity of Labour), a party whose leadership came predominantly from the *kibbutz* movement, and the *Rafi* party, who had originally split away from *Mapai* in the late 1950s after accusing the party elite of placing narrow party interests over those of the state.[12] The result was the establishment of the Labour party whose grip on government was strengthened further by the inclusion of the left-wing *Mapam* party. While keeping their independent identity, *Mapam* was included in what became known as the *Ma'arakh* or Labour Alignment. It was this broad labour coalition that dominated the Israeli political scene from 1948 to 1977, and acted as an equal partner in a series of national unity governments between 1984 and 1990. Under the leadership of Yitzhak Rabin, the Labour Alignment won a striking victory in 1992 that allowed for the formation of a centre-left coalition government independent of reliance on either right-wing or religious parties.

It was this government which explicitly recognised the Palestine Liberation Organisation (PLO) as the sole legitimate representative of the Palestinian people and signed the Oslo Accords of September 1993 which implicitly recognised the need to exchange land for peace as the basis for any resolution to the Israel/Palestine conflict. More recently, the Labour Alignment reinvented itself under the stewardship of Ehud Barak when it joined with *Gesher* – itself a refugee from the *Likud* bloc – and the doveish religious group *Meimad* (Dimension) to form *Yisrael Ahad* (One Israel) to contest the May 1999 national election. Barak consciously sought to move the new bloc beyond its traditional support base among Israelis of predominantly *Ashkenazim* background to appeal both to new and recent immigrants from the former Soviet Union, as well as the Oriental Jews. Indeed, Barak apologised publicly to the Oriental Jewish citizens for the ills that, however unwittingly, his party in its previous incarnations had visited upon them during the years it held the monopoly of political power in Israel. It was also an implicit recognition of how important ethnicity had been in determining political fortunes in the Jewish State.[13]

The politics of ethnicity

The character, norms and values on which the state of Israel was founded were very much the reflection of an *Ashkenazim* élite associated closely with Socialist Zionism. While all Israelis were accorded civil and political rights, the more prosaic issue surrounding equality of opportunity soon became entwined in the thorny issue of ethnicity. Between 1948 and 1962, the majority of those Jews who migrated to Israel were Oriental (also referred to as *Mizrachim* or *Sephardim*), Jews from North Africa, the Middle East, and south Asia. Unlike their *Ashkenazi* counterparts, the majority of the Oriental Jews were identified with low levels of education, socially conservative, and noted for their observance of Jewish tradition and rituals. Such a profile ensured that most of them entered Israel's economy as labourers and artisans, and had to mould their beliefs and expectations to the model of *mamlachtiyut* developed by an *Ashkenazim* élite. Accordingly, statism and democracy in the period 1948 to 1967 came to be bought at the expense of cultural alienation. This alienation took time to manifest itself in the electoral process, but its roots can be traced in part to deliberate policies of discrimination imposed by organisations such as the Jewish Agency. Journalist and historian Tom Segev uncovered material detailing housing policies weighted in favour of *Ashkenazim olim* over their Oriental counterparts. Housing units earmarked for the Oriental Jews were often reallocated to European Jewish immigrants, consigning Oriental Jews to the privations of *ma'aborot* (transit camps) for longer periods.[14] While the first generation of Oriental Jews continued to proffer support to the ruling *Mapai*-led coalition governments, future generations were not to prove so amenable. The stain of ethnic prejudice levelled against the embodiment of the *Ashkenazi* élite – the Labour Party and its cohorts in government-run and funded institutions – was seen as placing a glass ceiling on the upward mobility of the Orientals. In voting overwhelmingly for a Likud-led coalition government in May 1977, the latter hoped to shatter that ceiling.[15] Whatever their social and political desires, their electoral power changed Israel's political order, and was a major factor in diluting the consensus surrounding statism as conceived by the founding fathers of the Jewish State.

Revisionist Zionism

The antecedent of the *Likud* was the Revisionist Zionist movement. It was born out of a dispute over the tactics and strategy employed by the leadership of the *yishuv* – a leadership dominated by those closely affiliated to Labour Zionism – towards the British Mandate authorities. Whereas Ben-Gurion had been willing to accept decisions imposed by the British mandate authorities over restrictions on Jewish settlement in Palestine, regarding them as temporary setbacks, others within the broad Zionist movement rejected such restrictions as anathema to the historical legitimacy of the right of Jews to settle throughout *Eretz Yisrael* (The Land of Israel) that included the East Bank of the Jordan. Revisionist Zionists, first under the leadership of Zeev Jabotinsky, and later Menachem Begin, took great exception to the *yishuv* policy of failing to define the borders of a Jewish state. Revisionist Zionists opposed the UN partition plan of 1947, accepted by Ben-Gurion, and continued to agitate for the unity of *Eretz Yisrael*, territory that included at that time the East Bank of the river Jordan.[16]

Between 1948 and 1967 such debates were, for the most part, held in abeyance. The emphasis placed initially by Ben-Gurion on *mamlachtiyut* determined political discourse in Israel until the aftermath of the June 1967 war. As such, the *Herut* (Freedom) party, the main manifestation of the pre-state Revisionist Zionist movement, remained in political exile. In part this was due to the bitterness between Ben-Gurion and Menachem Begin. As the former leader of the *Irgun Zvai Leumi* (the National Military Organisation), Begin had been responsible for a number of terrorist actions aimed at undermining the British mandate that Ben-Gurion believed were detrimental to the wider interests of the *yishuv*.[17] In 1952, such bitterness was compounded still further by Begin's decision to oppose reparation payments by the Federal Republic of Germany to Israel for those Jews murdered in the Nazi holocaust. The reparations, totalling some 3 billion German marks, proved vital to Israel's economic well-being at a time of severe economic austerity. *Herut* only received a more popular legitimacy when, in 1965, it merged with Liberals who, while supportive of the Zionist endeavour, eschewed the central economic planning associated with Socialist Zionism. The resulting alliance, called *Gahal*, placed Begin in the political mainstream, allowing him to attract increasing numbers of Oriental Jews disillusioned with Socialist Zionism. With his inclusion in a government of National Unity formed on the eve of the June 1967 war, the stigma of political pariah was removed from Begin.

The eclectic profile of *Gahal* had a broad appeal. Many middle-class voters were attracted by its platform of free market liberalism which contrasted sharply with the traditional emphasis placed upon public sector industries and central planning by *Ma'arakh*. When combined with its increasing popularity among a working class comprising a disproportionately high number of Oriental Jews, the origins of the *mahapach* – the electoral upheaval of 1977 – can be discerned. In the summer of 1973, the *Likud* (Unity) bloc was formed which brought together *Gahal* with smaller parties such as the State List, the Free Centre, and activists in the Land of Israel Movement. While its economic policies remained decidedly libertarian, a refusal to countenance the return of the territories captured and occupied by Israel following the June 1967 war remained the core around which the bloc came to be organised. For some, this refusal was grounded in the strategic necessity to protect Israel proper in the absence of formal peace treaties with its Arab neighbours. For others, however, the historical claim to *Eretz Yisrael* remained the determining feature of the *Likud* political platform. While Israeli settlements in the Occupied Territories were condoned by successive Labour administrations following the June 1967 war, the election of the *Likud* under Menachem Begin witnessed a mass expansion of settlement activity throughout the West Bank and Gaza Strip. Settlements established under the Labour administrations had been agricultural *moshavim* and *kibbutzim* located in areas of low Palestinian population density. The trend after 1977, however, was for settlements to be established close to areas with a high Palestinian population density. By the end of the 1990s, some of these settlements had in fact developed into major conurbations with some, such as Ariel, boasting a Jewish population of some 30,000 people.

Preserving the territorial integrity of *Eretz Yisrael* on ideological grounds has also remained central to the platforms of smaller parties such as *Tehiya* (Revival), *Tsomet* (Crossroads) and *Moledet* (Motherland). *Tehiya* emerged in 1979 following the decision of the Begin government to return the Sinai peninsula to Egypt and offer a limited form of autonomy to the Palestinians as part of the Camp David Accords. *Tsomet* itself emerged from a split within *Tehiya* which resulted in the former Israeli Chief of Staff, Rafael Eitan, establishing his own party. *Tsomet* argued strongly for the retention of the Occupied Territories on strategic grounds alone but it was notable also for the strength of its anti-clerical agenda, a platform that appealed to those Israelis disillusioned with the growing hold exercised by religious parties over everyday life in Israel. *Moledet* proved to be the most extreme of the parties, its platform based openly upon the 'transfer' of Palestinians from the Occupied Territories. Land for peace, the standard formula touted regularly as the diplomatic palliative to the Arab–Israeli conflict, remained simply beyond the pale to these parties. As such, the signing of the Oslo Accords in 1993 undermined their very *raison d'être*. This crisis in ideological identity has been reflected in the fortunes of these parties since the 1992 elections. *Tehiya* was disbanded, *Tsomet* merged with the *Likud* bloc in 1996, while *Moledet* formed part of a new party, *Ha'Ihud Ha'Leumi* (National Union) in the May 1999 national elections which secured four seats.

The declining appeal of the ideology of *Eretz Yisrael* is, however, perhaps best demonstrated by the declining fortunes of the *Likud* bloc. In 1999 its percentage of the popular votes cast in the May election was 14.1 per cent, compared to 25.8 per cent in the 1996 election. This was only 1.1 per cent more than votes cast for *Shas* and resulted in *Likud* winning nineteen seats.[18]

The religious parties

'Israelis have lost but the Jews have won.' This aphorism, heard widely among secular Jews in Israel, encapsulates the resentment felt by many sections of Israeli society over the manipulation of the state's political structures by the non-Zionist *Haredim* or Ultra-Orthodox Jews. This resentment is based upon the fact that the *Haredim* remain ambivalent at best towards Zionism. Parochial concessions sought by the non-Zionist *Haredi* parties in the *Knesset* – long a feature of Israel's political scene – in exchange for supporting the wider platform of the coalition government of the day, have allowed minority interests to influence cultural patterns in Israel that impinge increasingly on the normative choices and preferences of many Israelis. Deferments from military service, the absence of civil marriage or divorce, public subsidies for *yeshivot* (religious seminaries), the virtual absence of public transport on *Shabbat*, and more recently, the insistence that conversions to Judaism carried out under Reform and Conservative

Judaism remain invalid – a position that has created bitter divisions with diaspora Jewry – are some of the more ostentatious examples of the power accrued by *Haredi* parties under Israel's electoral system. Such power over questions of identity and authenticity has led some commentators to warn openly of the emergence of a *kulturkampf* in Israeli society.[19]

The role that religion should play in defining the essence of the Jewish state has always remained a vexed issue, not least because of the antipathy demonstrated historically by the *Haredim* towards the whole Zionist enterprise. Zionism was regarded as an apostasy, a denial of the central tenet of Judaism that only the coming of the *Meshiach* could reunite the Jews with *Eretz Yisrael*. Throughout this process, Jews were expected to remain passive. Indeed, the main debates among the *Haredim* have centred on whether Jews could hasten the day of redemption through leading pious lives, or, alternatively, that this day has already been pre-ordained. As such, Zionism among the *Haredim* has been viewed as a usurpation of God's will, denying as it does the eschatological reasoning in Ultra-Orthodox thinking.

Such a world view was the antithesis of the *Mafdal* (National Religious Party or NRP). The origins of the NRP date back to 1902 when a group of Rabbis, sympathetic with the ideals of Zionism but not to the dominant secular ethos it placed upon education, founded the *Mercaz Ruchani* or spiritual centre. The idea behind this faction and its later reincarnations such as *Hapoel Mizrachi* was to provide political representation to working-class pious Jews who believed that Judaism should inform the process of state-creation. *Mafdal* emerged as a distinct political party by 1957. Aside from its insistence upon a separate religious education system, its working-class origins among Orthodox voters allowed it to coexist with all Israeli governments until 1967. With the capture of 'Judea, Samaria and Gaza' in June 1967, the *Mafdal* came to be associated with a religious nationalism that opposed any territorial compromise over land deemed to be the divine property of the Jewish people. Zionism, even as a secular creed, was seen as the beginning of the messianic process. In this sense, the founders of the state were, according to Rabbis associated with the *Mafdal*, the unknowing tools of God who were hastening the redemptive process by settling once more in *Eretz Yisrael*.[20] As such, the ideological sympathies of *Mafdal* came to be more closely attuned to those on the right of Israel's political spectrum, its constituency now encompassing Jewish settlers on the West Bank.

Differences of religious interpretation aside, both the *Mafdal* and *Haredi* parties have been a distinct feature of Israel's political landscape since the founding of the state. The very absence of a written constitution derived in large part from the lack of open consensus over the role religion should be allowed to play in determining the character of the newborn state. In drafting Israel's Declaration of Independence, many secular Zionists wanted all reference to God removed; Israel was to be a Jewish state in ethnic terms only. Given the need to avoid damaging splits among Jews as a polity, a compromise was condoned in which the declaration made reference to 'having faith in the Rock of Israel', a term taken from the *Torah*, and widely interpreted as refering to the presence of God.[21] What emerged through the dominant period of *mamlachtiyut* is what Alan Dowty has termed the 'ingrained habits of coexistence according to formulas that fit neither side's worldview squarely, but also did not unduly impinge on either group's basic way of life'.[22]

In the May 1999 Israeli general election, religious parties won 27 seats in the 120 seat *Knesset*. In forming his coalition government, Ehud Barak, as with previous Israeli premiers, remained sensitive to the needs of the two main non-Zionist parties, *Shas* and United Torah Judasim, who were both offered portfolios of varying seniority in the ministries of housing, religion, interior and social affairs. The allocation of such portfolios to religious parties reflected an entrenched political pattern in the formation of Israeli cabinets. From the perspective of the religious parties, such positions of power have always allowed for the defence of their particular values while exercising influence over the normative base of Israeli society out of all proportion to their constituent base. Examples of this abound: the absolute hegemony exercised by Rabbinical courts over marriage and divorce sits uneasily for many Israelis with the Declaration of Independence and its stated desire to ensure complete political and social rights for all of Israel's citizens, irrespective of religion, race or gender. The fact that none of the Basic Laws passed to date defines Israel as a democratic country, distinguishing clearly between the boundaries to be inhabited by the spiritual and the temporal, remains a point of bitter controversy for many Israelis.[23]

The influence of the religious parties has only increased in recent years. Demographic shifts, coupled with the declining hegemony exercised by the mainstream secular parties in Israel, have propelled religious parties to a position of political influence hitherto unknown. *Shas* (*Shomere Torah* – Torah Observing Sephardim), the main non-Zionist Orthodox party associated closely with *Mizrachim*, provides the most striking example. Formed in 1984 following a split within the ranks of *Agudat Yisrael* over the paucity of *Mizrachim* in the upper echelons of the party, *Shas* has continued to attract increased support away from mainstream political parties such as the *Likud* as well as the *Mafdal*. From winning four *Knesset* seats in 1984, *Shas* increased its representation in the *Knesset* over the next three elections, winning ten seats, one more than the *Mafdal*, in the 1996 election. Following the 1999 election, *Shas* won seventeen *Knesset* seats, twelve more than the *Mafdal* and only two fewer than the *Likud* bloc. The impact upon the *Mafdal* has been profound. The party now places greater emphasis upon consulting the rabbis of the Council of Torah Sages, previously the bastion of rabbinical authority of the non-Zionist *Haredim*, alongside greater adherence to the *Halachic* rulings of the Chief Rabbinate in the formulation and presentation of policy positions.[24]

On the question of the Occupied Territories, opinion among the *Haredim* appears set against further territorial concessions by Israel. They have come to accept the religious-nationalist argument of the *Mafdal* that retrenchment from the territories has not resulted in *pikuakh nefesh* – a concept derived from *Halacha* that allows the revocation of sanctified laws or edicts if it results in the saving of human life. As such, the signing of the Oslo Accords in September 1993 has only encouraged violence against Israelis in the form of suicide bombings. Further withdrawal from the Occupied Territories should therefore be discontinued. This is not to suggest that the *Haredim* *per se* have altered their position towards Zionism as antithetical to the realisation of the messianic era. Rather it is to suggest that greater Judaic piety on the part of the NRP, coupled with the belief that Arabs remain bent on destroying the Jews, has created a synergy of political interest among and between members of these two distinct religious traditions that would appear inimical to support for the peace process.[25]

Work conducted recently by two academics from Tel-Aviv University, Yochanan Peres and Efraim Yuchtman-Yaar, highlighted the extent to which Israel's democratic institutions and credentials remain anathema to the worldview of the *Haredim*. A poll conducted among 1,250 Israeli adults reflected the divergent attitudes held by the Ultra-Orthodox towards democracy. While 10 per cent of the poll sample were *Haredim* – twice their actual percentage of the Israeli population – 64 per cent of these believed unequivocally that Israel should be turned into a theocracy dominated by the strictures of *Halacha*. By comparison, 73 per cent of secular Israelis polled preferred democratic government, irrespective of whether particular policies pursued by the executive concurred with their own. In addition, some three-quarters of the *Haredim* polled believed that Israel belonged to the Jews only, a finding of some concern given the theological ambivalence demonstrated previously by the Ultra-Orthodox towards the Zionist enterprise. Noting that the structure of Israel's democratic system protected their rights, Peres and Yuchtman-Yaar concluded that Ultra-Orthodox support for the democratic process remained finite and dependent on the system's ability to propagate their particular interests.[26]

Some observers have argued that it is inaccurate to posit such a clear divide between the secular and religious communities in Israel. Charles Liebman, a leading authority on religion and politics in Israel, has estimated that up to 40 per cent of Israelis prefer the epithet *dati* (traditional), a term that encompasses a benign attitude towards Jewish rituals, but falls short of strict observance of Judaism as a religion.[27] Yet it cannot be denied that intercommunal relations in some areas are subject to strain. Secular Israelis have become increasingly resentful over what they perceive as petty restrictions imposed upon them. Public entertainments remain circumscribed on *Shabbat* and religious holidays, while much needed relief roads have in the past been delayed because the *Haredim* claim sanctity over land they believe to have been ancient burial sites. Indeed, the resentment is amplified by the fact that the spiritual leaders of the *Haredim* live outside of Israel and in some cases have never visited the Jewish State. Occasionally, such tensions have turned violent. In December 1997, clashes broke out between secular residents of Neve Rotem, a predominantly secular neighbourhood in the town of Pardes Hannah in northern Israel, and the *Haredim* from the adjacent district of Remez. Similarly, comments made by the spiritual leader of *Shas*, Rabbi Ovadia Yosef, that the apex of Israel's independent judicial system, the High Court of Justice, 'has no part in Israel's patrimony', and that its judges were 'worse than the laws of the goyim', a disparaging term for non-Jews, again suggests that many *Haredim* remain circumspect over conferring legitimacy on temporal structures that uphold Jewish ethnicity, rather than Judaic piety, as *the* motif of identity in the Jewish State.[28]

The Israeli Arabs

The question of identity has been most vexed for the Israeli Arabs. The very term 'Israeli Arabs' is a value judgement since, as Michael Wolffsohn has argued, it confers legitimacy on a sovereign entity called Israel in which a substantial Arab minority lives.[29] Other terms used are Palestinian Israelis, Palestinian citizens of Israel, or Palestinians in Israel, descriptions that are seen by some to question the legality of the State of Israel by laying clear stress on a Palestinian identity as the key communal reference point. Whatever description is used, the total number of Israeli Arabs – Sunni Muslims, Christians and Druze combined – totalled 1,074,200 people in 1997, some 18.2 per cent of the Israeli population.[30] Such population figures are remarkable if one considers that following the foundation of the State of Israel, only 160,000 Palestinians remained within the borders of the new Jewish State in 1949.[31] The majority are Sunni Muslim, with Christians constituting around 13 per cent of the Israeli Arab population. Small Circassian and Druze communities account for the rest. The high birthrate among Israeli Arabs is viewed with some alarm by many Jewish Israelis. On demographic grounds alone it is estimated that Arab and Jewish populations will reach a rough parity by around 2015. Thereafter, it has been estimated that 100,000 Jewish immigrants will be required each year to maintain any form of demographic parity.[32] Such statistics cut to the very core of Israel's viability as a Jewish state. The dramatic increase in the population is explained by a number of factors linked to a changed socio-economic milieu, and access to a modern state health service that reduced dramatically levels of infant mortality. By the 1960s the average Sunni Muslim family had ten children. By the 1990s this figure had dropped to five children per household, though this was still double the figure of 2.5 children given for Israeli Jewish households.[33]

Institutional discrimination against Israeli Arabs, however, proved a less savoury feature of *mamlachtiyut*, the legacy of which still haunts intercommunal relations between Jews and Arabs in Israel to this day. While given Israeli citizenship and the right to vote in parliamentary elections, from 1949 until 1966 Israeli Arabs remained subject to a number of draconian measures enshrined in military law. In part, these measures were a direct legacy of the war itself, the suspicion being that those Arabs who had not fled their towns and villages in the 1948 war represented something of a fifth column whose loyalties lay clearly with Israel's erstwhile foes. These measures included severe restrictions on travel between districts as well as land confiscation justified on the grounds of security and enshrined in the Absentee Property Law. This law allowed for the confiscation of territory by the Israeli state from those Arabs who had not been present on their land physically when the State of Israel came into being. Use of the Absentee Property Law and other legislation, some of it inherited from the British Mandate and even the Ottoman empire, had by 1970 resulted in over 300,000 acres of Arab land being expropriated by the state.[34] These measures had a particular impact on the Israeli Arab communities of the Galilee region, disrupting community-wide resistance to the establishment of settlements built to absorb new immigrants. These policies also changed the economic base of the Israeli Arabs. With increased land confiscation, many began to seek work in urban areas, resulting in 61 per cent of the wage-earning population working in Israel's larger towns and cities by the beginning of 1980, a stark contrast to the figure of 26 per cent in 1948.[35]

Such factors brought with them a degree of social mobilization that had been hitherto unknown. In the first decade of the State of Israel, the traditional *hamula* system – the old patriarchal system of extended families – continued to dominate the scope of political activity among Israeli Arabs. As Mark Tessler and Audra Grant note, this dominance suited Israel well since Israeli Arabs '[R]emained tied to local interests and identities, wedded to a particularism that discouraged any possibility of collective action on behalf of the [Israeli] Arab population in general'.[36] Up until 1966 Israeli Arabs developed under a system of benign neglect. It is undeniable that, in comparison with neighbouring Arab states as well as the Palestinians living in the West Bank and Gaza, Israeli Arabs began to enjoy a higher standard of living. But equally, Israeli Arabs suffered from consistent discrimination in funding for education, public housing construction and employment opportunities relative to their Israeli Jewish counterparts. Political activity, where allowed, tended to be carefully controlled by existing state institutions and parties. The *Histadrut* established a separate membership list for Israeli Arabs, a practice that was replicated by the main Zionist parties whose establishment of separate Arab party lists was driven more by the need to capture Israeli Arab votes as by any altruistic desire on their part to better the lot of the Israeli Arabs. As Tessler and Grant have argued, such political participation 'represented mechanisms of control as much as vehicles of integration'.[37]

When independent associations were formed from within the Israeli Arab community, punitive measures were introduced to forestall any expression of political identity that challenged Israeli sovereignty over territory. *Al-Ard* (The Land), an Israeli Arab organisation inspired by Nasserism, met such a fate. Established in 1959, its leaders were subject immediately to military harassment and/or detention and banned from participating in national elections. Land designated as closed military zones was often transferred to the Israeli Land Authority, thereby allowing its later development into *kibbutzim, moshavim* or development towns.[38] In 1966 military rule was lifted finally from Israeli Arabs but the issue of land continued to provoke political controversy. On 30 March 1976, in violent clashes between Israeli police and Israeli Arabs protesting against further land expropriations in the Galilee, several demonstrators were killed. Since this bloody event, their deaths have been remembered each year by Israeli Arabs on 'Land Day'. For those who participate, it is a reminder of the discrimination that they have suffered since 1948, as well as a clarion call for full equality – enshrined in Israel's own Declaration of Independence – with their Jewish counterparts.

Since 1966, the political fortunes of Israeli Arabs have been tied closely to parties of the centre-left of Israel's political spectrum. These have, for the most part, been secular in their orientation, the most notable being the non-Zionist *Rakah* or Israeli Communist Party, which in its modern-day variant, *Hadash*, won three *Knesset* seats in the 1999 election. Yet this represents a decline in the fortunes of a party that once received half the Arab vote in the 1977 election. Several reasons explain this erosion of their electoral support. First, the emergence of the Israeli right after 1977 and the expansion of settlement activity in the Occupied Territories saw increasing numbers of Israeli Arabs transferring their allegiance to the Labour alignment. This was seen as the most judicious use of their vote in countering the increasingly right-wing drift of the Israeli electorate. Secondly, the decline and subsequent collapse of the Soviet Union did much to disabuse Israeli Arabs of the veracity surrounding the ideological platform on which the *Rakah* had been based. Third, Israeli Arabs had come increasingly to identify with the Palestinian cause, a process that found expression in the foundation of the bi-national Progressive List for Peace in 1984 and, perhaps more importantly, the Arab Democratic Party (ADP) of Abdul Wahab Daroushe. Daroushe, originally a Labour *Knesset* member, had left the party in 1988 in protest at the brutal measures employed by the Israel Defence Forces (IDF) on the orders of Yitzhak Rabin – then a Labour defence minister in a government of national unity – to crush the Palestinian *Intifada*. It is perhaps ironic that Rabin came to rely heavily on the votes of the ADP in securing *Knesset* support in favour of the Oslo Accords between 1992 and 1995.

Israeli Arabs continue to face latent discrimination in the allocation of central government resources. Levels of unemployment are higher than among Jewish Israelis, though the Labour coalition government elected in 1992 authorised a three-fold increase in financial contributions to Arab local councils. While such largesse was welcomed, the suspicion remained that this increase represented official concern over the emergence of a relatively new political movement among many Israeli Arabs: the Islamist move-ment.[39] The genesis of the movement lies partly in the growing efficacy of political Islam in the Middle East throughout the 1980s, as well as the more immediate impact that the *Intifada* had upon the politicization of many Israeli Arabs. Its growing political clout, particularly in local politics, wit-nessed vociferous debates within the movement and among Israeli politi-cians over the exact relationship to be struck between the Islamist movement and the Jewish State. On the one hand, Islamists, having won control of several Arab town councils in 1989, faced increased pressure from many Israeli Arabs to run as a single party for the *Knesset*. This proposition was opposed by others in the movement on the grounds that this would be seen as acquiescence to, if not conferring outright legitimacy upon, a sovereign Jewish entity in Palestine. Equally, many Israelis called for the movement to be banned, given this self-same ambivalence towards the right of Israel to exist.

To date the issue has been somewhat fudged by both sides. In the 1999 election, Islamists stood as part of the ADP, securing five seats. It thus sidestepped the ire of its more militant support and managed to avoid provoking the wrath of right-wing parties in the *Knesset* while still securing some national influence, however circumscribed. Support for the Islamist movement does not extend, however, to predominantly Christian and Druze communities, particularly those located in and around the Galilee region in northern Israel. Its political appeal, based in part on a more pious adherence to the central tenets of the Sunni tradition, remains inimical to their cultural and religious outlook. Aside from such cleavages, Israeli Arabs have made enormous progress in social and economic terms since the *nakhba* – the disaster – of 1948. The suspicion remains, however, that the rights that they have accrued thus far have been gained through sufferance rather than through due legal entitlement. In this regard, their often ambivalent status among Jewish Israelis reflects both continued uncertainties regarding Israel's wider relationship with the Palestinians, as well as the continued difficulties inherent in Israel's claim to be both a Jewish state and a demo-cratic state.[40]

Israel, democracy and the Occupied Territories

In restrospect, Israel's military triumph in the June 1967 war proved *the* watershed in the democratic development of the Jewish State. The scale of Israel's victory – the destruction of three Arab armies and the capture of the West Bank of the River Jordan, the Sinai peninsula, the Gaza Strip and the Golan Heights – gave Israelis a territorial depth undreamed of previously. It also, at a stroke, placed nearly two million Palestinians under Israeli occupation, a situation that sharpened the distinction between the democratic tradition and the Jewish character of the State of Israel.

The strategic significance of the war was, however, but one part of the equation. Capture of the West Bank and East Jerusalem with its sacred Jewish sites witnessed the recrudescence of religious-nationalism in Israel, and with it the reaffirmation of a particularly Jewish identity that claimed a covenantal relationship between the 'People, God and the promised land'. David Hall-Cathala has argued that the June 1967 war marked the nadir of the universal values on which the Jewish State was founded, and with it the idea of an Israeli identity grounded firmly in secular, democratic values.[41] While such thinking within the *Knesset* came to be associated with the NRP, it was an extra-parliamentary movement formed in the aftermath of the October 1973 war, *Gush Emunim* (Bloc of the Faithful), that acted, with government approval, as the spearhead of the settlement drive.[42] As one-time member of *Gush Emunim*, Rabbi Yehuda Amital, stated:

> This [Religious-Nationalist] Zionism has not come to solve the Jewish problem by the establishment of a Jewish State but is used, instead, by the High Providence as a tool in order to move and advance Israel towards its redemption. Its intrinsic direction is not the normalisation of the people of Israel in order to become a nation like all nations, but to become a holy people, a people of living God, whose basis is in Jerusalem and a king's temple is its centre.[43]

The subtext of such thinking was clear; *Gush Emunim* regarded the State of Israel as constituting the means to achieve the sanctity of the Land of Israel – *Eretz Yisrael* – thus hastening the messianic era, rather than an end in itself. At its base level, *Gush Emunim* was placing the sovereignty of God as enshrined in sacred Judaic texts above that of the State. This was a clear rejection of the secular ethos of the state and a challenge to the centrality of *mamlachtiyut* that had determined the scope of political discourse in Israel until 1967. As long as successive Israeli governments – albeit on security grounds – continued to value Jewish control over the territories captured in the June 1967 war, a clear symbiosis of objectives existed with the religious-nationalists. Nonetheless, by regarding the land as central to the redemptive process of the Jewish people, it followed that any attempt to trade land for peace usurped the will of God, and therefore would be opposed. This position brought to the fore the centrality of *Halacha* – the doctrine, rules, and laws of Judaism – that through the centuries had been codified into juridical law. Constant reference to *Halacha* now defined the claims of *Gush Emunim* to Israel's continued control of the West Bank and Gaza Strip.[44]

The approbation heaped upon the maintenance and expansion of Jewish sovereignty by settler organisations such as *Gush Emunim* exposed a clear bifurcation in Israel's claims to be both a Jewish and a democratic state.

Whatever physical security the Occupied Territories bought, the price in terms of Israel's democratic culture proved high. Sudden ingestion of the Palestinians of the West Bank and Gaza, who by 1995 numbered 1,816,000, would clearly dilute the Jewish Zionist character of the state if (a) Israel annexed formally the Occupied Territories and/or (b) conferred Israeli citizenship upon its inhabitants.[45] Squaring this particular circle has dominated Israel's approach towards the Palestinians and, in turn, impacted upon its relations with the wider Arab world. Between 1967 and 1993, Israel denied political representation to the Palestinians beyond local elections which disenfranchised those affiliated to the PLO, thereby refusing to acknowledge the potency and resilience of Palestinian nationalism. This contrasted starkly with the settlers who continued to enjoy full political rights in the Jewish State, despite constituting at most 5 per cent of the population of the territories. Moreover, Israel, while refusing to annex outright 'Judea, Samaria and Gaza', imposed draconian restrictions upon most aspects of Palestinian daily life using a blend of rules and regulations that were often the legal legacy of Ottoman rule and the British mandate. These included, among others, land expropriations and, where deemed necessary, the destruction of property. Though justified in terms of ensuring strategic security against the Arab world, all Israeli governments recognised the importance of the occupation in providing a captive economic market on their doorstep, a cheap pool of labour, as well as strategic depth.[46] Such factors – aside from the ideo-theological determinism of the settlers – proved crucial in assuaging more normative concerns among many Israelis over the corrosive impact that occupation was having upon Israel's democratic credentials.[47]

The most visible example of how extreme religious-nationalism has challenged Israel's democratic structures, however, remains the assassination of Israeli premier Yitzhak Rabin on 4 November 1995 at the hands of a young religious-nationalist, Yigal Amir. Rabin's signing of the Oslo Accords in September 1993, an agreement which in effect condoned the formula of land for peace, remained anathema to a political community whose ideo-theological agenda remained mortgaged to a particularist interpretation of Judaic texts regarding the sanctity of *Eretz Yisrael*.

Civil society in Israel

If June 1967 witnessed the emergence of religious-nationalism as a powerful force in Israeli politics, it also served to focus attention on the development of civil society in the Jewish State. According to Augustus Richard Norton, the application of the term 'civil society' in the region has come to be associated with groups and organisations that are inclusive in their membership, and act as a 'buffer between the state and citizen'.[48] The development of an Israeli civil society does not fit this definition easily; *Gush Emunim* in particular proved an apposite example of an organisation located within Israel's civil society quite willing to support the state – providing it continued to facilitate the process of redemption – but according to its own rationale, remaining exclusionary in terms of membership. A more sophisticated framework for understanding the development of civil society in Israel is to be found in the work of Yael Yishai.

According to Yishai, the development of civil society in Israel has passed through two main phases and has now entered a third. The first phase, lasting from 1948 through to the late 1960s, was defined by 'active inclusion'. For Yishai, this was an era in which a popular consensus surrounding the aims, objectives and symbols of the state was manifest. It represented, in short, the apogee of *mamlachtiyut*. As Yishai notes:

> The ideological contours of the state were consolidated by a densely compact and institutionalised party structure. Although parties played a vital role in the provision of social services, they did not compete with the state but buttressed its power. The blurring of the line between state and parties turned the citizen into a subject, totally relying on authoritative agencies. Parties were insulated from public pressure owing to a highly structured organisational configuration. Their primacy circumscribed the emergence of an independent civil society.[49]

As evidence of this, Yishai cites the all-embracing power of the *Histadrut* trade union federation whose influence extended beyond representation of workers to include the establishment and control of economic and political institutions deemed vital to securing the state, thereby underpinning national sovereignty. In short, the demands of *mamlachtiyut* denied the political space required for alternative avenues of civic expression to fully develop.

The second phase identified by Yishai embraces the period from the late 1960s to the early 1980s. This is defined as 'active exclusion', a period in which increased national prosperity, coupled with increased rates of *aliyah*, led to an erosion of the monopoly exercised by the state over political discourse and organisation. Moreover, debates over the future of the territories captured and occupied by Israel in June 1967 moved beyond the confines of national security. Concern over the debilitating impact of the occupation on Israel's political culture and social fabric came to be expressed by peace groups within Israel. The most prominent of these remains *Shalom Achshav* (Peace Now), formed in 1978 by a group of reserve officers in the IDF, concerned at Prime Minister Begin's reluctance to invest the critical dialogue with President Sadat of Egypt with sufficient urgency. In an open letter sent to the Israeli premier, 350 soldiers, many of them decorated veterans of Israel's wars, declared that: 'A government policy that will encourage the continuation of control over approximately one million Arabs may damage the Jewish, democratic nature of the State and make it difficult for us to identify with the State of Israel.'[50] Long regarded as the 'sacred cow' of Israeli state and society, the outspoken attack by a sizeable caucus of Israel's officer corps was evidence of the challenge to the apolitical status of the IDF, the very symbol of *mamlachtiyut*. Located at opposite ends of the political spectrum, the emergence of Peace Now and *Gush Emunim* nonetheless highlighted particularities in the development of Israel's civil society that defied accepted norms surrounding its definition, particularly with regard to the study of politics in the Middle East.

Other groups that emerged during this period were more focused upon socio-economic issues and what they perceived to be the blatant ethnic discrimination of the dominant state and party structures. Organisations such as the *Panterim Shehorim* (Black Panthers), comprising young *Mizrachim*, mainly of Moroccan origin, dissatisfied with the socio-economic imbalance within Israel, did much to raise public awareness over social deprivation in the early 1970s.[51] Other organisations that emerged included a strong feminist movement that questioned the patriarchal structure of much of Israeli society, while other groups emerged from within the Israeli Arab community. The response of the state was to introduce legislation that sought to circumscribe the activities of such groups, hence the term 'active exclusion'. The Law of Associations, passed in 1981, required all associations to register with the Ministry of the Interior. Freedom of association and assembly remained enshrined in law, but the Law of Associations allowed the state to deny registration to those organisations deemed harmful to state security or the greater public good, thereby allowing the state to place clearly defined limits upon associational activity. As Yishai noted, this law 'reflects both the custodial role of the state and its ability to penetrate widely into society'.[52]

The third phase identified by Yishai and termed 'passive exclusion' stretches from the mid-1980s through to the present. Again, development of Israel's civil society is linked in part to continued economic growth, it being noted that accelerated privatisation resulted in the decline of the paternalistic leverage the government could exercise over key sectors of the economy. The result of such deregulation witnessed unprecedented growth rates in the Israeli economy and an average per capita income of nearly $17,000 by 1995. Such material well-being has unleashed the genie of consumerism among the Israeli public, but it has also seen Israelis become more actively engaged in associations and groups that have national, regional and international agendas. The 1990s have witnessed a plethora of environmental groups exerting pressure upon local councils and central government over poor urban planning and waste disposal. Interest groups with close links to political parties continue to operate across the spectrum of national political opinion. While Peace Now and *Gush Emunim* remain the most apposite examples, others include Women in Black and *Dor Shalom* who support broadly the idea of exchanging land for peace, while Women in Green and *Dor Ha'ameshech* remain their polar opposites in arguing against any Israeli territorial retrenchment in the Occupied Territories. All new organisations are still required to register under the Law of Associations but, as Yishai notes, the increase in independent organisations since the early 1980s has been enormous. In 1982, when the law was enacted, 3,000 associations were registered. By 1995, that number had risen to 23,000 covering the diverse range of human activity, ranging from taxi driver associations through to gay rights activist groups.

Such a broad range of activity has inevitably led to the decline of old statist institutions such as the *Histadrut*, which has seen its monopoly as *the* representative of blue-collar workers eroded throughout Israel as wage structures have come increasingly to be negotiated directly between employers and employees. Even the IDF, long regarded as the 'sacred cow' of the state, has not been immune from pressure groups. The monopoly that the IDF high command has exercised over matters of national security has, over the last decade, begun to fragment as increasing numbers of Israelis have come to question received wisdoms surrounding the use of the military. Parents have become more involved in the welfare of their sons and daughters conscripted to serve in the IDF. The most visible of these movements is *Ha'arba Imahud* – the Four Mothers Movement.[53] Established by women concerned at the mounting toll among Israeli soldiers serving in the last active 'hot front' of the Arab-Israeli war – the war in south Lebanon against *Hizb'allah* guerrillas – the Four Mothers did much to persuade a critical mass of Israelis to support a unilateral withdrawal from south Lebanon. Such was the appeal of the Four Mothers that Ehud Barak, previously identified as a hawk with regard to this limited if bloody conflict, made an Israeli withdrawal a central feature of his campaign in the May 1999 Israeli general election. Indeed, the success of the movement highlights the changing dynamic of civil–military relations in Israel today.

Civil–military relations

In the half century since the founding of the State of Israel no institution has played such a dominant role as the *Zvah Haganah Le Israel*: the Israel Defence Forces. It has been and remains the ultimate guarantor of Israel's security and is today the most powerful military force and certainly the most technologically advanced in the Middle East. But equally, the IDF was conceived by Ben-Gurion as a means to integrate a largely disparate population into a collective whole, thereby allowing a homogeneous national identity to be moulded. In this respect, the role assigned to the IDF reached beyond the immediate demands of national security to embrace the social, educational as well as economic development of the State. Mass conscription – currently three years for men and two years for women, as well as compulsory reserve duty – *milluim* – of one month per year for all fit males to the age of 55, have been the distinguishing features of a military system designed to extract optimal use from Israel's human resources. As such, the military in Israel has been the ultimate expression of *mamlachtiyut*. It has been a system that has served Israel well.

Meeting the needs of defence has, however, imposed a heavy burden upon the citizens of Israel. Aside from the human cost – some 18,000 Israelis killed in six Arab–Israeli wars as well as in a host of border clashes – defence expenditures on a per capita basis and as a percentage of gross national product have been consistently high. In the aftermath of the October 1973 war, defence spending consumed one-third of all government expenditure. The central role that the IDF has played in the development of the state has led to an intense debate over civil–military relations in the Jewish State. Israel has been described as a 'democratic garrison state' or as having a 'civilianised military'. The fact that so many Israelis have an intimate association with the military is seen as a bulwark against militarism undermining democratic government, since, to paraphrase a much used cliché, Israelis are soldiers who happen to be on eleven months leave a year. Civilian control over the military is set down in *Basic Law – the Army*. Less than a page in length, the law states in section 2a that 'The army is subject to the authority of the government', and in section 3b that 'The Chief of Staff is subject to the authority of the government and subordinate to the defence minister'.[54]

The legal basis of civilian control over the military would not, however, be enough by itself to secure the state against the threat of militarism. Rather, as Moshe Lissak has argued, the actual structure of Israel's military doctrine is inimical to the process of militarisation since it eschews the capture and occupation of territory solely for the purposes of ideological aggrandisement or expansion. Moreover, the IDF does not dominate the process of social interaction in Israel, thereby imposing its norms and values. As Lissak argues, Israeli society has 'powerful countercultures', themselves expressions of a vibrant democratic tradition, that act as alternative avenues of social and cultural expression.[55]

This view has been challenged. Uri Ben-Eliezer claims that Israel is a militaristic society, since 'the term is useful for describing a tendency to view organized violence and wars as a legitimate means of solving particular problems. It is a social and cultural phenomenon that usually has political consequences for the decision-making process. . . it is a belief in the inevitability of war'.[56] The argument put forward by Ben-Eliezer is that the existential demands of securing Israel against the animus of the Arab world has resulted in defence becoming the organising principle of Israeli society, and that it is a nation in arms. Accordingly, militarism in Israel has actually allowed a democratic tradition to flourish since the energies of the military have been directed towards ensuring external security, a goal achieved with the full support of the civilian establishment. As such, there is little need for usurpation of civil government since society is already militarised. Ben-Eliezer points to the concept of 'parachuting' as evidence of how the military have come to penetrate the civilian sphere of government. Israel is replete with former high-ranking officers who, having completed their military service, enter the political arena. Former Premier Ehud Barak is the most notable example, having served previously as Israel's Chief of Staff as well as being Israel's most decorated soldier. Others in the past have included Yitzhak Rabin, Yigal Yadin, Moshe Dayan, Rafael Eitan, Shlomo Lahat, Ezer Weizmann and Mattiyahu Peled.

Some Israelis have cast doubt on the effectiveness of these former generals in public life, the argument being that the certainties of a disciplined environment are poor preparation for the uncertainties of political life where compromise and bargaining inform everyday discourse. Gabriel Sheffer has argued that former military officers have often had a detrimental impact upon public policy by sustaining a 'huge defence budget, a considerable portion of which is earmarked to sustain the layers of fat that now cover the defence establishment'.[57] Sheffer argues further that the predominance of former military officers in politics prevents a fully fledged liberal democracy flourishing in Israel since they infuse the formulation of public and foreign policy with 'one of military belligerency'. While the performance of former generals in politics might not match their illustrious military careers, it is worth noting that army officers have supported parties and causes across the whole range of Israel's political spectrum. Indeed, the tendency in the past has been for generals to be more doveish in their views regarding territorial retrenchment and support for Palestinian self-determination than the wider Israeli public.[58]

For Ben-Eliezer, the real threat to democratic government comes from 'praetorianism', defined as 'a situation in which military officers play a predominant political role owing to their actual or threatened use of force'.[59] It is a phenomenon that is directed against the established order particularly when the threshold of external danger is deemed low and, consequently, the prestige of the military falls as the public question the rationale behind continuing high levels of defence expenditure. In the case of Israel, such a scenario is linked to continued progress in the peace process as well as a substantive shift in the social profile of the IDF.

The increasing sophistication of modern weaponry has provoked increased debate in Israel over the continued efficacy of the 'nation in arms'. Given the growing complexity as well as expense of weapon systems, increased calls for a smaller but smarter army have come to punctuate debate about the future of the IDF. The argument put forward is that Israel has to develop a professional army because conscription denies sufficient time to train a critical mass of soldiers to master the demands made by the weapon systems of the future.[60] But if technology provides an impetus to reform the structure of the IDF, another centres on the changing social profile of the IDF officer corps that Ben-Eliezer believes has the potential to nurture *praetorianism*. According to Peretz and Doron, an ethos of secularism marked the development of the officer corps. This was as a result of the disproportionately high number of officers – some 25 per cent – drawn predominantly from the *kibbutzim* and *moshavim*, although the population living on these agricultural collectives has never amounted to more than 8 per cent of Israel's total population.[61] This secular ethos has been challenged by the increasing numbers of officers now drawn from the religious-nationalist community. While religious-nationalists make up some 10 per cent of the Israeli populace, they now provide 40 per cent of the IDF officer corps and tend to do their military service in front-line combat units. Moreover, some 30 per cent of front-line troops now wear a knitted skullcap or *kippah*, a visible mark of affinity with religious-nationalism. Many combine military service with talmudic study in a religious seminary or *hesder yeshiva* where continued reference to *Halacha* in determining political positions continues to shape the territorial agenda of the religious-nationalist community. Ben-Eliezer argues that this development is disturbing, not least because it questions the ability of a significant part of the military to abide by the laws of the state over rabbinical injunction. Rulings by an organisation of right-wing rabbis – *Ichud Ha'Rabbanim L'Ma'an Am Yisrael Ve Eretz Yisrael* (Union of Rabbis for the people and land of Israel) – consistently deny the state any legality for uprooting settlements, even if condoned by the majority of Israelis. These rulings are serious because they challenge the national consensus surrounding the apolitical use of the IDF. In their bulletins, *Ichud Ha'Rabbanim* refer to the primary role of the IDF as being the defence of the land rather than the 'state', and call on soldiers to obey their religious conscience, rather than acting on orders, if and when told to expedite the evacuation of settlements.[62]

Cohen argues that such dangers, and by extension, praetorian tendencies among the new emerging officer corps, are exaggerated. The impact of Rabin's assassination, he notes, had a sobering impact upon the national-religious community which has now placed great stress upon the need to avoid *Halachic* injunctions that challenge the apolitical status of the army. Moreover, Cohen argues that the hierarchical structure of the army imposes a discipline upon troops which, irrespective of their individual beliefs or preferences, enforces the authority of legally binding orders.[63] Yet whatever terms one applies to describe the relationship between the IDF and broader Israeli society, it is clear that the military no longer enjoys the uncritical support it once commanded. As the very symbol of *mamlachtiyut*, the IDF has not been immune to broader changes in Israeli society. Indeed, in some respects it has become the mirror image of such changes, as concern over the political loyalties of soldiers holding religious-nationalist sympathies demonstrates.

Conclusion

In their annual report into state security released in July 1998, the Israeli internal security service, *Shabak*, warned of the growing threat of inter-necine violence between Jews should substantive territorial concessions to the Palestinians continue.[64] The very fact that the latent threat of violence has come to define political discourse in Israel says much about the decline in the politics of consensus nurtured by the demands of *mamlachtiyut*. The political *status quo* that formed the basis of statism and allowed for the development of democratic institutions could not, however, remain in a vacuum. Representing a military triumph of staggering proportions, the June 1967 war unleashed debates and tensions within Zionism that remain contrary to a democratic ethos. The irony remains that while encouraging greater political pluralism, the removal of the immediate existential threat to Israel's existence resurrected debates about the scope and nature of the Zionist enterprise that statism had held in abeyance.

To be sure, even during the period 1948 to 1967 Israel's democracy was highly stratified, its dispensation organised along dominant ethnic and political lines. The June 1967 war, coupled with the shifting demographic balance between *Ashkenazim* and Oriental Jews as well as Israeli Arabs, exposed cleavages between the universal aspiration of democratic governance and the reality of denial of those self-same rights implicit in the very act of occupation. This hybrid situation has continued to define the scope of a political debate in Israel, a debate in which locating an exact Israeli identity has become a contested issue. Israel's civil society, in this respect, has not necessarily led to a strengthening of democracy, since its constituent elements remain fragmented over the vexed question of national identity. It would be wrong to suggest that democracy in Israel is in terminal decline. In a region noted for its autocratic leaderships, political debate in Israel remains open, the judiciary independent and the press vociferous in its coverage of political debate. The portents for the long-term future, nonetheless, may not be so sanguine. As this chapter has shown, Israel faces a crucial decision over its very identity. How Israel's institutions deal with this issue will determine its very future.

Notes

1 Oren Yiftachel, 'Israeli Society and Jewish-Palestinian Reconciliation: "Ethocracy" and its Territorial Contradictions', *Middle East Journal*, Vol. 51, No. 4 (Autumn 1997), pp. 506–10.
2 Jillian Schwedler, 'Civil Society and the Study of the Middle East', in Jillian Schwedler (ed), *Toward Civil Society in the Middle East* (London: Lynne Reinner, 1995), p. 5.
3 Avner Yaniv, 'Introduction', in Avner Yaniv (ed), *National Security and Democracy in Israel* (London: Lynne Reinner, 1993), p. 1.

4 For the English translation of Israel's Declaration of Independence see Walter Laquer and Barry Rubin (eds), *The Israel–Arab Reader* (Harmondsworth: Penguin, 1984), pp. 125–8.

5 Such parties have included in the past those dedicated to gender equality, rights for the elderly, as well as environmental issues. See Peretz and Doron, op. cit., p. 73.

6 An example of this occurred in the composition of the government presented to the *Knesset* by Prime Minister Yitzhak Shamir on 11 June 1990. Rabbis Aryeh Deri and Yitzhak Peretz of *Shas* were given the portfolios of Interior Ministry and Absorption Ministry at a time when Israel was faced with the huge problem of *aliyah* from the former Soviet Union. It was claimed that Peretz in particular was not so much bothered with more Jews as with pure Jews, a reference to the concern held by the religious parties over the predominantly secular character of the Soviet Jews. See Clive Jones, *Soviet Jewish Aliyah 1989–92: Impact and Implications for Israel and the Middle East* (London: Frank Cass, 1996), pp. 132–40.

7 Yossi Beilin, *Israel: A Concise Political History* (London: Weidenfeld and Nicolson, 1992), pp. 61–2.

8 Avraham Brichta, 'The New Premier-Parliamentary System in Israel', *The Annals* (AAPSS), No. 555 (January 1998), p. 181.

9 Larry Diamond and Ehud Sprinzak, *Israeli Democracy under Stress* (London: Lynne Reinner, 1993), p. 4.

10 Brichta, op. cit., p. 186.

11 Peretz and Doron, op. cit., pp. 103–4.

12 Ibid., pp. 89–91.

13 Avishai Margalit, 'The Other Israel', *The New York Review of Books*, Vol. XLV, No. 9 (28 May 1998), pp. 30–5.

14 Tom Segev, *The First Israelis* (New York: Free Press, 1986), pp. 132–3. Widespread discontent over poor housing and employment opportunities led to widespread rioting among *Mizrachim* of Moroccan origin in the Haifa suburb of Wadi Salib in the summer of 1959. See Joseph Massad, 'Zionism's Internal Others: Israel and the Oriental Jews', *Journal of Palestine Studies*, Vol. XXV, No. 4 (Summer 1996), pp. 59–61.

15 See Lee E. Dutter, 'Eastern and Western Jews: Ethnic Divisions in Israeli Society', *Middle East Journal*, Vol. 31, No. 4 (Autumn 1977), pp. 451–68. See also Shlomo Swirski, *Israel: The Oriental Majority* (London: Zed Books, 1989), pp. 21–43.

16 For an excellent discussion of Revisionist Zionism see Colin Shindler, *Israel, Likud and the Zionist Dream* (London: I.B. Tauris, 1995).

17 It was not unknown for members of the *Haganah* or the Jewish Agency to pass on information to the British Mandate authorities regarding the activities of the *Irgun*, an act that still provokes much historical controversy in Israel today. See Naomi Shepherd, *Ploughing Sand: British Rule in Palestine 1917–1948* (London: John Murray, 1999), pp. 225–30.

18 Figures provided by James Sorene, Public Affairs Division, Embassy of Israel, London, UK in 'Israeli Election, 17th May 1999 – Results'. http://www.israel-embassy.org.uk/london

19 See for example Ilan Peleg, 'The Peace Process and Israel's Political Kulturkampf', in Ilan Peleg (ed), *The Middle East Peace Process: Interdisciplinary Perspectives* (New York: State University of New York Press, 1998), pp. 247–59; Nadav Shragai, 'Prisoners of their Dreams', *Ha'aretz*, 15 May 1998.

20 Clive Jones, 'Ideo-Theology: Discourse and Dissonance', *Israel Affairs*, Vol. 3, Nos 3 & 4 (Spring/Summer 1997), p. 30.

21 This example of religious compromise was highlighted during the course of a BBC interview with Dr Yehuda Ben-Meir, one-time member of the NRP. Gerald Butt, *God in the Palaces*, BBC Radio 4, 17 January 1993.
22 Dowty, op. cit., p. 29.
23 Shulamit Aloni, 'The Founders were Right', *Ha'aretz*, 23 November 1993. A recent camapign was launched by several Knesset members designed to promote legislation for a new Basic Law: Freedom from Religion. The proposed law would break the current monopoly held by the religious courts in Israel over marriage and divorce. While civil divorce courts in Israel decide on issues such as the division of property and custody of children, couples still have to undergo a religious divorce which includes the act of physically expelling the wife from the court. See the editorial, 'A Civil Option', *Ha'aretz*, 17 June 1998.
24 Yossi Klein Halevi, 'Democracy or Theocracy?', *The Jerusalem Report*, Vol. VIII, No. 23 (19 March 1998), pp. 22–6.
25 See Lili Galili, 'NRP: to the Right and to the East', *Ha'aretz*, 22 Febraury 1998; Shahar Ilan, 'Haredi Jews: out in the Right Field', *Ha'aretz*, 11 March 1998. In the survey quoted by Ilan, no respondents among the *Haredim* asked supported the idea of trading land for peace.
26 For a summary of the findings of Peres and Yuchtman-Yaar see Shahar Ilan, 'Who Needs Democracy?', *Ha'aretz*, 2 June 1998.
27 Liebman, op. cit., pp. 283–4. See also Charles Liebman and Bernaerd Susser, 'Judaism and Jewishness in the Jewish State', *The Annals* (AAPSS), No. 555 (January 1998), pp. 15–25.
28 For the full context of Ovadia's remarks see Ze'ev Segal, 'Shas and the Trampling of Justice', *Ha'aretz*, 8 February 1998.
29 Michael Wolffsohn, *Israel, Polity, Society and Economy 1882–1986* (New Jersey: Humanities Press International, 1987), pp. 155–6.
30 In 1997, the Israeli Central Bureau of Statistics gave the breakdown of Israeli Arabs by religion as follows: Sunni Muslims – 853,000; Christians – 124,700; Druze – 95,600. See www.cbs.gov.il
31 Mark Tessler, *The Israeli–Palestinian Conflict* (Indiana: Indiana University Press, 1994), p. 279.
32 Peretz and Doron, op. cit., p. 56.
33 Ibid., pp. 55–6.
34 Mark Tessler and Audra E. Grant, 'Israel's Arab Citizens: The Continuing Struggle', *The Annals* (AAPSS), No. 555 (January 1998), p. 101.
35 Wolffsohn, op. cit., p. 159.
36 Tessler and Grant, op. cit., p. 100.
37 Ibid., p. 100.
38 Adam Keller, *Terrible Days: Social Divisions and Political Paradoxes in Israel* (Amstelveen: Cyprus, 1987), pp. 89–103.
39 For an analysis of the rise of the Islamist movement among Israel's Arabs see Steve Rodan and Jacob Dallal, 'A Fundamental Gamble', *The Jerusalem Post Magazine*, 19 August 1994, pp. 6–10. See also Raphael Israeli, 'Muslim Fundamentalists as Social Revolutionaries: The Case of Israel', *Terrorism and Political Violence*, Vol. 6, No. 4 (Winter 1994), pp. 417–43.
40 For further information on the Palestinian citizens of Israel, see Nadim N. Rouhana, *Palestinian Citizens in an Ethnic Jewish State* (New Haven: Yale University Press, 1997); Noah Lewin-Epstein and Moshe Semyonov, *The Arab Minority in Israel's Economy* (Boulder, Colorado: Westview Press, 1993); Raja Khalidi, *The Arab Economy in Israel* (London: Croom Helm, 1988); Aziz Haidar, *On the Margins: The Arab Population in the Israeli Economy* (London: Hurst, 1995); and Jacob Landau, *The Arab Minority in Israel 1967–1991* (Oxford: Clarendon Press, 1993).

41 David Hall-Cathala, *The Peace Movement in Israel 1967–87* (London: Macmillan, 1990), pp. 4–5.

42 For a useful collection of essays dealing with *Gush Emunim* see David Newman (ed), *The Impact of Gush Emunim: Politics and Settlement on the West Bank* (London: Croom Helm, 1985).

43 Amital's comments were quoted in Ehud Sprinzak, *The Ascendance of Israel's Radical Right* (Oxford: Oxford University Press, 1991), p. 116. It should be noted that Amital has since renounced his links with *Gush Emunim* and is a founding member of *Meimad* (Dimension), a religious-nationalist movement but one that takes a more benign view towards the issue of territorial compromise.

44 Jones (1997), op. cit, pp. 32–3.

45 For a breakdown of Palestinian population figures see Elia Zureik, *Palestinian Refugees and the Peace Process* (Washington, D.C: Institute for Palestine Studies, 1996), p. 14.

46 Ruth Margolies Beitler, 'The Intifada: Palestinian Adaptation to Israeli Counterinsurgency Tactics', *Terrorism and Political Violence,* Vol. 7, No. 2 (Summer 1995), pp. 55–6.

47 This point is made forcibly by Oren Yiftachel. He argues that the peace process has heightened the socio-economic stratification of Israel along ethnic lines. The middle classes in Israel, usually associated with the *Ashkenazim*, see the peace process as a means to advance their own particular commercial interests by attracting inward investment. *Mizrachim*, on the other hand, have felt excluded from this process and have yet to accrue, at least from their particular standpoint, any economic benefits from the Oslo process. Accordingly, *Mizrachim* have favoured retention of the territories largely on socio-economic grounds, preventing from their perspective a return to being the underclass of Israeli society. Evidence exists that such views became entrenched further by the mass migration of some 800,000 Jews from the former Soviet Union from 1989 onwards, well educated and predominantly of European origin. Many *Mizrachim* feared the demographic usurpation of their hard-won political power and status. See Yiftachel, op cit., pp. 506–10 and Jones (1996), op. cit., pp. 143–8.

48 Augustus Richard Norton, 'The Future of Civil Society in the Middle East', *Middle East Journal,* Vol. 47, No. 2 (1993), p. 211.

49 Yael Yishai, 'Civil Society in Transition: Interest Politics in Israel', *The Annals* (AAPSS), No. 555 (January 1998), p. 149.

50 Hall-Cathala, op. cit., p. 40.

51 Peretz and Gideon, op. cit., pp. 167–8.

52 Yishai, op. cit., p. 155.

53 See the booklet, *The Four Mothers: Leaving Lebanon in Peace* (in English, Nof Yam, Israel 1999). In terms of gender the Four Mothers represents something of a breakthrough in the traditional male-dominated discourse of national security. Men, many of them veterans of Israel's war in Lebanon, have become members of the movement, proclaiming that they are proud to called 'Four Mothers'.

54 See Yehuda Ben-Meir, 'Civil-Military Relations in Israel', in May Chartouni-Dubarry (ed), *Armée et Nation en Israel: Pouvoir Civil, Pouvoir Militaire* (Paris: Institut Français des Relations Internationales, 1999), p. 40.

55 Moshe Lissak, 'The Unique Approach to Military Societal Relations in Israel and its Impact on Foreign and Security Policy', *Davis Occasional Papers No. 62,* The Leonard Davis Institute for International Relations, Hebrew University of Jerusalem, Israel (September 1998), pp. 14–15.

56 Uri Ben-Eliezer, 'Rethinking the Civil-Military Relations Paradigm', *Political Studies,* Vol. 30, No. 3 (June 1997), p. 360.

57 Gabriel Sheffer, 'Time to Get the Military out of Politics', *Ha'aretz,* 13 February 2000.

58 Peretz and Doron, op. cit., pp. 157–8.
59 Ben-Eliezer, op. cit., p. 360.
60 Stuart Cohen, 'Societal Military Relations in Israel', in Ilan Peleg (ed), *The Middle East Peace Process: Interdisciplinary Perspectives* (New York: State University of New York, 1998), pp. 111–12.
61 Peretz and Doron, op. cit., p. 156.
62 See 'Psak Halakhah: The Evacuation of Jews from their Homes in Eretz Yisrael', *Secretariat of Ichud Ha'Rabbanim* (in English), Jerusalem 1997 on http://www.virtual.co.il/orgs/orgs/ichud/evacuate.htm
63 Stuart Cohen, 'The Scroll or the Sword? Dilemmas between Religion and Military Service in Contemporary Israel', in Chartouni-Dubarry (ed), op. cit., pp. 63–7.
64 Ze'ev Schiff, 'Jews could fight Jews, Shin Bet predicts', *Ha'aretz*, 10 July 1998.

3   Trials, triumphs and tigers

Introduction

In the early 1990s, the Israeli economy was being described by many analysts as an emerging *tiger* economy. Rapid growth, diversified exports, a technology-intensive industrial base, a thriving stock market, an extensive liberalisation programme and a per capita GDP comparable to the margins of Western Europe,[1] all fuelled arguments that this was a mature post-industrial economy on the verge of taking off. A slow-down in activity in the mid-1990s was attributed largely (but incorrectly) to the stalling of the Arab–Israeli peace process, but there can be little doubt that the overall performance of the Israeli economy over the past 50 years has been profoundly impressive. The path to economic prosperity has not, however, been smooth. Indeed, Israel's economy has suffered from severe structural weaknesses for most of its life, some of them remaining to this day. The principal reason for this has been that economic policy has always been determined first and foremost according to political objectives. The two most significant imperatives have been the desire to absorb relatively enormous numbers of immigrants while maintaining a standard of living that is high enough to attract and keep those new arrivals, and the need to maintain high levels of defence expenditure to ensure the security of the state. That having been said, economic policy was low on the list of priorities for Israel's politicians until well into the mid-1980s. For the most part, Israeli public debate has been traditionally dominated by security issues. Economics was not on the political agendas of politicians until the crisis that found its expression in terrifying hyper-inflation. Economic concerns have since played a strong role in election outcomes, although prime ministers still tend to 'observe an unstated tradition of lack of interest in economic matters'.[2]

At the regional level Israel stands out from its neighbours to the extent that Arab fear of Israeli economic domination has been a contributing factor to the failure to realise any meaningful comprehensive regional co-operation, let alone integration. Growth of the Zionist economy has been achieved in spite of – one might almost argue because of – the comprehensive boycott imposed by Arab and Muslim states after 1949. Deprived of regional markets, Israel turned westwards to Europe and the United States, developing profound trading, investment and financial aid ties that have served to move Israel rapidly up the industrial ladder. Today Israel has achieved developed nation status and is almost fully integrated into the global economy. Problems remain in the form of an inflated public sector, a legacy of bad public sector debts, a political bias in favour of excessive budgetary spending, incomplete structural reforms and a continuing heavy defence burden. On the whole, however, the long-term outlook is promising regardless of political improvements or failures in the regional environment.

The roots of the economy

The origins of the Israeli economy are usually traced to the pre-state *yishuv*.[3] Before the large-scale waves of immigration began at the end of the nine-teenth century, the Jewish community, known as the 'old settlement' (*Yishuv Ha Yashan*), played only a peripheral role in the Palestinian econ-omy. For the most part, the Jews were engaged in primarily religious activ-ities and were dependent for their survival on charitable donations from the Jewish *diaspora*. There were some efforts to encourage the 'productivisation' of the Jews, notably from European Jewish philanthropists who cultivated agricultural communities, but the majority lived in urban poverty.

Successive waves of Jewish immigration in the late nineteenth and early twentieth centuries brought a rapid increase in the Jewish labour force. The immigrants, whose motivations in settling in Palestine were more diverse than those of their established co-religionists, engaged in new economic activities and developed institutions and modes of interaction to support their collective endeavours.

Rapid population growth provided the primary resource for the Jewish economy, with an increase in the Jewish population from 24,000 in 1882 to 600,000 in 1948. The bulk of this, around 72 per cent, was accounted for by immigration, which fluctuated considerably year by year but which none-theless introduced a steady stream of new manpower and capital to the Jewish economy. The majority of immigrants (84 per cent) were under the age of 44, were literate[4] and had previous experience or training in agricul-ture, crafts, industry or the professions. In the later years of the Mandate, as they arrived from Europe, the immigrants brought substantial amounts of capital with them, which was supplemented with capital transfers via the World Zionist Organisation and other Jewish institutions. These transfers facilitated both imports and investment and the Jewish economy grew cor-respondingly and proportionately much faster than its Palestinian Arab equivalent.[5]

As the waves of immigration grew larger in the 1920s and 1930s, the productive base of the Jewish economy changed. While the early immigrants from Russia and Eastern Europe (the third *aliyah*, 1919–23) had either been farmers themselves or were committed to making a living from the soil, the later immigrants were largely middle-class shopkeepers and artisans who preferred an urban lifestyle. The fourth and fifth *aliyahs* (1924–28 and the 1930s) also brought well-educated German and Austrian Jews who contributed to industrial growth and investment in infrastructure construction. The much publicised and controversial efforts to buy land resulted in Jewish ownership in 1947 of less than 7 per cent of the land of Palestine, and employment and investment were concentrated in urban rather than rural areas. Jewish agriculture nonetheless thrived, particularly due to British support for citrus products in the 1920s and 1930s and demands for mixed food production during the 1939–45 war years.

The majority of Jewish-held land was privately owned but a proportion was bought by the Jewish National Fund (JNF) and leased to Jewish farmers as part of the inalienable Jewish patrimony. It was on such land that the first collectivist farms, the *kibbutzim*, were established. These small-scale operations fused progressive socialist aspirations with a desire for Jewish redemption via a return to labouring on the land. While the *kibbutzim* took collective living to the extreme, the *moshav ovdim* (also known as *moshavim* or workers' co-operatives) allowed farmers to settle on JNF land, buy their equipment, sell their produce and run their communities collectively, while maintaining their own family lives and individual incomes. Although life was harsh and their survival was precarious until well into the 1930s, the *kibbutzim* and *moshavim* assumed immense social importance as vanguards of the utopian way of life, symbolising the social equality and voluntarism to which the growing Jewish community aspired.

Collectivisation also operated in the cities, with collectivist laundries, kitchens and workshops springing up around the country. For the most part, however, industry was – like agriculture – founded on private capital. The single most important Jewish industry was construction – by 1927 as many as 45 per cent of workers in Tel Aviv were employed in the building trade.[6] Jewish companies bid for, and won, contracts for large-scale infrastructure projects such as the construction of power stations from the British. They also established large factories for the production of salt, flour, oil, soap, textiles, stone, cement, lumber, chemicals and other goods. Generally, however, the industrial sector comprised small workshops employing a handful of workers.

The growth of Jewish industrial and agricultural production occurred simultaneously with the development of Jewish political and social institutions that would serve to fuse Jewish economic activity into a distinct entity. The British government, in true colonial fashion, was determined that the occupation of Palestine should not lead to any demands on their own treasury. Efforts to develop the basic services and infrastructure of the country should be paid for through taxation of the local population. While this did provide for improved transport, communication and legal systems, it was not enough to bring educational and health standards up to the level required by the Jews. Britain had authorised the World Zionist

Organisation to assist in developing the Jewish national home and it was the various agencies of this body that channelled funds into Palestine for independent Jewish hospitals and schools, for land purchases, business loan capital and housing. The British had also allowed the creation of the *Va'ad Leumi* (in effect a provisional Jewish government) to administer to the needs of the community and thus, in the collaborative efforts of the Jewish organisations inside and outside Palestine, a quasi-public sector was born.

Rudimentary workers' organisations, established in the late nineteenth century, took advantage of the expanding industrial base and the interest and influence of emerging political parties, to advance the interests of the growing urban workforce. In 1920 the leftist trade unions joined together to form a single labour federation, the *Histadrut*, which campaigned to prevent Jewish employers from taking on non-Jewish labour and thereafter to improve the conditions under which Jewish workers laboured. The *Histadrut* quickly developed its role further by forming a holding company, the *Chevrat Ovdim*, which served as an umbrella for the *Histadrut*'s own enterprises. The labour federation was soon engaged in retailing, banking, renting out housing, running bus services and even operating hotels and restaurants. It also established a health fund (the *Kupat Cholim*), an autonomous school network, a newspaper and an arts network, but its greatest contribution to development was perhaps the establishment of major industrial companies such as the *Solel Boneh* construction company.

> As early as 1930 [then], the multitude of these activities drew into the Histadrut fold three-quarters of the Jewish working population of Palestine. Nearly all phases of a man's life, and the life of his family, were embraced by the vast canopy of the workers' organisation. By the eve of World War II, the Histadrut had become much more than a powerful institution in Jewish Palestine. For a majority of the Yishuv, the Histadrut was all but synonymous with Jewish Palestine itself.[7]

All the Jewish organisations and institutions could not, however, protect the emerging Jewish economy from the impact of wider economic change. British occupation brought with it exponentially increasing exposure to the world capitalist economy and both Arabs and Jews found themselves vulnerable to global economic conditions, even as new opportunities for material wealth were presented. The *yishuv*, backed by international Jewish capital and equipped with greater educational and technical skills, was able to benefit disproportionately from this exposure. But although growth was rapid (net domestic product grew by around 20 per cent annually between 1922 and 1935), the economy proved vulnerable to changing international conditions and suffered a series of boom and slump cycles which the British administration proved unable to prevent. For all that they were convinced that overall growth in Palestine depended on a healthy

Jewish economy, the British were committed to free trade and the market economy. In the interests of development, they nonetheless found themselves giving preferential and protectionist treatment to Jewish agricultural and industrial producers, enacting pro-Jewish employment policies and granting greater political autonomy to Jewish economic institutions.

In effect, British economic policy served to widen the gap between the Jewish and Arab economies in Palestine.[8] However, the notion that there existed a wholly distinct and autonomous Jewish economy should be treated with caution. The *yishuv*'s political leaders would undoubtedly have liked that to be the case, but the reality was one of interaction between Jewish, Arab and colonial economies. For example, Jewish development drew upon Arab resources. In the 1930s, between 8 and 10 per cent of Arab agricultural produce was purchased by the Jewish community.[9] Arab agricultural labour serviced Jewish cash-crop production for export, and the sale of Arab lands facilitated Jewish settlement and agricultural production. Thus there were unquestionably areas of overlap between the Jewish and Arab economies under British administration. The nature of this overlap is open to debate. The relational paradigm discussed in Chapter 1 acknowledges the reciprocal impact of events in each economic entity upon the other. The colonial paradigm considers the impositions of the Jewish and colonial economies upon the Arab, while versions drawing on Marxist or Dependency theories consider the implications of capitalist intrusion on an indigenous, predominantly pre-capitalist mode of production. It is beyond the remit of this chapter to elaborate on the relationship further, but it is important to bear in mind that 'while it is true that the various separate enclaves of Jewish activity did tend to coalesce into something, which, by 1936, could reasonably be called "a Jewish economy", this entity had many more points of contact with the different sectors of the wider Palestinian economy than some writers generally allow'.[10]

Economic policy in the early years of statehood

Statehood brought both challenges and opportunities for the economy. In the immediate term, the Israeli government had to meet a number of major demands. Firstly, significant funds had to be directed towards the country's defence. Secondly, the state was both ideologically and practically compelled to absorb over 340,000 immigrants who arrived within the first two years alone from neighbouring Arab countries or from displaced persons camps in Europe. The new immigrants had to be housed and provided with food, clothing and ultimately with work. Thus the creation of a national infrastructure, of basic services and of employment opportunities was also high on the agenda. Social justice and equality were also to become principal goals of policy-makers and politicians were keen to stress their commitment to maintaining and even improving the standard of living across the board. This was not only out of practical considerations regarding attracting and keeping immigrants, but also to differentiate Israel from its poorer, economically backward Arab neighbours. As one *Mapai* leader put it:

> Israel is a poor country. And precisely because we are poor we must have a certain minimum standard of living – unless we are prepared to drop to the level of our Arab neighbours. And that we are not willing to do. . . . We . . . believe that in the long run a progressive community such as ours will achieve – will be forced to achieve – productivity high enough to maintain its services. On the other hand, a socially backward community would fail to develop Israel's economy. . . . Even our military superiority over the Arabs comes from our technical skills and our advanced system of education, our better diet, the superior environment we provide our children.[11]

The sheer magnitude of the tasks facing the government encouraged it to take a profoundly interventionist role in the economy. To begin with, strategic natural resources such as water and potash were nationalised. Large tracts of land, which the government claimed had been abandoned by fleeing Arabs, were expropriated by the state, which either held them itself or passed them to the Jewish Agency for leasing to Jews. Since trade with Israel's neighbours was embargoed by the Arab states, oil supplies dried up (particularly the pipeline supply from Mosul to Haifa), and the government had to seek out new supplies and establish new companies for subsequent distribution. Similarly, the need for cheap mass pre-fabricated housing for new immigrants led to the creation of the *Amidar* corporation. Hence large state-owned companies were formed which benefited from monopoly status. The government took over the electricity corporation, although it left the water company in the management of the *Histadrut* and limited some of its activities to joint partnerships with either the *Histadrut* or the Jewish Agency.

Necessity being the mother of invention, the early years saw the establishment of a large number of other national institutions such as the civil service, the central bank, a national insurance institute and an employment agency. To some extent pre-state *yishuv* institutions were simply enlarged and formalised to become national bodies. As early as 1920 the Zionist Congress had established the fundamental principle that economic colonisation depended upon public capital supporting collective pioneering settlement and this was a natural evolution as far as the Israeli leadership were concerned. However, one important difference was that, in line with Ben-Gurion's statist preferences, national state planning and organisation would replace the voluntarism that had characterised the institutions of the *yishuv*. The net result was a rapidly expanding public sector with a bureaucracy to match, but it was nonetheless in line with the socialist leanings of the political leadership as a whole, as well as the Keynesian economics of the post-war era in general.

Direct fiscal intervention in the economy took two forms. On the one hand, the government lacked the necessary finances to meet all the demands made upon it. With a relatively small tax base, the government was forced to borrow money, either from the commercial banks or in the form of issuing dollar-based bonds to citizens in return for seizing their foreign currency assets or floating bonds in the USA. When this proved to be insufficient, it simply printed the money it needed. To try to hold back inflationary pressures and direct resources to where they were most needed, a policy of severe austerity and rationing was also introduced. Price controls would hold back inflation while rationing and import controls would constrain private consumption. Private sector activity was not actively discouraged, but the heavy hand of government intervention served to deter foreign investment even as it encouraged strategic production rather than the manufacture of consumables. Priority was given to investment in agriculture rather than industry, the idea being to concentrate on decentralising the population and developing food self-sufficiency. Immigrants were relocated to agricultural settlements around the country, and budget finances were used to provide housing, infrastructure (including water, transport, communications and energy provision) and agricultural inputs.

The programme met with mixed success. It did manage to facilitate the rapid absorption of a massive population influx, and to establish the basic institutions and infrastructure of the economy. It also managed to prevent a very sudden rise in unemployment and to temporarily suppress demand-surplus inflation. In the longer term, however, it was unsustainable and created as many problems as it resolved. With domestic production geared towards import substitution rather than exports, and with the massive government spending nonetheless fuelling consumption of imports, the country soon suffered from a chronic shortage of foreign exchange as well as rising balance of trade and budget deficits. Living standards for the established population declined (despite the growth of a thriving black market) while the new immigrants complained of the harshness of their own resettlement. Despite its efforts, the government could not create employment sufficiently quickly to accommodate the growing workforce, fuelling dissatisfaction with the absorption programme. Moreover, underlying inflation was pushed steadily upwards so that by 1952 it was clear that a new economic strategy was needed.

The years of rapid growth

The change came in the form of a New Economic Policy declared after the General Zionists won increased representation in the government in the 1952 elections. Their more liberal economic inclinations encouraged the government to cease its inflationary financing, to devalue the currency and to remove price controls. The immediate impact was to bring the suppressed inflation into the open (the Consumer Price Index rose by 56 per cent in 1952 and 28 per cent in 1953) and allow unemployment to climb even higher. On the positive side, however, a conscious decision to moderate the rate of immigration (if not the ultimate objective) reduced the budget demands on the government, while devaluation helped to diminish the currency crisis.

The following decade was one of rapid economic growth, with the national product rising by an average of 10 per cent per annum. Israel was soon able to satisfy its food requirements with local production and, with the existing constraints on the availability of both land and water, agricultural growth slowed to around 5–6 per cent per annum. The government now switched its attention to encouraging industrial growth through investment grants, subsidised credit, and trade protectionism. Immigrants were directed to new industrial development towns rather than to the agricultural *moshavim* and the state invested heavily in manufacturing state-owned enterprises (SOEs) that would provide both employment and consumer goods.

But although the heavy regime of price controls had been formally lifted, the government's preference for import taxes and export subsidies over further devaluation created *de facto* a multitude of exchange rates, distorting prices and resource allocation. The controversial receipt of reparations from the Federal Republic of Germany, amounting to $850 million, private transfers from Jews abroad, and the government issuance of cost-of-living linked bonds all served to fuel consumption and inflation. This was only made worse by the growing power of the *Histadrut* and its ability to exert strong upwards pressure on public sector wages which was soon replicated in the private sector.

The deepening structural problems were only partially disguised by rising consumption and impressive growth rates. Between 1945 and 1972, for instance, growth averaged 9–10 per cent a year, but even this was not enough to offset a widening trade deficit. In 1966 it was decided that government investments had to be reduced and exports improved if the economy was to pay for itself. Recessionary policies were introduced, growth and consumption slowed and unemployment began to rear its ugly head. An increase in government defence consumption after the 1967 war, and the availability of cheap labour from the Occupied Territories, jump-started the economy once more. Despite its good intentions to rein in spending, protests against the growing socio-economic inequalities within Israel spurred the government to a new round of subsidies and social transfers, funded partly by increased taxation but also by a round of devaluations which served to fuel inflation further. With the political and ideological consensus supporting the predominant *Mapai* grouping beginning to crumble, the government was unable to resist union demands for higher wages and subsequent subsidies to private industry to enable them to compete for labour. The political fear of renewed recession, combined with defence requirements and the taboo against inhibiting immigration in any way, were enough to dampen enthusiasm for any serious reform of the paternalistic economic structure, although a limited privatisation programme in 1968–72 indicated that many economists already recognised the dangers of continuing on the same path.

Outside of the government, however, enthusiasm for the free market was growing, not least among the young Oriental immigrants who were unburdened with ideological commitments to the collectivist past and regarded the *Ma'arakh* leadership as self-privileging. Their socio-economic grievances, combined with a rising tide of hawkish nationalism and the political fall-out from a number of scandals that tarnished the upper echelons of *Ma'arakh*, led to the election in 1977 of the first *Likud*-led government, ending a 30-year reign by the Labour élite. The new Minister of Finance, Simha Ehrlich, introduced a 'turnabout' in policy, liberalising foreign exchange holdings and initiating a new round of privatisations. Unfortunately any serious intentions for reform were scuppered by the prime minister's disinterest in matters economic. Menachem Begin was wholly absorbed, first with the peace-process with Egypt and later with the invasion of Lebanon. As a result of the war, defence costs soared, paid for by the tripling of gross foreign debt from $11.5 billion in 1977 to $30.5 billion in 1985, requiring a third of GNP to be spent every year in interest payments and debt repayment.

The government proved unwilling and unable to take on the mighty *Histadrut* to rein in wage increases. By now, the *Histadrut* represented more than 70 per cent of the workforce,[12] including some 450,000 public sector workers and 700,000 private sector employees. The business empire of the *Histadrut* accounted for 25 per cent of all economic enterprises in the Israeli economy and itself employed around 15 per cent of the labour force.[13] With wage increases linked to the cost of living, and as public sector employment rose from 20 to 30 per cent of the labour force, the public sector deficit peaked at 17 per cent of GDP. By the mid-1980s the public sector accounted for 25 per cent of the GNP and nearly 30 per cent of employment. Public and private sector consumption soared, and the balance of trade steadily worsened to over $5 billion (not least due to the massive hiking of energy costs), creating a foreign currency reserve crisis. In 1984 and the first half of 1985, inflation spiralled upwards at a dizzy monthly rate of between 10 and 25 per cent. Growth, after briefly seeming to halt altogether in 1982, hovered at around 3 per cent per annum, way below the levels to which Israelis had become accustomed. Even then, it was not growth based on production so much as the evolution of the financial sector to cope with the consequences of hyper-inflation. In 1983 a crisis hit even that sector when it became clear that the banks had been artificially manipulating their own share prices to compete with government bonds. Sudden massive sales of those shares as the public, anticipating devaluation, switched to foreign currency purchases, caused the collapse of the banks and a crisis in the Tel Aviv Stock Exchange. In short, by 1984 it was clear that Israel was mired in a profound structural crisis and that the era of rapid economic growth had not only come to an end but now had to be accounted for.

It was evident that Israel suffered from a combination of deep-rooted problems, all of which could be traced back to the unique manner of its establishment. Firstly, the continuing failure to establish peaceable borders meant that defence assumed a disproportionate role in government spending. Public sector consumption was further boosted by the requirements of providing for immigration. This entailed not simply direct material provision for their immediate absorption, but a general commitment to maintaining high living standards and low unemployment. This remained a political prerequisite for sustaining popular support for the process and countering the negative effects of territorial insecurity on the impetus for immigration. A third problem was the over-inflated size and influence of both the public and *Histadrut* sectors. Israel had never been a truly socialist state, despite the popular image presented abroad by the utopian *kibbutzim* life. The public sector and *Histadrut* had assumed a major role in production due to the perceived necessity for directing scarce resources where they were most needed. Their firms, despite being heavily subsidised and inefficient, were nonetheless run on profit-making bases, much like the private sector. The growing overlap between the Labour élite on the one hand, and the public sector machinery and *Histadrut* management on the other, dating back to the *yishuv* years, had become the mainstay of *Ma'arakh*'s political grip over the economy. By the time *Likud* had come to government, the organisations and institutions of the public and quasi-public sectors had developed a life of their own, exerting tremendous power and able to resist any political will to diminish their status. Thus, the government lacked autonomy in policies relating to labour, wages, public investment, welfare and social transfers. Living standards could only be sustained by supplementing the productive capacity of the country with foreign borrowing, deficit financing and repeated devaluations. Inflation was out of control, the economy was proving inordinately susceptible to world recession, populist policies were being pursued over economic interests, and it was clear that the potential of import substitution had been exhausted. In sum, a new approach to the economy was again urgently needed.

Stabilisation and reform

In September 1984 a government of national unity was formed when neither a *Ma'arakh* (formerly *Mapai*) nor *Likud*-led bloc was able to construct a coalition on their own. A series of 'package deals' between the government, the *Histadrut* and the Manufacturers' Association (representing employers) restricted wages and prices in the immediate term, but the following year a team of economists was mandated to draw up an Emergency Stabilisation Plan (the ESP). Essentially the ESP introduced a number of drastic austerity measures, including cutting the budget deficit by $1.5 billion (7.5 per cent of GDP), a 20 per cent devaluation of the shekel, and reduced export subsidies and import duties. The Cost of Living Adjustment (COLA), whereby the government and employers had been committed to annual wage increases relative to the price index since 1941, was temporarily suspended and the liquidity of dollar-linked financial instruments was drastically reduced. The whole package was supported by American aid worth a total of $2.8 billion, conditional upon what became known as 'Herb's Ten Points', a document outlining the measures drawn up jointly by American and Israeli economists. The net effect of the measures was to curb public and private consumption. The public sector deficit was not only reduced but was ultimately reversed, showing a surplus in 1987 and indicating that, far from pumping the economy full of money, the government was actually extracting money from it. Inflation fell accordingly, from 444.4 per cent in 1984 to just 20 per cent in 1986. Yet the ESP failed to address the structural problems of the economy and its successes were limited accordingly. Indeed, the austerity measures were soon subverted by the Labour Alignment's promises of financial assistance for public sector industries in difficulty, as well as for two *Histadrut* giants, *Solel Boneh* (construction) and *Kupat Cholim*. Between them, the companies demanded a total of $2 billion – or 9 per cent of GNP – just to cover their debts, and *Ma'arakh* promised renewed help just before handing over the reins of government (and responsibility for the consequences of the decision) to the *Likud* party.

The new Prime Minister, Yitzhak Shamir, was ultimately forced to concede the rescue packages in return for a new tripartite agreement on a twelve-month wage and price freeze. He also tried to initiate some structural reform, slashing personal taxes[14] while broadening the tax base through a new Corporate Tax law, reducing the national insurance burden, opening up domestic capital markets and embarking upon the long-awaited privatisation programme. There were by now some 200 SOEs including major national monopolies such as *Bezeq* (telecommunications), *El Al* (the national air carrier), Israel Chemicals, and Oil Refineries, and their sale was to be the flagship of Shamir's liberalisation efforts. He soon came up against a number of problems. There was substantial political opposition to the sale of what were considered to be strategic assets, and existing cartels were able to utilise their influence with and in the *Histadrut* and the *Ma'arakh* to block sales that would reduce their own privileged status. Moreover, most SOEs were heavily in debt, making them unattractive to foreign investors who were already deterred by the heavily interventionist role of the government in the economy. Tel Aviv's own stock exchange had a limited capacity and successful privatisation relied upon foreign investment, yet the *Knesset* insisted on vetting potential buyers to assess their Zionist credentials. The government did attempt in some instances to either restrict the sale to 49 per cent of equity or to retain a 'golden' share, but neither was conducive to making the sales more attractive to potential buyers. The bottom line was that, although the need for privatisation was recognised, neither the public nor the *Histadrut* sectors were ready to take the difficult decisions that consequently arose. The programme was therefore slow to take off and little of the $5 billion that it had been expected to realise was actually forthcoming.

The ESP undoubtedly caused a recovery but one which soon proved to be short-lived. In 1986 GDP rose by 3.6 per cent, and in 1987 by 6.5 per cent, the highest growth rates since the 1973 war. Unemployment began to fall slowly and investment grew. The economy was assisted by a fall in the price of fuel, a shift away from financial to productive activities as inflation dropped, and the withdrawal from Lebanon and the consequent easing of the defence burden. Ultimately, however, it proved impossible to get inflation back to single digit figures, and overall productivity remained low. High interest rates, which had been used to curb domestic demand but which did not stimulate domestic savings, caused a crisis for many of Israel's uncompetitive and unproductive enterprises, while the pegged exchange rate caused a steady erosion of the real exchange rate. By 1988, the country was plunged into an unforeseen recession which was to last until the end of 1989. Although the *Intifada* in the West Bank and Gaza Strip included some measures of economic warfare, its effect was far more damaging for the Palestinian economy than the Israeli, and it cannot reasonably be blamed for the slide into recession. The problem was rooted instead in the failure to genuinely reform the economy and the application instead of piecemeal and almost *ad hoc* policy-making to address short-term difficulties. By 1988 the government had resumed the policy of making frequent devaluations, pushing inflation back up to 25 per cent.

The pressures for serious reform were increased with the arrival in Israel of a new *aliyah* of immigrants from the former Soviet Union in 1990 (Table 3.1). The public sector would clearly be unable to provide employment for the estimated 500,000 immigrants expected to arrive within two years. In September 1990, it was estimated that the GDP would have to grow by 8.5 per cent a year if the economy was to accommodate all the immigrants and the business sector alone by 10 per cent.[15] The Bank of Israel, in a major policy document released in 1991, stated categorically that the only way forward was stringent reform to improve the profitability and competitiveness of the private sector so that it could grow at a pace that would enable it to absorb the enlarged work-force. Given that at least 600,000 jobs would have to be created over five years just to maintain existing employment levels, the urgency for reform was evident. Additional pressure for liberalisation of trade, capital and labour markets, and for accelerated privatisation, was levied by the IMF which was at the time in the process of lending Israel $20 billion to assist with immigrant absorption.

Table 3.1 Immigration into Israel (000s and annual average)

	000s	Annual average
1882–1903	20–30	–
1904–14	35–40	–
1915–30	116.8	7.3
1931–38	197.2	24.6
1939–45	81.8	11.7
1946–48	56.5	18.8
1948–51	686.7	171.7
1952–54	54.1	18.0
1955–57	164.9	55.0
1958–60	75.5	25.2
1961–64	228.0	57.0
1965–68	81.3	20.3
1969–79	484.0	44.0
1980–84	83.6	16.7
1985–89	70.3	14.0
1990–91	375.5	187.7
1992–98	502.8	71.8

Sources: Yair Aharoni, *The Israeli Economy: Dreams and Realities* (London: Routledge, 1991), p. 104. State of Israel Ministry of Industry and Trade, *The Israeli Economy at a Glance* (Jerusalem, April 1999).

The era of liberalising reforms

Successive governments, whether Labour or *Likud*-led, have since then sustained the general direction of reform, although with varying degrees of rigour. Yitzhak Rabin (prime minister from 1992–95) attempted to revitalise the privatisation process by setting up a privatisation committee together with the Finance and Justice Ministries and bypassing resistance from within his own cabinet and the Labour establishment.

In the event, the programme still failed to meet projections for sales and revenue generation. Between 1986 and 1996 a total of sixty-eight companies ceased to be state-owned, as well as holdings in another twelve, raising just $3.6 billion. The pace accelerated in 1997 and 1998 under Netanyahu's government, boosted by sales of bank shares, increasing the number of companies sold to seventy-five, and raising a further $7.1 billion for the treasury.

Privatisation of the banks has been a pivotal part of the overall reform of the financial services sector. In the early 1990s the government assumed ownership of the bulk of the equity of the four largest banking groups after the banks proved unable to repay the government loans that had bailed them out of the 1983 crisis. Originally the shares were due to pass to the government in 1988, but what was in effect a nationalisation of the major banks was viewed as highly undesirable in an era when the state was actually trying to divest itself of such assets. From 1989 it therefore sought to equalise voting rights of shares so that future privatisations would be more attractive propositions. More difficult to manage was the profitability of the banks, which were simultaneously being forced to write-off huge debts owed by industry and agriculture as part of rescue, reform and rescheduling operations in those sectors. In May 1993 the first bank privatisations went ahead, with 23.1 per cent of the equity of Bank Hapoalim and 13.4 per cent of Bank Leumi being sold on the Tel Aviv Stock Exchange. Further sales, scheduled for 1994, were delayed by stock market falls in that year, but 1995 saw 26 per cent of United Mizrahi Bank being sold to a group of investors. In 1997 a controlling stake of 43 per cent of Bank Hapoalim was sold to an American-Jewish investor, along with further stakes in Bank Leumi and the Israel Discount Bank. Small, profitable subsidiaries of the banks were also put up for sale independently. Of course, privatisation is not in itself enough.

In 1995 a range of banking reforms was launched, designed to reduce the grip of the big banks on both the financial and non-financial services sectors. The privatisations had introduced foreign ownership of shares in the major banks and relaxation of foreign exchange controls encouraged Australian, American and European banks to move into what had previously been effectively closed markets of corporate finance and investment banking. Meanwhile banks were given new freedoms to operate in foreign currencies, to guarantee loans raised overseas, to make loans to Israeli firms from overseas branches and to engage in limited pension fund provision in moves which were intended to open the sector to greater competition while enhancing its utility to private sector corporations. The banks were also forced to reduce their shares in holding companies. Bank Hapoalim in particular was forced to sell its stakes in major *Histadrut*-linked industrial firms, diminishing its control over around 8 per cent of the Israeli economy through non-financial holdings.[16] Overall, however, the banking sector remains heavily concentrated, with the five largest banks accounting for over 90 per cent of the sector. Following the 'universal banking' model, they 'operate as retail, wholesale, and investment banks, as well as being active in all the main areas of capital market activity, brokerage, under-writing and mutual and provident fund management.'[17] Not all aspects of the sector are yet open to competition and there is as yet no overall super-visory body to regulate it, and analysts have argued that the albeit signifi-cant strides that have been made towards liberalisation need to be supplemented with a more comprehensive approach to policy-making and regulation.

The liberalisation of trade has made more systematic and comprehensive progress since 1985, when it was decided to progressively eliminate all trade barriers, export subsidies and import licences. Traditionally import licences, taxes and customs duties were levied most heavily on consumer goods but only lightly on raw materials and capital imports. Exports were meanwhile encouraged by means of heavy state subsidies. The first movement towards free trade had actually been in 1964, when Israel signed its first Free Trade Agreement with the European Community. This was renewed in 1967, upgraded to a five-year preferential trading agreement in 1970 and expanded in 1974. In 1977 Israeli industrial products entered the European Community free of tariffs. When another Free Trade Agreement with the United States was reached in 1985, totally eliminating reciprocal customs duties by 1995, Israel was well on the way to establishing open trade with its major markets. Non-tariff barriers to trade with other markets, notably Eastern Europe and Asia, were replaced in 1991 with a system of customs duties that were reduced to an 8–12 per cent band in 1996 and then progressively phased out. By 2005 the Israeli economy will be almost completely open to all goods imports.

Trade liberalisation has been aided by the staged lifting of foreign exchange controls. In 1977 the *Likud* government had attempted to lift foreign exchange restrictions but the government was forced to abandon the policy in 1983–84 due to a balance of payments crisis. In 1987 the government tried again, instituting a five-year programme of deregulation. By 1992 controls on current account operations and those applying to the business sector had been lifted, Israeli firms were free to invest abroad and households could purchase foreign securities or real estate. Allowances for travel and study abroad had been increased and the levy on the purchase of services abroad reduced for individuals and abolished for firms. Importantly, Israeli companies were now free to seek investment loans from overseas, improving credit prospects for the private sector. In May 1998 most remaining foreign exchange restrictions were removed and the New Israeli Shekel (NIS) became almost fully convertible.

The means of determining the exchange rate has also been adjusted to facilitate flexible adjustment. In 1985 the NIS was introduced, replacing the old shekel which had effectively devalued by 25,000 per cent against the US dollar in the preceding five years due to the effects of hyperinflation. From 1986 the NIS was valued against a basket of currencies and a first devaluation of 10 per cent was introduced in 1987. From 1988, and in order to sustain export competitiveness, a policy of frequent value adjustments was introduced. This led to some turbulence in the economy, however, as firms and financial agencies sought to continually pre-empt anticipated or impending devaluations. In 1991 the system was refined with the introduction of the so-called crawling-peg 'diagonal line' system, whereby the rate was set through daily floating adjustments. The shekel floats against a basket of currencies within a bank (similar to the EMU), the upper and lower limits of which are allowed to float around a mid-point that is set daily by the Central Bank of Israel. An annual target is set for alterations in the mid-point, and since 1994 there has been an additional annual adjustment which aims to correct the representation in the basket in line with the volume of trade. In June 1997 further changes meant that the band within which the rate could float was broadened from the previous plus or minus 7 per cent from the mid-point to plus or minus 14 per cent.[18]

The lifting of exchange rate controls and the liberalisation of financial markets also served to invigorate the Tel Aviv Stock Exchange. The TASE is nearly 70 years old, with over 400 companies being quoted on it by 1994. Once foreign investors were given the freedom to engage in transactions, and as more Israeli companies began to list their shares on the New York Stock Exchange, the TASE became an interesting market for international capital. Despite a rather rocky decade in the 1990s, with confidence rising and falling due to the combination of structural reforms, privatisation, inconsistent domestic growth, the stops and starts of the peace process, and turmoil in international financial markets, the TASE is now considered to be a truly promising emerging market.

The progress of liberalising reforms has not always been steady. Yitzhak Rabin was generally committed to liberalising trade, exchange rates, capital and labour markets, but while he was initially able to press ahead with reforms, assisted by renewed demand on the back of the wave of ex-Soviet immigration, by 1994 he faced strong opposition to his peace process policies and was forced to raise public expenditure in a bid to improve his party's position in the run-up to the next election. Large public-sector wage rises and increased spending on social services were intended to harden leftist and centre support for his government. Since tax revenues fell unexpectedly in 1995, the net result was a larger than hoped-for budget deficit. The higher spending had fuelled a rush of imports, leading to a deterioration in the balance of payments and a hike in inflation. On the positive side, however, demand was fed by the requirements of over 700,000 new immigrants. In 1990 alone, some 200,000 new immigrants arrived in Israel, and another 178,000 the following year, representing an overall increase in the population of around 8 per cent. A further 240,000 arrived in the next three years, all of whom demanded housing, food, services and consumption goods, with a knock-on effect on demand for investment goods to increase productive capacity.[19]

The dramatic agreement reached with the PLO in Oslo in 1993 created a tremendously positive atmosphere, as foreign companies that had previously held back from dealing with Israel now rushed to do business with the strongest economy in the Middle East. With the lifting of the secondary boycott by the Arab states, international firms were no longer to be penalised for their relations with Israeli counterparts, and major multinationals such as General Motors, Westinghouse, Salamon Brothers, Cable and Wireless, Daimler Benz and Siemens were among the first to move in. For the most part they were interested in joint ventures with high-tech Israeli firms or in using the Middle Eastern economy as a gateway to markets further afield in Asia. They were encouraged in this by the speed with which countries around the world, which had previously refused to establish diplomatic relations with the Zionist state, now queued up not only to open reciprocal diplomatic missions but also to sign trade, investment and joint-production protocols. Israel focused its own efforts on developing economic ties with East Asia. Relations were established with China, India, Mongolia, Vietnam, Cambodia and Laos in 1992 and 1993 and the Prime Minister toured China, Japan, Singapore, both Koreas, Thailand, the Philippines and Malaysia in 1994. As a result, in the first nine months of 1994 Israeli exports to Asia increased by a third, accounting for 12.4 per cent of total exports, and trade with individual countries in the region grew by as much as 69 per cent.[20] Finally, Israel was able to cash in on the shift from military to civilian goods production. Forty years of heavy educational, defence, and research and development investment had generated a capacity for developing state-of-the-art technology that was transferred to the civilian productive sector. Once political conditions allowed, foreign investors were quick to find niche markets where Israel could maintain a qualitative edge. Firms such as Intel and Motorola provided venture capital for joint stock companies, and Israel was able to rapidly earn itself a name as a global centre for the production of high-tech electronic and software products for export. None of this would have been possible without the continuing process of trade and financial sector liberalisation that opened Israel to the global economy. After the recession of 1988–89, growth picked up steadily, averaging 6 per cent between 1990 and 1995, making it one of the fastest growing economies in the world.

The Netanyahu government which was elected in 1996 initially returned to a tight monetary policy, cutting spending and reducing the budget deficit despite the fact that the economy was beginning to slow down of its own accord. The first flood of immigrants was waning, reducing domestic demand. Security problems were having a negative effect on tourism, and high interest rates were strengthening the shekel and diminishing exports. This was partly compensated for by a surge in foreign investment capital, although the short-term element was reduced when the financial crisis in East Asia affected general confidence in emerging markets. Net foreign investment in 1992–94 had averaged between $500 and $800 million a year. In 1996, 1997 and 1998 it amounted to $2.9 billion, $3.6 billion and $2.5 billion respectively. By 1999, however, it was clear that Netanyahu's intransigent policies towards the implementation of agreements reached with the Palestinians were damaging foreign confidence in Israel. Foreign investment plummeted, the shekel lost ground against the dollar and the TASE index went into decline. The government was forced to introduce a sharp hike in interest rates, squeezing business credit.

Not all was doom and gloom. The slowdown in growth, to 4.4 per cent in real terms in 1996, and to less than 2 per cent in 1998, was matched by a drop in inflation to just 4 per cent in 1999 and in the budget deficit to less than 2 per cent. In short, fiscal and monetary policy were kept tightly in hand, although the government was never able to reduce public sector spending as a proportion of GDP to the levels it would have liked.[21] Like his predecessors, Netanyahu found himself a hostage to small party coalition partners who angled for greater public spending in the direction of their own support bases in return for continued political alliance. Thus spending on settlements, education, health and transfer payments rose rapidly and the budget deficit was only kept down by increasing revenues (notably from privatisation) and by keeping defence expenditures at a stationary (if still high) 10 per cent of GDP. As the 1999 election drew near, Netanyahu abandoned his austerity programme altogether and embarked on a spending spree. Free pre-school education, heavy subsidisation of medical costs, the scrapping of proposed cuts to pensioner benefits and the sale of public housing at substantial discounts cost the state an additional NIS 2.5 billion a year but failed to win the prime minister a second term.

Ehud Barak came to office, therefore, to find a number of heavy economic burdens awaiting his attention. Unemployment had risen under Netanyahu's administration to 9.4 per cent, with widening income differentials being seen as one root cause of social grievances. To maintain a coalition that included *Shas,* he was quickly forced to pump funds into health, social welfare and the party's own bankrupt educational network, appeasing Oriental perceptions of economic inequalities. His first full budget in 2000, however, set the aim of reducing further the budget deficit (to 2.5 per cent from 2.75 per cent in 1999) in line with European competitors. The general goal of stimulating renewed growth was to be achieved through creating the conditions under which the private sector could flourish rather than by injecting cash into the economy. Savings would be made by withdrawing the army from its occupation of Lebanon and by reversing Netanyahu's commitments to settlement expansion. With the government focusing on maintaining inflation at 3–4 per cent for two years, it was also hoped that the Central Bank would see fit to reduce the interest rate (from 8 per cent in 1999). Following the European model of supply-side economics, government policy would also target existing monopolies, introducing new structural reforms to break up cartels and foster competition in both the domestic and international markets. New product standards were to make goods competitive in international markets and further capital market reforms would improve the conditions of Israel's exposure. Barak's ambition was to achieve 3 per cent growth in 2000 and 4–5 per cent annually thereafter. By the end of the decade per capita GDP may be as high as $25,000, with a vibrant and competitive Israel fully incorporated into the global economy.

How real is the Israeli tiger?

The net achievement of past policies and performance has been the establishment of a modern, developed, industrialised and globally integrated economy. Some of the structural weaknesses have been remedied by the prolonged if incomplete process of reform, and Israel today can rely on two fundamental strengths: the diversified and high-tech nature of its productive base on the one hand, and the scale and spread of its trading relations on the other.

The productive base

While the early years of the state saw production geared, under the guiding hand of the state, towards self-sufficiency and import substitution, the process of structural reform and liberalisation has seen a reorientation towards producing for export. A simultaneous and related process has been the transfer from an agricultural bias to a sophisticated high-technology and services-based economy. Israel lacks raw materials in either quantity or variety. Since it must also import virtually all its energy requirements, low value-added manufactured products are uncompetitive in international markets. Given that Israeli labour is highly skilled but also expensive, the economy is best placed to take advantage of high value-added production, be it in industry or agriculture (Table 3.2).

Manufacturing contributes around a third of business sector GDP. Since the mid-1980s both the sector and individual firms have been busy restructuring and adjusting to the increasing domestic and international competition. Many companies have successfully branched out into new high-tech industries, albeit at the expense of traditional manufacturing activities such as textiles. This has been the result of the withdrawal of protectionist measures on the part of the government on the one hand, and an increasing ability to capitalise on Israel's highly educated labour force and the heavy public investment in research and development on the other. As well as the overflow of technological innovation from the military-industrial complex, Israel has among the highest civilian R & D expenditures in the world, second only to Japan and Germany.[22] Between 1969 and 1985, civilian R & D increased by 1300 per cent. More recent evidence of the government's recognition of the importance of R & D to industrial development, particularly in the high-tech sectors, came in the multiplying of R & D grants

Table 3.2 Composition of gross domestic product at factor cost, 1995 (percentage of total)

Agriculture, forestry and fishing	2.3
Manufacturing, mining and quarrying	18.6
Construction, electricity and water	10.3
Public and community services	25.3
Transport, storage and communications	6.9
Trade and private services	38.1
Subsidies for various industries	0.2
Errors and omissions	−1.7

Source: Central Bank of Israel, *Statistical Abstract of Israel.*

from $100 million to $500 million a year between 1990 and 1997. Israel also has by far the highest number of scientists and technicians per head of population,[23] boosted not least by the flow of highly educated immigrants from the former Soviet Union in the early 1990s. Israeli governments have always prioritised education in their budgets, with education accounting for twice the expenditure on health and coming second only to defence or, on occasion, labour and welfare payments.

Israeli companies currently lead the world in industries such as multimedia, computer software, computer telephone integration (CTI), fibre optics, digital technology, computer security systems, thermal-imaging night-vision equipment and automatic or robotic production systems. These industries effectively 'took off' in the mid-1990s as the removal of capital and exchange restrictions facilitated foreign investment via venture capital funds. Many of the firms still have relatively inefficient capital bases, and Israeli labour is comparatively expensive, but Israel undoubtedly has the technological edge over many emerging market competitors and can benefit from its preferential access to American markets. Indeed, there have been a number of cases where Israeli technology has become a world-beater by utilising American finance and being marketed through American firms. Israeli technology has even allowed it to put its own satellites in space,[24] placing it among the few space-age nations on earth. Less laudable has been the rapid growth of technology 'piracy'. Due to lax intellectual property rights, Israel is fast becoming 'a distribution hub in a multi-country network' for pirated video games, computer programs and compact discs.[25] While legitimate high-tech exports contribute some $3 billion a year to the Israeli economy, the prevalence of pirate business is threatening to undermine the confidence of international business in Israeli policies of non-disclosure, the net effect being to discourage joint-venture capital. The net effect of structural reform in the sector has inevitably been a reduction in the numbers employed, both in absolute terms and relative to the workforce as a whole (Table 3.3), an effect which has also been seen in the agricultural sector.

The romantic imagery of the barefoot pioneer turning the desert green is a far cry from the reality of Israeli agriculture. Today's sector is capital and technology intensive. After a financial crisis in the mid-1980s due to a lack of budgetary control, over-spending and bad investment decisions, the sector – including the *kibbutzim* and *moshavim* – was forced to rationalise, albeit with considerable reluctance. In the 1990s the *kibbutzim* submitted to a series of debt rescheduling and restructuring packages which have led them to rely more on their industrial and service operations and less on agricultural production. The system of mutual guarantees that had developed between settlements was abandoned, and the large bureaucracies of the marketing organisations were cut back, their monopoly powers being either reduced or eliminated. The sector, which has a powerful farming lobby drawn from the overlap between *kibbutzim* personnel and the labour estab-

Table 3.3 Labour force by sector, 1985 and 1998 (percentage of total and 000s)

	1985		1998	
	%	000	%	000
Agriculture, forestry and fishing	5.3	72.1	2.1	48
Industry, mining and manufacturing	22.9	309	17.1	390
Electricity and water	0.9	12	1.0	20
Construction and public works	5.4	72	6.0	131
Trade and food services	12.4	168	15.4	352
Transport, communications and storage	6.4	86	5.4	124
Business, finance and personal services	16.3	220	12.7	290
Public services	29.2	403	29.7	675
Total labour force		1350		2272

Source: Economist Intelligence Unit.

lishment, nonetheless remains heavily subsidised, through cheap water supplies, minimum farming prices and protected markets. This ensures some protection of food production, as well as sustaining the ideological motif of the Zionists' return to the land. Perhaps most importantly of all, the agricultural settlements provide the rural outposts of the country, ensuring a Jewish population in strategic locations.

Around 22 per cent of Israel's land is cultivated today, nearly 50 per cent of which is irrigated. The sector produces around 5 per cent of net domestic product (only a quarter of the share of manufacturing) and employs 2.1 per cent of the workforce.[26] In the early years of statehood, the drive for food self-sufficiency established cereals as a major focus of production, as well as citrus fruits that could be exported to Europe. In recent years the emphasis of production has switched to exotic fruits, winter vegetables and flowers, all of which benefit from irrigation and technology inputs and find ready markets in Europe.

The two sectors that have seen employment rise proportionately over the last 15 years have been trade and food services on the one hand (both of which have benefited from the opening of the economy to investment, markets and imports) and public services. Ironically, for all the talk of privatisation, organisational restructuring and spending cuts, the reality has been a public sector that just won't get any smaller. This remains a serious problem, although there has been a significant alteration in the ethos of that employment. As Michael Shalev puts it: 'Privatisation and deregulation, although incomplete, have putatively lowered both the scope and the sheltered quality of employment in public corporations, military industries, infrastructural monopolies, and the former *Histadrut* enterprises'.[27]

Although privatisation has not advanced at the rate initially hoped for, its effects – and those of more general liberalisation – have been felt deeply in the labour market, and not least in the *Histadrut* sector. Having accepted the abandonment of wage indexation and 'framework agreements' for wages negotiated with the private sector in the wake of the 1985 stabilisation plan, and following tremendous internal political turmoil in the 1990s, the *Histadrut* found itself under attack from all corners. Successive governments have reduced its ability to manipulate its pension funds to refinance itself. The Labour élite has cast it adrift politically out of frustration over repeated demands for debt write-offs and reschedulings. Reduced subsidisation forced the sale of many of its own holdings, and finally, its inability to resist lay-offs in both the private sector and its own firms has weakened its credibility as a trade union. It is currently seeking to reformulate its role as primarily a trade union, but even here its bargaining power is relatively reduced by the influx of foreign workers imported as cheap manual labour. Since the 1967 war, Israel has taken advantage of captive Palestinian labour from the Occupied Territories to staff its low-paid casual labour demands. The *Intifada* abruptly ruptured this relationship and recent security-related and political demands for the separation of the two economies has led since 1993 to a preference for the import of some 200,000 Turkish, Eastern European and Asian labourers. Such labour, in contrast to Palestinian workers, is not heavily regulated by the state – indeed much of it remains technically illegal. Responsibility for recruiting and facilitating that labour has been delegated to the private sector, breaking the historical and ideological precedents of Hebrew labour and signifying an internationalisation of Israel's labour market.

A further sign of the internationalisation of Israeli production and asset ownership has been the territorial dispersal of the private sector, which has taken advantage of opportunities presented by liberalisation. Examples include the relocation of textile firms to neighbouring Jordan where labour is cheaper than in Israel itself, and the establishment of a Moroccan subsidiary of the Israeli water company, *Tahal*. Israeli direct investments overseas have boomed since the 1990s, amounting to over $1 billion worth of equity in the period 1994–96 alone.[28] In exchange, over seventy technology-led Israeli companies were being quoted on the New York Stock Exchange by 1996.[29] The relationship between American and Israeli ownership is particularly strong; in 1999 there were over 170 Israeli companies operating subsidiaries in the USA and 100 major US companies operating subsidiaries in Israel. It should be noted, however, that there are negative aspects to this relationship. High-tech firms, eager to take advantage of their technical head-start over international competition, still find domestic taxes overly burdensome and the regulatory environment relatively cumbersome. Consequently, there has recently been a tendency for Israeli firms to register in the United States rather than at home, even though their productive assets remain in Israel. This move is often demanded by the foreign suppliers of investment capital who find Israeli ownership laws too restrictive. Furthermore, since so much of the market for Israeli high-tech goods lies in the United States, some firms have been encouraged to relocate entirely. The government has promised significant reforms of the tax and corporate laws, but until they are forthcoming Israel risks losing its technical start-up revolution to the United States.[30]

Nonetheless, foreign direct investment (FDI) into Israel in recent years has been forthcoming – indeed Michael Shalev has called it 'the most novel and noticed element of Israel's contemporary integration into the world economy'.[31] From being virtually insignificant and almost entirely dependent on philanthropic gestures by Jewish businessmen, investment rose to a peak of $3.6 billion in 1997. A note of caution should be included here; the interests of multinational corporations in Israeli high-tech production and infrastructure expansion have been encouraged as much by the lapse of the Arab secondary boycott as by liberalising trends – in fact Shalev has noted that FDI opportunities are 'softened' with generous state subsidies and the easy availability of financing from Israeli banks.[32] Moreover, the Israeli government frequently imposed 'offset' structures where foreign investors must sub-contract or make purchases amounting to a given percentage to or from Israeli firms.

Trade

Trade has perhaps been more comprehensively liberalised, with impressive results (Table 3.4). Following the 1948 war, Israel was cut off from commercial ties with its Arab neighbours, who imposed a comprehensive boycott on all aspects of trade with Israel. The fledgling state, in urgent need of

Table 3.4 Israel's main trading partners by volume of trade, 1998 (percentage of total)

Country	Exports	Imports	Contribution to export growth 1990–98
North America	36.3	20.8	43.4
EU	30.7	48.5	25.5[a]
Central and Eastern Europe	4.8	3.8	7.8
EFTA	1.8	5.8	–
Asia (incl. Central Asia)	13.9	12.4	11.6
Africa	2.1	1.3	2.7
Oceania	1.2	0.4	1.4
Latin America	3.8	1.4	5.0

Source: *The Israeli Economy at a Glance 1998* (Jerusalem: State of Israel Ministry of Industry and Trade, 1999).

[a]Figure relates to Western Europe.

capital and consumer goods, focused on developing trade relations with Europe and the United States and taking advantage of historical and *diaspora* business ties. The twin processes of trade liberalisation and the post-1993 peace process have served to open up the economy to a greater variety of trading partners, as well as to rapidly increase the volume of trade. While America and Europe remain the major trading partners, there has been a sharp increase in trade with Asian partners such as Japan, Hong Kong and India. Prior to the financial crisis of 1998, Asian partners received almost 20 per cent of Israeli exports. Israel seeks to project itself as a gateway for products and technology travelling between the East and the West, a vision far grander than the aspirations for regional economic hegemony which Arab neighbours suspect.

Trade with its own region continues to elude Israel. This is partly due to the political impediments arising from the ongoing Arab–Israeli conflict but there are also severe structural impediments. At the moment, neighbouring Arab states have little that is competitive to sell to Israel other than energy and cheap agricultural goods. While Israel has been happy to purchase oil (and in the future, gas) from Egypt, it has pursued a policy of source diversification in response to its dependence on energy imports, looking as far afield as Australia, South Africa and the UK for supplies. An agreement for the sale of natural gas from Qatar to Israel was frozen in response to the Netanyahu government's provocative settlement policies. In the long term, however, such agreements are likely to be revived, with Israel seeking competitively priced energy on its own doorstep. Agricultural trade is also an increasing fact of life for Arabs and Israelis. Since 1997 Palestinian agricultural produce has theoretically had unlimited access to the Israeli market (although this has not been the case in practice) and Jordan has been granted duty-free access for 50,000 metric tons of fresh and processed agricultural products. One interesting arrangement was that concluded in 1995 whereby Egypt and Israel agreed on a joint exporting and marketing formula which would allow Israeli produce to penetrate Gulf markets while Egypt benefited from Israel's superior distribution and marketing infrastructure. Israel's own production is increasingly oriented towards large sophisticated consumer markets. So far, the Middle East countries can provide only a limited market for high-tech, service-intensive products. In the long term, however, and assuming the removal of political obstacles to trade, Israel might be able to act as a local supplier of telecommunications systems, irrigation equipment and technology, chemicals and chemicals technology and high-quality agricultural products to the wealthier Gulf states. Thus, while there is potential for Arab–Israeli trade, issues of global competitiveness and product specialisation make it unlikely that Israel would flood the Arab world with 'dumped' low value-added goods. Equally, while there may be considerable room for Israeli-owned productive units being located within those Arab countries in which labour is cheap, the globalised nature of Israeli capital means that it can as easily and perhaps more profitably seek out labour in the Indian sub-continent or the Far East. Meanwhile the much vaunted free trade zone agreement with Turkey, which many Arabs feared would create a hegemonic non-Arab economic bloc within the Middle East, has in reality played only a supporting role in the economic relationship between Ankara and Tel Aviv. The real hub of commercial links has been the sale of Israeli military hardware, technology and upgrading services to back up a military-strategic alliance.

In line with its global approach to trade, in 1995 Israel ratified the Uruguay Round Agreement and became a member of the World Trade Organisation, with the WTO regime being implemented from 1 January 1996. It still retains two unique forms of protection for locally produced goods. *Harama* is a system of 'uplifting' the pre-duty value of invoice prices for imports (allowed under the Brussels Definition of Value or BDF), and the TAMA is a post-duty uplift which converts cost insurance freight (c.i.f.) value plus duty to an equivalent wholesale price for purposes of imposing purchase tax. There are also some remaining purchase taxes on specific goods, and the removal of discriminatory measures against some other goods has been slow and uneven. The manipulation of standards requirements has obstructed the entry of goods that are also domestically produced, notably those imported from the US which has consistently complained against this bias. On the whole, however, and with the final phasing out of almost all export subsidies, Israel is well and truly 'open for business'.

One consequence of this opening has been a dramatic rise in the volume of trade. This is evident from the increases in the dollar value of trade as illustrated in Table 3.5. While exports grew rapidly in the 1990s on the back of the high-tech industries, new markets and the implementation of various free trade agreements, imports grew faster. The dramatic increase in the population as immigrants flooded in from the former Soviet Union, and

Table 3.5 Balance of payments current account, 1990 and 1997 (US$ millions)

	1990	*1997*
Exports of goods free on board (f.o.b.)	12,133	21,894
Imports of goods f.o.b.	−15,149	−27,742
Trade balance	−3,016	−5,848
Exports of services	4,308	8,426
Imports of services	−4,930	−11,068
Balance on goods and services	−3,638	−8,490
Other income received	1,890	2,067
Other income paid	−3,611	−4,858
Balance on official and private transfers	5,931	6,266
Current balance	574	−5,014

Source: *Europa Yearbooks: The Middle East and North Africa*, 1994 and 2000.

the high rates of economic growth consequently generated, had created a massive surge in demand for production inputs, consumer goods and capital imports. Furthermore, with few natural resources of its own, Israel is highly vulnerable to price movements in raw materials, commodities and energy. Since over 80 per cent of its exports are manufactured goods, the trade profile is also weakened when the prices of manufactured goods fall relative to commodity prices – as they did in the mid-1990s (accounting for some of the trade deficit). During that period the value of the dollar also fell and, since exports are measured in dollars due to the size of the US market for Israeli sales, the relative value of exports to imports was also heavily disguised.

In short, the widening trade deficit at this point in time reflects a number of circumstantial features of the period as much as any chronic failure of the economy to sell enough to pay its way. Moreover, like other emerging 'feline' economies such as India, Thailand, Singapore and Turkey, Israel maintains a trade deficit with a high ratio of investment goods and production inputs, signifying economic confidence and potential future growth rather than present weakness (see Table 3.6).

In fact exports are not only growing at a satisfactory rate,[33] they are also diversifying, with manufactured goods far outstripping any other export sector apart from diamonds. As Table 3.7 illustrates, Israel exports a range of manufactured and industrial goods, with the fastest growth being seen in electrical goods, electronics, chemicals, rubber goods and plastics.

The aid debate

Given the endemic trade deficit, it would be inexcusable to ignore the contribution of private and official transfers to the current account, although Table 3.5 shows that even the heavy subsidisation of the economy which

Table 3.6 Composition of imports (US$ millions, including cost, insurance and freight)

	1985	1998
Consumer goods	621.0	3,875
Non-durable	389.3	2,146
Durable	231.7	1,729
Production inputs	6,278.9	18,488
Diamonds	1,285.5	3,839
Fuel	1,510.2	1,800
Other	3,483.2	12,849
Investment goods	1,413.7	4,550
Total imports	8,313.6	26,913

Source: Economist Intelligence Unit, *Country Profile: Israel and the Occupied Territories.*

Table 3.7 Composition of industrial exports (excluding diamonds), 1980 and 1998 (US$ millions)

	1980	*1998*	*Increase (%)*
Electrical and electronics	490	7,415	1530.2
Chemicals, rubber and plastics	851	3,851	452.5
Metal and machinery	761	2,102	276.2
Textiles, clothing and leather	473	1,063	224.7
Food and beverages	298	475	159.3
Mining and quarrying	175	443	253.1
Other	292	778	266.4

Source: *The Israeli Economy at a Glance* (Jerusalem: State of Israel Ministry of Industry and Trade, 1999).

these represent is not enough to balance the account. In recent years, the combination of grants, loans and private transfers has amounted to around $7 billion a year, around $3 billion of which come in the form of military and economic assistance from the United States, $2.8 billion in private remittances and the remaining $1.2 billion from the Jewish Agency and other institutions. Much of the American aid is used to service existing foreign debts (mostly to the USA itself) of around $25 billion, although the debt servicing burden has fallen in recent years due to rapid GDP and export growth,[34] or to purchase American-made military goods. Since the mid-1980s the ratio of aid to arms has hovered at around 2:1, and since 1992 Israel has been able to take advantage of American government loan guarantees to raise a further $10 billion worth of loans. This combination provides the Israeli government with credit-worthiness in international capital markets and the flexibility to adjust its defence budget up or downwards without impacting upon the budget deficit. It has furthermore been of great value in cushioning the processes of first stabilisation and then structural reform. Some critics have argued that it is time for Israel to wean itself off this annual injection of cash, not least since the debt profile is relatively long-term and could probably be serviced from economic and export growth in the coming years. They argue that 'no strings attached' aid has artificially boosted living standards for too long and distorted economic structures. Others point out the ongoing benefits of technology transfers via privileged access to military purchases and the freedom which the guaranteed source of income gives the government to invest in infrastructural growth. Either way, it is incorrect to assume that Israel is either dependent on the aid or weakened by it. The experiences of Malaysia and South Korea both demonstrated that aid, when used to enable governments to invest in industry-oriented infrastructure, actually strengthens a developing economy. In this context, one can point to the fact that investment as a percentage of GDP in Israel (24 per cent in 1996) is higher than in either Germany or the United States and almost on a par with Japan. The combination of economic and export growth on the one hand, and the freeing of resources made possible by economic assistance, allowed Israel to enjoy an investment splurge in the mid-1990s, with major new transport and energy facility construction and educational growth, the benefits of which will be seen in future production and exports.

Conclusion

Michael Shalev has summarised Israel's comparative performance in liberalising its economy as follows:

> An educated guess is that, relative to trends in other countries, Israel has gone particularly far in cutting [non-social] public expenditure and in deregulating the state's role in capital markets; is around the average with respect to trade and foreign-currency reforms and privatisation; and ranks below the average in terms of welfare state retrenchment.[35]

This assessment reflects a number of features of the present economy. Firstly, there is a general consensus among politicians and economic agents that liberalisation is the only road forward. The gains that have accrued so far have reinforced this perception among the élite, but the failure to make really profound progress in either reforming the welfare state or cutting the size of the public sector indicates that resistance remains at the level of beneficiaries and employees. This is in no small part the result of the paternalistic legacy surviving from the era of *mamlachtiyut*, when the state was both powerful over and responsible for the corporate interests of the population. Secondly, Israel has been cushioned from the most painful effects of structural adjustment by a combination of external economic assistance and a large influx of highly educated and sophisticated labour in the form of immigrants from the former Soviet Union. Indeed, the latter would have been a far greater burden on the Israeli economy if American loan guarantees and aid had not been forthcoming. In the event, foreign transfers enabled the state not only to absorb the labour but also to provide the infrastructural growth needed to utilise it effectively to enhance growth and exports.

There remain tensions within Israel between the winners and loser of economic reform which obstruct some aspects of liberalisation. But while these are generally common to liberalising economies, the Israeli government must also deal with the implications of its own political uniqueness. Coalition bargaining usually results in budgetary hand-outs for politically significant groups but does not necessarily provide reciprocal economic benefits. Zionist imperatives demand high levels of expenditure on maintaining the conditions that will attract and keep immigrants, although the fact that the Russians are probably the last great *aliyah* will inevitably mean that this dynamic diminishes in the future. As collectivism and the role of the state are steadily eroded by the twin processes of economic liberalisation and post-Zionist politics, and as alterations in the international environment reduce American political will behind economic assistance, the Israeli economy may come to more closely resemble other developed economies. Alternatively, in the absence of solidaristic corporatism, and as the market economy takes over, ethnic and religious diversity may yet assume class configurations. Secular Jews may find the financial burden of the state subsidy-dependent *Haredim* communities to be increasingly unacceptable, fuelling political antagonisms over the Jewish identity of the Israeli state. Oriental Jews may yet find the economic power in the free market to challenge the political domination of the *Ashkenazim*. Similarly, globalisation and the internationalisation of production, trade and labour will undermine concepts of Hebrew exclusivity and territorial attachment. Thus, while the post-ESP era has been one of deep-rooted change for the Israeli economy, it may well be that the greatest upheavals are yet to come.[36]

Notes

1 In 1998, per capita GDP was $16,404.
2 Howard Rosen, 'Economic Relations Between Israel and the United States', in Robert O. Freedman (ed), *Israel Under Rabin* (Boulder, Co.: Westview Press, 1995), p. 211.
3 See, for example, Yair Aharoni, *The Israeli Economy* (London: Routledge, 1991), p. 56.
4 In 1931, 93.4 per cent of Jewish males aged 7 years and over were literate and 78.7 per cent of women. See Nadav Halevi and Ruth Klinov-Malul, *The Economic Development of Israel* (New York: Praeger, 1968), p. 17.
5 Ibid.
6 Howard M. Sachar, *A History of Israel* (Oxford: Blackwell, 1977), p.155.
7 Ibid., p. 159.
8 For elaboration on this point see Barbara J. Smith, *The Roots of Separatism in Palestine: British Economic Policy, 1920–1929* (London: I.B. Tauris, 1993).
9 Baruch Kimmerling and Joel Migdal, *Palestinians: The Making of a People* (The Free Press: New York, 1993), p. 59.
10 Roger Owen, 'Economic Development in Mandatory Palestine' in George T. Abed, *The Palestinian Economy* (London: Routledge, 1988), p. 14.
11 Yosef Almogi, quoted in Howard M. Sachar, op. cit., p. 413.
12 *The Independent*, 14 July 1993. Some estimates have been as high as 90 per cent, including *Newsview*, 10 January 1984, p. 16.
13 In 1990 the *Histadrut* accounted for 12 per cent of all economic activity and more than 30 per cent of industrial output. It was the parent company for more than 400 industrial *kibbutzim* plants, several dozen *kibbutzim* hotels, 77 per cent of *kibbutz*-produced agricultural exports and the largest bank in Israel.
14 The top rate of tax on personal earned income was reduced from 60 to 48 per cent, leviable on income over $25,000.
15 *Financial Times*, 29 May 1990.
16 Reducing cartel activity in financial services was not confined to the banks. The insurance sector even saw a number of legal trials and forced resignations, while new (including foreign) firms moved into the market.

17 Economist Intelligence Unit, *Country Profile: Israel and the Occupied Territories 1996–97* (London: EIU, 1997), pp. 23–4.
18 The pre-planned rate of depreciation of the lower edge of the band was also changed from 6 to 4 per cent annually, effectively resulting in a further widening of the band.
19 An explanation of the linkages between immigration, demand, supply and growth can be found in Ben-Zion Zilberfarb, 'The Israeli Economy in the 1990s: Immigration, the Peace Process, and the Medium-term Prospects for Growth', in *Israel Affairs*, Vol. 3, No. 1 (Autumn 1996), pp. 1–12.
20 In 1993, trade with South Korea grew by 50 per cent. In 1994 exports to Thailand grew by 69 per cent and those to India by 54 per cent.
21 In 1997, the ratio of government spending to GDP was 47 per cent. http://www.state.gov/www/issues/economic/trade_reports/neareast9//
22 *Guardian*, 10 February 1996.
23 In 1996, Israel had 138 scientists and technicians per 10,000 workers. This compared with the next highest figure of 80 per 10,000 workers for the United States. Ibid.
24 In 1995 the Ofeq I and II satellites were launched for non-civilian use and the Amos I was launched on the French Ariane rocket.
25 *Financial Times*, 6 May 1999.
26 Economist Intelligence Unit, *Country Report: Israel and the Occupied Territories 1998–99* (London: EIU, 1999).
27 Michael Shalev, 'Have Globalisation and Liberalisation "Normalised" Israel's Political Economy?' in *Israel Affairs*, Vol. 5, Nos 2 & 3 (Winter–Spring 1999), p. 142.
28 Ibid., p. 132.
29 With a total capitalisation in excess of $8 billion (1996 figures).
30 *Financial Times*, 1 June 2000.
31 Michael Shalev (1999), op. cit., p. 131
32 'The Israeli government actively solicits foreign private investment, including joint ventures, especially in industries based on exports, tourism and high technology. Foreign firms are accorded national treatment in terms of taxation and labour relations, and are eligible for incentives for designated "approved" investments in priority development zones. Profits, dividends and rents can generally be repatriated without difficulty through a licensed bank.' http://www.state.gov/www/issues/economic/trade_reports/neareast9//
33 In the early 1990s, exports grew by an average of 10 per cent a year, and by 8 per cent in 1995.
34 The ratio of net debt to GDP fell from 73 per cent in 1985 to 23.2 per cent in 1995. Debt servicing fell from 18.3 per cent of export revenues in 1991 to 12.9 per cent in 1995. *Country Profile: Israel and the Occupied Territories 1996–97* (London: EIU, 1998).
35 Michael Shalev (1999), op. cit., p. 147.
36 For an excellent analysis of the political economy of transition in Israel, see Ephraim Kleiman, 'The Waning of Israeli Etatism' in *Israel Studies*, Vol. 2, No. 2 (1988).

4   A place among the nations

Introduction

Foreign policy in Israel has always remained subordinate to the demands of ensuring national security. Having been involved in six major conventional conflicts in its half century of existence (in addition to innumerable border clashes of varying intensity), the culture of national security remains central to the conduct of Israel's foreign policy. Maintaining a powerful military, as well as ensuring strong ties with Washington, have become the enduring themes of Israel's search for security. It is an approach determined by the logic of a security dilemma particular to a state that lacks substantial human resources, strategic depth and, until recently, any tangible regional alliance.

Despite the seismic shifts in the contours of the international system since 1991, the old mantra that 'Israel has no foreign policy, only a defence policy' remains the dominant prism through which the Jewish state views its immediate external environment. It would be churlish to ignore the formal peace treaties Israel has signed with Jordan and Egypt, or, more immediately, the recognition of Palestinian national rights, however circumscribed, under the Oslo Accords. But equally, Israel's burgeoning strategic relationship with Turkey, its concerns expressed forcefully over the acquisition – real or otherwise – of weapons of mass destruction (WMD) by Baghdad and Tehran, as well as the continued importance placed upon the special relationship with the United States, delineate a continuity of thinking seemingly immune from changes in the broad arena of global politics.[1] While Israeli foreign policy has become synonymous with the external demands of national security, this fails to capture the domestic context of foreign policy decision-making peculiar to the Jewish state. This is important because, since the 1980s, the consensus among Israelis over what constitutes national security began to fragment under the impact of Israel's invasion of Lebanon in 1982 and the outbreak of the Palestinian *Intifada* in 1987, events that were entwined with the fate of the territories captured and occupied by Israel in the June 1967 war.[2]

As discussed in Chapter 2, a popular consensus over the strategic threat faced by Israel among a hostile Arab world held in abeyance ideological debates within Zionism over territory to be claimed as part of a Jewish sovereign state. But since 1967, Israel's domination of the physical and political space in the West Bank and Gaza Strip has not only appeared incongruent with Israel's democratic tradition, but exposed deep rifts in a society that even seasoned observers of Israel's political scene have come to believe contain the future seeds of internecine conflict.[3] In this respect, Israel's foreign policy is as much about defining the political boundaries of Zionism, as it is about determining the future physical borders of the Jewish state.

Domestic determinants of Israel's foreign policy

In his seminal study, *The Foreign Policy System of Israel*, Michael Brecher describes the dominant Jewish character of the state as the prism through which all foreign policy decisions are made. He declared, 'For Israel's high policy elite, as for the entire society, there is a primordial and pre-eminent aspect of the political culture – its *Jewishness*: this pervades thought, feeling, belief and behaviour in the political realm'.[4] Israel remains one of the few states worldwide to encourage immigration on ideological grounds alone irrespective of constraints imposed by resources or geographical space. Because of the emotive appeal of fulfilling the highest ideal of Zionism, the state continues to actively promote the value of *aliyah* throughout the Jewish diaspora and among governments able to facilitate Jewish immigration to Israel. Accordingly, such activity has become a foreign policy *value* rather than just another foreign policy objective, given the decimation of European Jewry during the Second World War.

Brecher noted that Ben-Gurion regarded the population of the State of Israel and those Jews living in what was termed *galut* (exile or the *diaspora*) as indivisible. In perhaps the most explicit declaration of the Jewish state's *raison d'être*, Israel's first premier declared that: 'The two groups are interdependent. The future of Israel – its security, its welfare, and its capacity to fufil its historic mission – depends on world Jewry. And the future of world Jewry depends on the survival of Israel'.[5] It is this claim to be the protector of heterogeneous Jewish communities worldwide, irrespective of their national allegiance, that is perhaps unique to Israel in the construction of its national identity. It should be noted, however, that defining the *internal* character of the Jewish state and, in particular, the exact balance to be struck between religious and secular identities remains, as the assassination of Rabin demonstrated, a contemporary issue of bitter debate.

Israel has gone to extraordinary lengths to rescue *diaspora* communities deemed to be under threat. The airlift of 35,000 Jews from the Yemen between May 1948 and November 1949 provided a template for similar operations involving Ethiopian Jewry in 1984 and 1991. More recently, some 1,000 Jews were smuggled out of Sarajevo in 1994 by representatives of the Jewish Agency and the Israeli intelligence agency *Mossad* during the

Bosnian war.[6] Such actions are, according to the Israeli journalist and historian Tom Segev, entirely consonant with the core belief of Zionism that 'Jews can live in security and with full equal rights only in their own country and that they therefore must have an autonomous and sovereign state, strong enough to defend its existence'.[7] The irony for Segev, however, is that given the tensions that have been engendered by the creation of the State of Israel, far safer places exist elsewhere in the world for Jews now to live.

The policy-making elite

Determining what constitutes *the* national interest, and indeed the core beliefs of Zionism, remains a vexed question. In the case of Israel, core values – the need to secure the Jewish state against external threat while preserving a Jewish majority internally – provide a framework in which the process of inductive reasoning determines the national interest. As such, ideological, pragmatic and geo-strategic dispositions of key decision-makers – attitudinal prisms – remain key variables in determining policy preferences. This is not to suggest that such prisms vary markedly between decision-makers over a period of time. From 1967 through to 1987 Israeli foreign policy was marked more by continuity than change in its approach towards the Arab world, as well as the need to ensure strong ties with Washington.

The emphasis upon security is influenced in no small part by the individual background of those charged with maintenance of Israel's national security, with key decision-makers having been, to quote Efraim Inbar, 'socialised in the defence establishment'.[8] Such socialisation is best personified by the figure of Yitzhak Rabin, who held both the portfolios of Prime Minister and Minister of Defence twice, having already served as the Israeli Defence Force (IDF) chief of staff and Israel's ambassador to Washington. Other key individual decision-makers steeped in the ethos of Israel's military culture have included Yigal Yadin, Ezer Weizmann, Moshe Dayan, Yigal Allon, Ariel Sharon, Ehud Barak and Yitzhak Mordechai, all former generals who at one time or another occupied the portfolios of either foreign affairs or defence.

This process of socialisation has, however, proven to be problematic to a premier lacking a perceived 'grounding in or experience over' security issues. Levi Eshkol, Israel's premier on the eve of the June 1967 war, faced strong pressure from his Chief of Staff, Yitzhak Rabin, to turn the Defence Ministry – a portfolio held by Eshkol himself – over to former Chief of Staff Moshe Dayan, thereby creating a critical mass within the cabinet for the option of launching a pre-emptive strike against Egypt. More recently, the permissive environment invoked by the need to ensure national security allowed Ariel Sharon, as Israeli Defence Minister in 1982, to manipulate both cabinet opinion and Prime Minister Begin into authorising Israel's invasion of Lebanon.

Given this process of socialisation, it is not suprising that foreign policy in Israel has been viewed as complementing, rather than determining, the value placed upon ensuring the maintenance of Israel's military superiority. This is perhaps best illustrated by the fact that the Israeli *Knesset* committee system, based on the Westminster model, convenes such a cross-party forum on both foreign affairs and defence combined, rather than treating them as distinct areas. The influence, however, that such committees have on preference formation in foreign policy remains limited. Indeed, once the horse-trading involved in the formation of a coalition government has been completed, the *Knesset* remains circumscribed from any real input into the decision-making process.

As such, foreign policy decision-making remains a restricted process in Israel, and one in which strong personalities can emasculate the role of bureaucracies charged with formulating and implementing foreign policy. David Ben-Gurion, Golda Meir and Yitzhak Rabin based their leadership in government upon highly stratified lines with relatively few people party to broad policy formulation beyond their respective 'kitchen' cabinets. Nowhere is this demonstrated more visibly than in the role played by the Ministry of Foreign Affairs. In the competition for influence within the Israeli cabinet, the views of the Foreign Ministry have carried less weight than either the views expressed by the Prime Minister's Office or the Defence Ministry. Indeed, even though Uri Savir, Director General of the Foreign Ministry, was responsible for brokering the negotiations that led to the signing of the Oslo Accords, senior representatives of the Defence Ministry and the IDF dominated negotiations over implementation of the Accords once they were signed. As one former ministry official opined:

> This phenomenon can only be understood in the Israeli context. All of Israel's interests are determined according to security considerations, and that's why the security establishment became dominant in defining the state's vital interests. . . political considerations were pushed aside. It was so in the talks with the Palestinians, as well as the contacts that preceded the signing of the peace treaty with Jordan.[9]

Moreover, prime ministers have often combined the duties of their primary office with that of foreign minister, denying sufficient representation of Foreign Ministry views on policy making at cabinet level. Accordingly, the Foreign Ministry has all too often been left to deal with issues of presentation rather than substance.[10] In this hierarchy of influence, the intelligence services hold considerable sway in defining Israel's key foreign policy interests, a position that has led to a process of cognitive dissonance whereby alternative avenues of diplomacy have been downgraded.

Three main intelligence agencies exist in Israel: military intelligence (*Agaf Modi'in* or AMAN), the *Mossad* (*HaMossad LeModi'in U'Letafkidim Meyuhadim* – Institute for Intelligence and Special Duties), and *Shabak* (*Sherlut Bitachon Kalali* – General Security Service or GSS). Of these, AMAN carries the most weight, with the Director of Military Intelligence and the head of AMAN's assessment division serving as intelligence advisors to the Israeli cabinet. They remain subordinate to the Minister of Defence and Chief of Staff of the IDF, who attend all cabinet meetings. Mossad and the GSS operate under the auspices of the Prime Minister's Office and coordinate intelligence gathering and assessment with AMAN through the *Varash* (*Va'ad Rashei Sherutim* – the Committee of the Chiefs of the Services). Yet assessing the objectivity of attitudinal prisms through which an intelligence assessment or 'product' is presented to the consumer, in this case the Prime Minister or Israeli cabinet, can prove particularly problematic. On assuming office in 1996, former Prime Minister Netanyahu believed that as appointees of the previous Rabin/Peres government, the heads of the intelligence services had become politicised into an uncritical acceptance of the Oslo process and, as such, 'tended to ignore military intelligence, Mossad and GSS warnings that the likelihood of war increased as the peace process moved towards a dead end'.[11]

Suspicions of political bias in formulating policy preferences are not new to a state where ideological disposition has influenced decision-making. Accordingly, much debate surrounded the establishment by Netanyahu of a National Security Council (NSC) based on the American model. The creation of an NSC was first recommended by the Yadin–Sharaf committee in 1963, set up following the intelligence scandal surrounding the Lavon Affair in the mid-1950s. Intermittent calls for the establishment of an NSC were met with entrenched bureaucratic resistance from the heads of the existing intelligence bureaucracies and government ministries. It was the failed Mossad attempt on the life of a Hamas activist, Khalid Meshal, in Amman in September 1997 that finally broke this resistance. The NSC is supposed to be a forum for balanced assessment of foreign policy aims and objectives, but evidence to date suggests that its areas of responsibility remain circumscribed. Established in March 1999, the NSC has been tasked with combating regional proliferation of WMD, rather than acting, as was the original intention, as a co-ordinating body overseeing objective assessment on a broad range of foreign policy issues, including continued negotiations with the Palestinians.[12]

Extra-parliamentary actors

If bureaucracies and personalities dealing with national security dominate the actual foreign policy decision-making process, the actual arena in which that process operates has been influenced heavily by pressure groups or grass-roots activists representing a distinct ideological, ethnic and religious outlook associated with policy towards the Occupied Territories. The immediate strategic threat Israel faced between 1948 to 1967 held in abeyance debates inherent within the very concept of Zionism over the exact territory to be claimed as part of a Jewish sovereign state. The demands of *mamlachtiyut* – not least the need to build a coherent polity from a largely immigrant society – as well as the continuous demands of ensuring external security, offset potentially divisive debates over the normative character of Zionism. While successive Israeli governments remained convinced that the ceasefire lines established following the 1948–49 Arab–Israeli war remained indefensible, Zionism *per se* had never reached a consensus over defining the territorial dimensions of the Jewish state. While a cross-party consensus justified retention of territories captured in the June 1967 war both on strategic grounds and in the absence of peace overtures from surrounding Arab states, a confluence of interest emerged between Revisionist Zionists, who believed *a priori* in the unity of *Eretz Yisrael* on historical grounds, and religious-nationalist Zionists, who regarded the capture and settlement of the Occupied Territories in eschatological terms.[13]

Gush Emunim (Bloc of the Faithful), formed in 1974, became the most high profile of such groups. Indeed, between 1977 and 1983, *Gush Emunim* enjoyed a symbiotic relationship with the government of Menachem Begin. Settlements associated with the movement were accorded the same status as *kibbutzim*, a move that allowed public money to be used in the process of ideological construction while suggesting that *Gush Emunim* were now seen officially as the true inheritors of the pioneering ideals behind Zionism. In 1980, *Yesha* (Council of Jewish Settlements in Judea, Samaria and Gaza), an umbrella organisation representing all settlements and settlers in the Occupied Territories, was formed. There is little to distinguish *Gush Emunim* from *Yesha* but, if anything, *Yesha* is more influential in terms of the direct influence it can exert upon government policy towards the territories. This is because several of its members represent nationalist parties in the *Knesset* that have included in the past *Tehiya* and the NRP.

The discourse surrounding the issue of the territories continues to be cloaked in the language of national security. Certainly, for organisations representative of the ideological and religous right in Israel, policy towards the territories remains internal to the Jewish state. Recognition of the future status of the Occupied Territories as constituting a foreign policy issue negates claims over sovereignty inherent within the very concept of *Eretz Yisrael*. In this regard, the emphasis placed upon national security disguised the core debates surrounding the West Bank by justifying settlement policy in terms of protection against the 'other', rather than dealing with the recrudescence of a debate concerning the very identity of the Jewish state. It is such concerns over the debilitating impact of the occupation on Israel's political culture and social cohesion that first led to the emergence of peace groups in Israel such as *Shalom Achshav*. The emergence of such organisations has proved to be symptomatic of a broader evolution away from the traditional demands of self-sacrifice incumbent within the original concept of *mamlachtiyut* and continued during the *Intifada* as questions of moral rectitude undermined the mantra of national security as justification for Israel's brutal response to violent – though for the most part non-lethal – expressions of Palestinian identity.[14] As such, the Oslo Accords were as much about the need to assuage increased tensions within Israeli society, as any attempt to deal with the national aspirations of the Palestinians in the West Bank and Gaza. The Accords represented, in effect, an attempt by Rabin's government on behalf of the State of Israel to seek security from itself.

Israel's foreign relations 1948–1993: the search for security

Ever since the establishment of the Jewish state in 1948, all Israeli governments have, as Shibley Telhami notes, followed a duel strategy in their foreign relations. With regard to its immediate environment, Israel always sought strategies that would prevent the Arab world uniting both politically and militarily. In this regard, divisions in the Arab world have always been viewed as advantageous to Israel. At the apex of this strategy was the desire to see Egypt, the clear hegemonic leader in the Arab world, removed as a threat to the Jewish state. Secondly, Israel has always sought the patronage, if not outright support, of a great power.[15] This dual strategy was designed to ameliorate what were perceived as Israel's key vulnerabilities: its small geographical space, vulnerable borders, finite economic resources, few natural resources, and vast demographic asymmetries with surrounding Arab states.

While Israeli leaders always regarded close ties with the United States as the best guarantor of Israel's security, several factors impeded the development of the 'special relationship' that today marks bilateral ties between the two countries. Washington had been the first state to offer *de facto* recognition of Israel on 14 May 1948, and had agreed to lend Israel $100 million the following year. Yet at a time when the Cold War had begun to shape global politics, Israel's first Prime Minister, David Ben-Gurion, remained acutely aware that much of the Jewish *diaspora* remained behind the Iron Curtain. Moreover, many within the new-born polity held open sympathies for the position of the Soviet Union, partly out of ideological affiliation and partly out of recognition of the huge suffering incurred by Moscow in its struggle to crush the nemesis of the Jewish people, Nazi Germany.

By 1950, however, Israel had begun to openly identify with the West. With the outbreak of the Korean war, Ben-Gurion considered seriously the dispatch of a small military contingent as a means to cement closer ties with Washington, while offers were also made to the United States that would allow for the pre-positioning of American military supplies in the Negev desert.[16] All were rebuffed by Washington. The initial grace that had met the establishment of the Jewish state under the Truman administration – a position influenced heavily by the need to harness the American Jewish vote to the Democratic party cause – gave way to a sober reassessment of United States foreign policy interests in the Middle East with the election of the Republican candidate, Dwight D. Eisenhower, to the White House in 1952. His new Secretary of State, John Foster Dulles, argued that the ability of Washington to contain Moscow in the Middle East and ensure the unfettered flow of oil to the West had been undermined by Truman's support for Israel. In short, attempts by Washington to cohere the Arab states into some form of anti-Soviet alliance could not be reconciled with Israel's own security interests.

Accordingly, the 1950s was marked by periodic tensions in bilateral relations between Washington and Tel Aviv. Israel's policy of cross-border incursions into neighbouring states brought sharp rebukes from the United States. While justified by the Israelis as response to terrorist assaults against civilian settlements, the scale of the retribution exacted by the IDF was often out of all proportion to the initial attacks. Such attacks were met with vocal condemnation from Washington, mindful that such attacks undermined its attempts to promote an anti-Soviet alliance among the Arab states.[17] Ben-Gurion, realising that access to American arms and security guarantees remained a distant prospect in the short to medium term, looked increasingly to an alliance with France to secure his military requirements. Paris was able to supply Israel with advance fighter aircraft and armour, but it was in the field of nuclear technology that French aid proved crucial. Under help and guidance offered by Paris, Israel constructed its own nuclear test facility at Dimona in the Negev desert. While maintaining that its function remained directed towards peaceful purposes, overwhelming evidence exists that Dimona has, since its construction in 1957, been used by Israel to develop its own nuclear weapons capability.[18]

Both Paris and Tel Aviv remained concerned at the direction of Egyptian foreign policy under President Gamal Abdul Nasser, who had taken over the reins of power in Cairo in 1954. A man of extraordinary charisma, Nasser's brand of Arab nationalism struck a popular chord throughout the Arab states of the Middle East and North Africa. While never forged into a coherent ideology, 'Nasserism' remained inimical to what was perceived as the continued colonial usurpation of Arab rights and sovereignty. Israel was commonly perceived through this popularist if simplistic mindset, but such ideas also began to influence the struggle against French rule in Algeria. In short, both Israel and France had a shared interest in cutting Nasser down to size. In an episode that still provokes fierce historical controversy today, Israeli military intelligence initiated sabotage operations against both American and British targets and property in Egypt in 1954, in the infamous 'Lavon Affair'. Aside from the historical controversy of an operation initiated without formal Israeli government approval, the episode is of note because it undermined secret contacts between Israeli foreign ministry officials acting on behalf of the new Israeli Prime Minister,

Moshe Sharett, and emissaries representing Nasser. The Egyptian President, believing at the very least that Sharett could not control his own defence ministry, promptly broke off these exploratory talks and looked to strengthen Egypt's own defence posture.

The resulting Czech arms deal of September 1955 – so called because Moscow used the Communist government in Prague as a front for the deal – was perceived by Israel as a clear threat to its national security. Ben-Gurion, having once again become Prime Minister in November 1955, believed war remained the only viable option for Israel if its national security were not to be permenantly undermined. Time was of the essence since the Chief of Staff, Moshe Dayan, believed that Israel had to strike against the Egyptian army before it could master the Soviet weaponry. Moreover, Ben-Gurion believed that Washington would not supply Israel with the types of weapons Israel believed necessary to offset the scale of the Czech arms deal. As Yaacov Bar-Siman-Tov notes, Ben-Gurion now felt free to 'disregard US calls for Israeli self restraint'.[19]

Other international and regional factors pointed increasingly to the use of force as the best means to secure Israel's position. While the Eisenhower administration remained distant from Tel Aviv, its relations with Cairo had become tense. Washington and London had agreed originally to provide loans to Cairo to facilitate the construction of the Aswan Dam, a key infrastructure project for Nasser if the modernisation of Egyptian agriculture and industry was to progress. With Nasser's decision to recognise the People's Republic of China, both the United States and Britain withdrew their financial backing. In response, Nasser decided to nationalise the Suez Canal company, the majority shares in which were held by the British and French governments. The belief in both London and Paris that Cairo would never be able to operate the company effectively – its revenue was earned by ensuring the safe navigation of international shipping through the canal – was soon disabused. Military force to deal with Nasser was viewed with increasing favour by Britain and France. It was a position that conflated neatly with the policy aims of Israel, who believed that decisive military action against Nasser had now become essential following the signing of a tripartite military agreement with Jordan and Syria.[20]

On 29 October 1956, Israel invaded the Sinai peninsula in secret collusion with London and Paris. British and French troops occupied the canal basin around Port Said. While successful militarily, the operation soon turned into a political fiasco. Under severe financial pressure from the United States, London was forced to withdraw its troops, soon to be followed by Paris. The Suez crisis marked the end of British paramountcy in the Middle East, but the outcome was more propitious for the Jewish state. Firstly, Israel had seized all of the Sinai peninsula, including the Straits of Tiran that had previously guarded access to the Red Sea and the Israeli port of Eilat. These Straits had been closed to Israeli shipping, making it difficult for Israel to develop both the port and alternative trade roots to Asia and

Africa. Secondly, the IDF had captured or destroyed massive amounts of Soviet weaponry, thereby undermining the modernisation of the Egyptian military. Thirdly, while Eisenhower used financial as well as political leverage to force an Israeli withdrawal from the Sinai, Tel Aviv made important political gains. Washington, albeit grudgingly, recognised Israeli concerns over freedom of navigation, thus ensuring that the Straits of Tiran could not be closed to Israeli shipping. Golda Meir, then Israel's Foreign Minister, made it clear that any future closure of the Straits would be seen as an act of war by Israel and that the Jewish state would act accordingly. Moreover, Israel gained the partial demilitarisation of the Sinai, with a United Nations Observer Force stationed along the border between Israel and Egypt.

These gains aside, Israel drew one important lesson from Suez. Power in the Middle East no longer lay in the European capitals but with the United States. While relations were to remain close with France until at least the mid-1960s, Israel began to court the United States more assiduously, a process that included supporting more vigorously lobby groups on Capitol Hill that could influence United States foreign policy towards the region. Most notable among these, the American–Israel Public Affairs Committee (AIPAC) was to play an increasingly influential role in determining Washington's policy towards the Arab–Israeli conflict. Today, AIPAC is reckoned to be second only to the National Rifle Association in the influence that it can exert over senators and congressmen in Washington.

The phrase 'dormant war' was used by Yitzhak Rabin to describe Israel's external relations with the surrounding Arab states between 1957 and 1967. In the immediate aftermath of Suez, Nasser's position at the apex of Arab politics remained unassailable. The recipient of substantial Soviet aid, Nasser appeared set upon laying the foundations for wider political unity among the Arab states. Yet the formation of the United Arab Republic (UAR) in 1958, seen as the first concrete step towards this goal, foundered upon inter-state rivalries. Syria, a supposedly equal partner in the UAR, proved unwilling to accept the increased domination of its political structures by Cairo. By 1961, the experiment in greater unity had collapsed. Moreover, Nasser's intervention in the Yemen Civil War in September 1962, brought about by the overthrow of the Royal Family by Yemeni army officers holding Republican sympathies, highlighted the bifurcation of inter-Arab politics. Monarchical or dynastic regimes, most notably Saudi Arabia and Jordan, rallied to support the deposed Imam, while Egyptian intervention on the side of the Republicans included the dispatch of 50,000 Egyptian troops. Poorly trained and ill equipped to cope with the insurgency tactics of the Royalist forces, the Egyptian army soon found itself mired in a conflict it could not win.

The splits in the Arab world only served Israel's interests. Allegations have been made that Israel, through third parties, helped supply Royalist forces in the mountains surrounding the Yemeni capital San'a.[21] Whatever the truth, the debilitating impact of the war upon Egypt certainly benefited

Israel. During this period, the IDF underwent both modernisation and expansion, with emphasis placed upon building up the air force and armoured corps. Politically, however, Israel had begun to forge closer ties with Washington. In this they were undoubtedly aided by the election of the Democrat John F. Kennedy into the Oval Office in 1960. For Kennedy, the perception of Nasser as a close ally of the Soviet Union and a threat to conservative Arab states, reduced the risk of Arab opprobrium as Washington approved closer ties with Tel Aviv. Kennedy, moreover, acknowledged Israel's security dilemma, though his willingness to discuss arms sales to Israel was in part driven by a desire to use weapon sales to disuade Tel Aviv from 'going nuclear'.[22]

Under Kennedy, the first steps were taken towards the establishment of their special relationship with the sale of Hawk surface to air missiles to Israel. Kennedy was also the first American President to give open verbal assurances regarding Israel's security, declaring that the United States would come to the aid of Israel if the Jewish state were to be the victim of aggression. Such support, while welcomed by Israel, was contingent upon Tel Aviv recognising that Washington had its own interests in the region and that, accordingly, Israel should refrain from undertaking policies that would threaten those interests.[23] The assassination of Kennedy in November 1963 did little to alter the upward trajectory of bilateral ties between Washington and Tel Aviv. The new incumbent at the White house, Democrat Lyndon Baines Johnson, remained alarmed at Cairo's drift into the Soviet orbit, a process underlined by the conclusion of a $500 million arms deal between Egypt and the Soviet Union in June 1963.

The result was a massive boost to Israel's conventional arsenal. Levi Eshkol, the Israeli premier, gave assurances over Israel's nuclear development. In return, Washington authorised the sale of armour and aircraft to Israel. It should be noted that Eshkol's assurances regarding Israel's nuclear activity were not conclusive. The IDF High Command in particular remained wary of agreements that in any way impeded Israel's ability to undertake actions or policies designed to ensure its own security independent of any other actor. This has become an enduring theme of Israeli national security. Even today, Israel has still to conclude a formal strategic alliance with the United States, fearing the terms of such an alliance would constrain any latitude for independent action. Accordingly, while allowing some limited inspection of its nuclear facilities, Israel adopted the position that it would not be the first state to introduce nuclear weapons to the Middle East, an opaque statement that remains crucial to Israel's policy of nuclear ambiguity.

Between 1965 and 1967, Israel received some 210 M60 tanks and 100 Skyhawk jets from the United States. This weaponry helped give Israel a qualitative edge that it was to deploy with devastating effect in the June War of 1967. Like much else in the Middle East, the origins of the war remain the subject of bitter debate. Tension on the Syrian–Israeli border had resulted in a number of armed clashes from late 1966 onwards. Israel accused Syria of deliberately shelling *kibbutzim* in the Galilee region, while Damascus argued that Tel Aviv was provoking such attack by encouraging Israeli farmers to plough in the demilitarised zone that had separated the two sides since 1949. Whatever the cause, the intensity of these clashes resulted in rising tension between Egypt and Israel. Nasser, stung by Syrian criticism of inaction in the face of Israel's belligerency, increased his rhetorical threats against Israel. In retrospect, it seems that Nasser had no clear intent to go to war, but hoisted by his own petard and acting on Soviet reports of Israeli troop movements that proved totally inaccurate, the Egyptian President blundered into a crisis that was to lead to war.[24]

According to Telhami, Israel felt it could not allow such provocative statements to go unchallenged 'lest other Arab states be emboldened to follow suit'.[25] Indeed, Nasser's decision to close the Straits of Tiran and order the removal of UN observers from the Sinai was viewed by Tel Aviv as a *casus belli* for war. A central tenet of Israel's foreign policy has been to prevent an effective alliance among Arab states emerging to challenge its sovereignty. The conclusion of a military pact between Jordan and Egypt on the eve of hostilities presented Israel with just such a scenario. The IDF, aware of the asymmetry it faced in terms of manpower and resources, as well as the vulnerability of its borders, argued that Israel only had a limited 'window of opportunity' in which to launch a decisive pre-emptive strike before mass mobilisation began to cripple the economy.[26] On the eve of the war, Meir Amit, head of the Israeli intelligence agency *Mossad*, was sent to Washington to gauge Johnson's opinion regarding the crisis. According to United States Defence Secretary Robert McNamara, Israel was told that 'if it acted alone, it would be alone. It was a very clear statement'.[27]

The June 1967 war proved to be one of the most devastating military campaigns of the twentieth century. Between 5 and 10 June 1967 Israel captured the whole of the Sinai peninsula, the Gaza Strip, the West Bank of the River Jordan including East Jerusalem, and the Golan Heights. Overnight, Israel more than doubled the size of the territory under its control. While it was a traumatic event for the Arab world, Israel emerged as the dominant military power of the region, a position that witnessed its ties with Washington grow ever closer. The Arab states presented little in the way of a viable military challenge. Indeed, Abba Eban, then Israel's Foreign Minister, recalled how many within his ministry expected a phone call from the Jordanian monarch, King Hussein, offering to open negotiations over the return of the West Bank.[28] But if June 1967 remains Israel's greatest moment of triumph, securing as it did a strategic depth it had hitherto not known, it also contained the seeds of internal dissent that has come to mark Israel's domestic political agenda.

Until 1967, Israel's foreign policy was determined by the need to survive among the animus of a largely Arab Middle East. The clear external dangers and the demands of *mamlachtiyut* had limited the extent to which domestic factors influenced foreign policy. After the June 1967 war this position began to change. Debates over the captured territory were initially dominated by strategic concerns, but increasingly, groups and organisations such as the Land of Israel Movement began to lobby against the return of territory, particularly the West Bank, which was seen as the cradle of Jewish civilisation. It was between 1967 and 1970 that the first Israeli settlements in the Occupied Territories were established. While for the most part these were collective farms, located in the sparsely populated area of the Jordan Valley, they set a precedent for the establishment of a permanent Israeli presence in the Occupied Territories that has come to bedevil relations between Israel and the Arab world. Indeed, the fate of over one million Palestinians now living under Israeli occupation changed the dynamic of conflict in the region. From 1948 to 1967 the Arab–Israeli conflict had been dominated by inter-state rivalries. Now, with the issue of the Palestinians to the fore and with it, irreconcilable claims to sovereignty over the West Bank, East Jerusalem and the Gaza Strip, Israel faced an intra-state conflict, the conduct of which came increasingly to dominate its relations with the Arab world and beyond.

Still, the regional hegemony that Israel enjoyed between 1967 and 1973 negated any serious attempt to find a diplomatic solution to the Arab–Israeli conflict. While faced with a rejuvenated Palestine Liberation Organisation (PLO), as well as a bitter war of attrition with Egypt along the banks of the Suez Canal between 1968 and 1970, Israel's regional supremacy was never seriously challenged in this period. While United Nations Resolution 242, passed in November 1967, called explicitly for Israel to return territories captured in June 1967 in exchange for Arab recognition of the Jewish state, few politicians on either side appeared willing to accept the resolution as the basis for settlement. Certainly, Israel felt sufficiently strong to rebuff attempts by William Rogers, the US Secretary of State, to link Israeli territorial retrenchment to Tel Aviv's requests for more advanced American weaponry. Rogers' plan, based on UN Resolution 242, was also undermined from within the White House. A new President, Richard Nixon, had been elected in 1969 and with his preoccupation with the Vietnam War, the formulation of policy towards the Arab–Israeli conflict came to be influenced heavily by his National Security Advisor, Henry Kissinger.

Kissinger very much saw the Arab–Israeli conflict through the prism of the Cold War. In the aftermath of the June 1967 war, both Washington and Moscow had undertaken massive arms supplies to their respective clients in the region. Kissinger saw Israel as a reliable ally and a regional power whose strength was key to undermining Soviet influence in the region. According to Bar-Siman-Tov, Kissinger felt that: 'Only when the Arab states, particularly Egypt, realized the futility of the military option and of Soviet military aid would they choose the diplomatic option'.[29] That diplomatic option was reliance upon the United States to secure a resolution to the Arab–Israeli conflict.

By 1973, therefore, Washington had come to regard Israel as a strategic asset in its competition with Moscow. The strong geo-political ties with the United States that Tel Aviv had always desired had come to fruition as a result of the exigencies of the Cold War. Between 1971 and 1973 American aid to Israel totalled $1.5 billion, the bulk of which was earmarked for military purposes. The strength of Israel's ties with Washington was certainly noted by Cairo. The death of President Nasser in September 1970 brought Anwar Sadat to power. Sadat, anxious to rebuild the Egyptian economy as well as regain the Sinai peninsula, made tentative diplomatic overtures towards Washington. The United States failed to appreciate the true significance of Cairo's moves, even when it expelled the bulk of Soviet advisers from Egypt in the summer of 1972. Early the following spring, Sadat began to draw up joint plans with Syrian President Hafez al-Assad for a simultaneous attack on the Sinai and the Golan Heights. For Sadat at least, recourse to the use of force had become the only means to break the diplomatic impasse.

Both Israel and the United States failed to see the coming war. Israel, perhaps blinded by perceptions of its own military superiority, only mobilised its reserve forces on the eve of the joint Egyptian and Syrian attack. Some have suggested that Tel Aviv's preoccupation with Palestinian terrorism, and in particular, tracking down those deemed responsible for the murder of Israeli athletes at the 1972 Munich Olympic Games, had blinded Israel's intelligence services to the dangers of war.[30] On 6 October 1973, the eve of Judaism's holiest day, *Yom Kippur*, Egyptian troops stormed across the Suez Canal, breaching Israeli defences and inflicting severe losses upon the IDF. The success of these initial assaults was matched by Syrian forces who came within an ace of breaking through to Lake Kinneret. After three weeks of bitter fighting, Israel had regained the upper hand, crossing the Suez Canal and encircling the Egyptian Third Army. Having pushed Syrian forces off the Golan Heights, the IDF came within 40 kilometres from Damascus before a ceasefire came into effect.[31]

Both Moscow and Washington undertook extensive resupply operations to their respective allies, but it was the United States which was to accrue the greater diplomatic advantage at the cessation of hostilities. Washington had already demonstrated its power to control the Israelis by threatening to transfer its support to Cairo should the IDF attempt to destroy the trapped Third Army. Such leverage set the pattern for the diplomatic moves following the cessation of hostilites. Egypt, its tarnished military honour much restored, found Washington more receptive to its demands in the aftermath of the war. Undoubtedly, the energy crisis in the winter of 1973 and 1974, and Cairo's ability to influence the oil-producing states of the Arabian Gulf, helped focus Washington's attention on Egypt's wider aims. It was a diplomatic shift that had implications for Israel's standing in wider United States foreign policy. From Washington's perspective,

[T]he special relationship with Israel had compelled the Arabs to appeal to the United States, but once that was accomplished, Israel's strategic importance declined. Israel again became a special US client, but only because its control of the territories made it crucial in US strategy. The United States valued Israel not for its military strength, but for its readiness to make territorial concessions that would reduce the Arab–Israeli conflict and establish US dominance in the region.[32]

In an effort to induce such territorial concessions, American aid to Tel Aviv totalled $5.4 billion between 1974 and 1976, much of it used by Israel to maintain, and indeed increase, its qualitative edge militarily. But if such aid was meant to induce greater Israeli flexibility towards territorial concessions, developments within Israel dictated otherwise. First, many within the Jewish state realised that tremendous pressure would be placed upon any Israeli government over territorial retrenchment. Already, under the 1974 disengagement agreements brokered by Washington, Israel had conceded control of roughly one-third of the Sinai peninsula. For many in Israel this set a dangerous precedent. In response, settler organisations such as *Gush Emunim* were established to forestall any such concessions. Secondly, the balance of power in Israeli politics shifted dramatically with the election of Israel's first right-wing coalition government in May 1977 under Menachem Begin. With his core belief in the sovereign unity of *Eretz Yisrael*, Begin's politics were, in appearance at least, inimical to further territorial concessions. This view seemed confirmed following the shock visit of President Anwar Sadat to Israel in November 1977. The first open visit by an Arab head of state to Israel, and one still technically in a state of war with Tel Aviv, Sadat's visit was met with rapturous approval by the Israeli public. Yet the approbation heaped upon the Egyptian leader in his attempt to break the impasse in negotiations over the Sinai failed to move Begin.

Begin, however, now had to deal with Jimmy Carter, the new Democratic President. Elected into office in November 1977, Carter favoured closer ties between Cairo and Washington. Many within Washington policy circles, including officials in the Pentagon, had come to question the perceived wisdom of Israel as a strategic asset.[33] Certainly, Carter believed in Israeli territorial retrenchment and a comprehensive solution to the issue of the Palestinians and believed that Israel should be more forthcoming towards the dramatic overture of President Sadat. A clear paradox was now apparent in Israel's position. Through mediation by Washington, it was on the verge of securing a formal treaty with the most powerful state in the Arab world, thereby dealing a grave blow to a united Arab front against Israel. However, the price that would be extracted from Tel Aviv, territorial retrenchment, was clearly inimical to the ideological disposition of Prime Minister Begin.

In an attempt to frame an agreement, Carter hosted talks between Sadat and Begin at the Presidential retreat at Camp David, Maryland, in

September 1978. After tortuous negotiations in which Carter linked continued American military aid to greater flexibility on the part of Israel over
territorial concessions, a deal was finally struck. The Camp David Accords,
signed on 26 March 1979, did much to cement closer ties with Washington.
The United States pledged to take any measures deemed necessary to ensure
the security of the Jewish state should the treaty be violated. This included
protecting Israel's freedom of navigation in international waters. In return,
Israel agreed to return all of Sinai to Egyptian sovereignty by 1982 while
promising autonomy for the Palestinians of the West Bank and Gaza Strip
as an intermediate solution before final negotiations commenced on the final
status of the Occupied Territories.

Throughout the whole of the Camp David process Begin proved to be
recalcitrant. It was only the urging of Foreign Minister Moshe Dayan and
Defence Minister Ezer Weizmann that finally persuaded him to part with
the Sinai.[34] But with regard to the autonomy proposals for the Palestinians,
Begin prefered to place the emphasis upon 'civil' rather than 'political'
autonomy. The fact that the PLO rejected the Camp David Accords out
of hand spared Israel the outright opprobrium of the international community as it continued to expand settlement construction throughout the
Occupied Territories. Indeed, it was securing the future of the West Bank
as part of Israel's dispensation that now determined the contours of Israel's
foreign policy.

The atrophy that marked relations between Moscow and Washington in
the early 1980s provided a more permissive environment for Tel Aviv to
pursue an aggressive foreign policy. Carter, humiliated by the Iranian revolution and the American hostage crisis, had been replaced by Republican
Ronald Reagan. On entering the White House in 1981, Reagan made clear
his determination to contain and 'roll back' the Soviet threat globally, a
policy that entailed active support for regional allies facing Soviet client
states. The result was the signing of the November 1981 Strategic Co-operation Agreement between Washington and Tel Aviv that provided for joint
military co-operation, the pre-positioning of American military supplies in
Israel, and increased grants for military research and development. The
agreement was not a formal military alliance, however, as Tel Aviv continued to eschew any agreement that would circumscribe its freedom of action.
As Israel's bombing of the Iraqi nuclear reactor at Osirak on 6 June 1981
demonstrated, recourse to unfettered unilateral action remained central to
Israel's national security.

The close strategic ties with Washington, coupled with the peace treaty
with Cairo, now produced an ideal environment in which Israel hoped to
deal with the PLO. While never threatening the survival of the Jewish state,
the presence of the PLO in southern Lebanon had produced periodic bouts
of high tension and violent confrontations along Israel's northern border. In
June 1981, Begin won a second national election. His new cabinet included
Ariel Sharon, a former general and now Defence Minister, who made clear

his intention to deal a crushing blow against the PLO in Lebanon. It was felt that such a blow would achieve a number of political objectives. Firstly, by driving the PLO from Lebanon and removing the Syrian military presence, Israel could reassert Maronite Christian domination of Lebanon's political structures. Israel would then have a dependable Lebanese ally. Secondly, by destroying the PLO in Lebanon, Israel would be freed from any serious obligation to invest the Palestinian autonomy proposals under the Camp David Accords with the diplomatic energy required. Thirdly, and closely connected, it was hoped that the very destruction of the symbol of Palestinian nationalism would be so total, that a more pliant Palestinian leadership would emerge in the Occupied Territories that would accept Israel's ingestion of the West Bank in return for some limited form of autonomy.[35]

Israel's invasion of Lebanon on 6 June 1982, 'Operation Peace for Galilee', achieved none of these objectives. In a war that bitterly divided public opinion, the IDF succeeded in forcing the removal of the main body of PLO fighters from Lebanon but failed to realise its grand strategy. Sharon distorted the true aims of the invasion, claiming military necessity had forced Israel not only to clear PLO forces to a line 40 kilometres from Israel's northern border, but to engage Syrian forces on the Beirut–Damascus highway. Given that this was a war of Israel's choice, the steady flow of casualties appeared incongruent in what was portrayed as a defensive operation.[36] This inconsistency was further underlined following the massacre of over 2,000 Palestinian men, women and children by Christian militiamen in the refugee camps of Sabra and Chatilla. The fall-out from this appalling crime, carried out under the noses of IDF troops, led to a mass demonstration of 400,000 Israelis organised by Peace Now against the war. Such was the scale of popular opposition to the war – both among civilians and a high proportion of the troops serving in Lebanon – that Ariel Sharon was forced from office and an official enquiry, the Kahan Commission, was established to ascertain the level of Israeli culpability in the massacre. The scale of Israel's invasion served only to undermine any attempt at the restitution of Christian hegemony. The assassination of Israel's chosen President elect, Bashir Gemayel, sparked bitter intercommunal fighting which served only to radicalise the competing communities or confessions in Lebanon. The origins of *Hizb'allah* (the Party of God) can be traced directly to the impact that Israel's invasion had upon a Shi'a community already affected by the radical influence of the Iranian revolution. Far from achieving a grand strategic design, the invasion of Lebanon polarised political opinion, exposing rifts within a society previously assuaged by the more immediate exigencies of national security.

The removal of the PLO from Lebanon undoubtedly proved a sobering experience for Palestinians in the Occupied Territories. While Shlomo Gazit has noted that it dealt a final blow to the efficacy of the 'armed struggle', it did not make Palestinians any more inclined to accept the Israeli occupation as an enduring reality.[37] The outbreak of the Palestinian *Intifada* throughout the Occupied Territories in December 1987 demonstrated the futility of Israel's attempts to solve the Palestinian issue by military means. A popular uprising born of frustration at the impasse in any tangible peace process, the *Intifada* was also a clear demonstration of a vibrant Palestinian nationalism that Israel had refused to recognise. It was a conflict where the enduring image of Palestinian youth confronting the IDF with little more than stones did much to erode the perception of Israel as a bastion of liberal-democratic values amid the otherwise autocratic regimes of the Arab world.

The *Intifada* served only to deepen political cleavages still further over the efficacy of territorial compromise. From 1983 onwards, a series of national unity governments (NUGs) had effectively stymied any tangible peace initiatives on the part of Tel Aviv. Following the resignation of Menachem Begin, leadership of the *Likud* passed to Yitzhak Shamir, a man who had opposed the Camp David Accords and whose belief in the integrity of *Eretz Yisrael* effectively denied the exchange of land for peace as the diplomatic palliative to the Arab–Israeli conflict. Attempts by Shimon Peres, leader of the Labour Alignment, who occupied the portfolios of Prime Minister and Foreign Minister in NUGs throughout the 1980s, to pursue a negotiated agreement with Jordan over the future of the West Bank foundered precisely over such differences. The *Intifada* was to drag on for at least another five years, but new geo-political realities were to create regional conditions that proved instrumental in breaking the political impasse in Israel.

At the international level, Soviet leader Mikhail Gorbachev brought about the retrenchment of Moscow's position in the Middle East, removing what remained of any ideological threat posed by the Soviet Union to the region. The change brought with it both benefits and potential costs for Israel. Of benefit were the growing numbers of Soviet Jews who were now allowed to emigrate. While championing their right of migration, the decision of the United States to impose strict immigration quotas meant that Israel remained the only viable destination. But equally, with the demise of the Cold War, Israel's role as a key strategic asset for Washington came to be questioned by events elsewhere in the Middle East.

On 2 August 1990, Iraq invaded Kuwait. The resulting crisis divided the Arab world as the United States assembled a multinational coalition to initially defend Saudi Arabia and access to its oil fields, and later, to expel Iraqi forces from Kuwait. In Washington, any Israeli involvement in the conflict was seen as counterproductive to the stability of the coalition. It was clear that in this crisis, Israel was a clear strategic liability for the United States. Accordingly, attempts by Baghdad to fragment the coalition by launching missile attacks on Tel Aviv and Haifa in January and February 1991 resulted in the United States exerting enormous political and financial leverage on Prime Minister Yitzhak Shamir to desist from retaliation. For many Israelis, the failure of their government to respond in kind to Iraq's attacks undermined both Israel's deterrence capability as well as conceding Israel's defence to another sovereign power. But Israel was also struggling to absorb over 200,000 new immigrants from the Soviet Union and required financial support from the United States to fund the costs of absorption.

Prior to the Gulf crisis, the government of Yitzhak Shamir had been refused loans of $400 million by President George Bush because of the acceleration of settlement construction in the Occupied Territories. The Bush Administration proved unusually tough on Israel and Washington's refusal to authorise the money without a prior cessation in Israeli settlement activity was described by Shamir as tantamount to a declaration of war.[38] Now, in recognition of Israel's restraint in the face of Iraqi missile attacks, the Bush Administration authorised the release of the money but Secretary of State James Baker made it clear that any further requests for funding would be conditional upon Israel adopting a more forthcoming attitude towards any future peace process. Baker was well aware that progress towards some resolution of the Arab–Israeli conflict had to be addressed in the aftermath of the Gulf conflict. Washington's insistence on Iraqi compliance with a whole raft of UN Security Council resolutions sat uneasily with what was perceived as a reluctance to enforce Israeli compliance with UN Resolution 242 or UN Resolution 425, passed in 1978. This resolution called for a full Israeli withdrawal from the security zone that it had established in south Lebanon in conjunction with surrogate Lebanese militia forces.

In the wake of the the Iraqi defeat, Baker engaged in an intensive round of shuttle diplomacy in a bid to convene an international peace conference to deal with the Israeli–Palestinian issue. Shamir had tried to resist a conference which he knew would place considerable pressure upon Israel to at least entertain the real possibility of territorial compromise. Moreover, Shamir opposed the idea of an international conference that would result in Israel having to engage in multilateral talks with all Arab states, rather than conducting talks on a bilateral basis as Israel had always preferred. The idea that Israel would sit down at a conference table with Palestinians who openly represented the PLO was anathema to Shamir and contrary to Israeli law which proscribed contact with what was still deemed to be a terrorist organisation. But the immediate financial burden imposed by the continuing *aliyah* from the Soviet Union proved beyond Israel's ability to cope. The spring of 1991 saw Israel submit a request for loan guarantees worth $10 billion to fund the absorption of Soviet Jews. The scale of the request allowed Baker to make access to such loans conditional on Israel at least attending the proposed international conference. Even so, Shamir extracted what he considered to be two key concessions from Baker: that the Palestinian representatives, drawn from the Occupied Territories, should not be affiliated with the PLO and would only attend as part of the Jordanian delegation. In addition, after the preliminaries of the conference were over, the multilateral forum would give way to bilateral discussions with Israel negotiating on an individual basis with those Arab representatives present.[39]

On 30 October 1991, the Middle East Peace Conference opened in Madrid. While mutual rancour marked the opening speeches of some of the delegations – most notably those of Israel and Syria – the Madrid conference at least paved the way for further talks. Between October 1991 and June 1992 a further five rounds of talks were held in North America, Europe and Japan. It was clear, however, that the maximum Israel was willing to place on the negotiating table did not meet the minimum demands of the Palestinian delegation. For example, during talks held under the Madrid framework in February 1992, Tel Aviv proposed self-rule for Palestinians in the Occupied Territories but failed to include any proposal for the election of a Palestinian authority to oversee the transition to self-rule. Nor did the proposal include an Israeli military withdrawal from the West Bank or the dismantling of settlements. In short, Israel's plans were seen by the Palestinans as a mechanism to legitimise Israel's continued rule over the Occupied Territories.[40] It is doubtful if Shamir was ever sincere over Israel's participation in the Madrid process. Nonetheless, the fact that Israel, under pressure from Washington, was at least discussing the possibility of exchanging land for peace proved too much for some of Shamir's more extreme right-wing allies in his coalition government. The *Tehiya* and *Moledet* parties resigned from the coalition, forcing Shamir to bring forward the date of the next national election from November to June 1992.

The result of the election of 23 June 1992 has been described as a *mahapach* – an upheaval that changed the whole dynamic of the Israel–Palestine conflict. Under the leadership of Yitzhak Rabin, a reinvigorated Labour Alignment won enough seats to form a government without reliance upon the more extreme national or religious parties in the *Knesset*. Rabin's victory resulted from several factors. According to David Kimche, Israelis had tired of the Occupied Territories and the incumbent security burden imposed by the *Intifada*. Indeed, the scale and intensity of the Palestinian uprising did much to disabuse Israelis of the sagacity of *Likud*'s concept of *Eretz Yisrael*. In short, there could be no going back to the situation that existed before 1987.[41] Moreover, the social dislocation caused by the mass migration of Soviet Jewry allowed parties of the centre-left to highlight the apparent disparity between continued investment in settlement construction in the Occupied Territories and the lack of housing and employment opportunities in Israel proper. One of Rabin's first acts as Prime Minister was to freeze construction of new settlements, a move that prompted Washington to allow Israel access to the $10 billion in loan guarantees requested previously.[42]

Rabin had promised that he would reach an autonomy agreement with the Palestinians within six to nine months of taking office as well as advancing negotiations with Syria and Jordan. The Madrid process, however, had not produced the hoped-for breakthrough. It was clear to Rabin's Foreign

Minister, Shimon Peres, that the previous Israeli strategy of only dealing with regional state actors to achieve peace remained flawed. Peres realised that until the issue of the Palestinians was addressed, Arab states would never accept the legitimacy of the Jewish state. Moreover, the profile of the ongoing *Intifada* gave Israelis grave cause for concern. The days of mass clashes between IDF troops and stone-throwing youths in the Occupied Territories had given way to more deadly confrontations with *Hamas* (*Harakat al-Muqawama al-Islamiyya*), the radical Palestinian Islamist movement.

Rabin realised it was easier to deal with the secular nationalists of the PLO than with *Hamas*, who rejected the very idea of a Jewish state. Indeed, the Israeli premier knew that in spite of the façade of a joint Jordanian–Palestinian delegation, the Palestinian representatives to the Madrid process represented the PLO. In November 1992, Rabin had ordered the mass deportation of 400 alleged *Hamas* activists to south Lebanon following the murder of an Israeli border policeman. The growing appeal of *Hamas* with its network of social services contrasted sharply with the fortunes of the PLO. It was an organisation on the verge of bankruptcy, both financially and politically, weakened by Arafat's support for Saddam Hussein during the Gulf crisis. The growing strength of *Hamas,* particularly among young Palestinians, produced a symbiosis of interest with Israel to ensure that some tangible gain emerged from the peace process.[43]

Secret contacts had already been made between Israelis acting on behalf of Shimon Peres and representatives of the PLO in July 1992. Rabin had hoped that the Madrid process would lead to an agreement with the Palestinian delegation, but it was clear by the spring of 1993 that the positions of the two parties, operating under the public gaze of the international community, remained far apart. The Palestinian delegation, for example, insisted on full territorial autonomy and that UN Resolution 242 be applied to East Jerusalem. While Rabin acknowleged the need for autonomy proposals to go beyond the confines of the Camp David proposals, the Palestinian position was clearly unacceptable to Israel. Indeed, when Arafat informed the Palestinian delegation that they should temper their demands, three members of the delegation threatened to tender their resignations in protest.[44]

Realising that the Madrid process was moribund, Rabin agreed to invest diplomatic capital in the secret channel that had been established by Peres. From January to August 1993, tight secrecy surrounded fifteen separate meetings between representatives of the PLO and Israel held outside the Norwegian capital Oslo. Israel's parliamentary opposition was never informed of the discussions lest it mobilised public opposition to any agreement. Indeed, the Palestinian delegation to the Madrid talks remained oblivious to the secret negotiations. It was also noteworthy that Washington was excluded entirely from these negotiations. The choice of Norway helped create a level playing field where both sides could 'dispense with dramatic posturing' and try to tackle the substantive issues in a more benign environment.[45]

On 13 September 1993, Prime Minister Yitzhak Rabin and Yasser Arafat formally signed the 'Declaration of Principles on Interim Self-Government Arrangements between Israel and the PLO', or more simply, the Oslo Accords, in Washington. Just prior to the signing of the Accords, the PLO and the Israeli government had exchanged notes of mutual recognition. The Accords themselves were not a formal peace treaty, but laid down principles and confidence-building measures designed to facilitate agreement towards such a treaty. Israel agreed to evacuate an enclave around Jericho as well as most of the Gaza Strip. The more substantive issues – East Jerusalem, water rights, the return of Palestinian refugees, the location of borders, the future of Israeli settlements – were to be discussed in final status negotiations no later than the third year after the signing of the agreement.

The basis of the Accords has been tested severely since 1993. Religious extremists on both sides have perpetrated atrocities, while Rabin himself fell victim to a young religious zealot following a peace rally in Tel Aviv on 4 November 1995. Opponents of the Oslo Accords were quick to point out that more Israelis had been killed in terrorist acts between 1993 and 1996 than in the fifteeen years prior to the signing of the accords. Given that maintaining national security remains an enduring theme in Israeli politics, the rash of suicide bombings represented a strategic threat to the very basis of the Oslo Accords. The ferocity of such attacks did enough to persuade Israelis, albeit by a tiny majority, to elect a right-wing *Likud* government to power in May 1996. The new premier, Binyamin Netanyahu, known for his antipathy towards the Accords while in opposition, made further progress on Israeli territorial concessions contingent on the Palestinians doing more to 'fight terrorism'. Against what criteria this was to be measured remained vague, allowing Netanyahu to apply a subjective criterion in determining the extent to which further concessions, if any, should be given to Arafat.

If the Oslo process is still to produce a final agreement between Israel and the Palestinians, it certainly created a more benign regional environment for the Jewish state. A full peace treaty with Jordan signed in October 1994, as well as low-level but open contacts with Arab states stretching from the Atlantic to the Gulf, would not have been possible but for the Oslo Accords. Even the difficult progress made in negotiations with Syria over future sovereignty of the Golan Heights would not have occurred without the Oslo Accords. Throughout, Washington has remained a staunch supporter of the Accords, faciliatating and occasionally pushing the process forward. Beyond this, it has remained fully supportive of Israel's search for security. It is a search that is now determined as much by domestic constraints, as it is facilitated by external opportunities.

Israel's foreign relations in the contemporary world

While acknowledging the unipolar character of the post-Cold War world and the subsequent Arab loss – at least among the so-called 'radical Arab states' – of a superpower patron, Israelis regard the Middle East as a region still wracked by turmoil in which, despite the strides made towards regional accommodation, recidivist tendencies still determine inter-state relations. As Efraim Inbar has argued:

> [A]ttempts to establish a new Middle East order have failed and it is still a region where the use of force is widely considered a policy option and one which receives popular support. The negative effects of the systemic changes on the international arena and on the Middle East have been similarly overlooked. Israel's [security] predicament has hardly changed. It is still a small state facing various challenges from powerful regional foes.[46]

It remains a moot point as to whether continuity, rather than change, does indeed define Israel's security predicament in the post-Cold War age. But the efficacy of this perception has meant that all Israeli governments continue to place the utmost emphasis upon maintaining Israel's technological superiority in weapons procurement and deployment. It is in the area of nuclear weapons that Israel remains the regional power *par excellence*. All Israeli governments since the 1960s have embraced 'nuclear ambiguity' by stating that the Jewish state will not be the first to introduce such weapons to the region. Such opacity aside, Israel is believed to possess some 200 nuclear weapons and appears set on developing a survivable deterrent capability. Apart from advanced delivery platforms based upon the indigenous Jericho 3 ballistic missile system and American supplied F15I strike aircraft, Israel has taken delivery of three Dolphin class diesel attack submarines from Germany. The importance of these boats is that the IDF is thought to be developing a sea-launched nuclear cruise missile system which, if fitted to the Dolphins, would give Tel Aviv a survivable nuclear triad and thus enhance its deterrent capability vis-à-vis the second and third circles of Arab and Muslim states.[47] Given the belief that nuclear weapons compensate Israel for the demographic and territorial asymmetries it faces in the Middle East, it is unsurprising that Israel has yet to become a signatory to the 1968 Nuclear Non-Proliferation Treaty.

Israel has also developed its own space-based *Ofek* (Horizon) satellite systems. By harnessing its missile capability to provide a launch platform, Israel now has three *Ofek* satellites in geosynchronous orbits, allowing real-time intelligence to be gathered. It is a capability unique to Israel among the states of the Middle East and is meant to give warning of impending attacks, particularly from missiles. Indeed, the threat posed by missile attacks, as demonstrated during the Gulf war, would appear to be the main preoccupation of Israel's defence planners. Countering this threat has led Israel to develop the Arrow *(Chetz)* anti-ballistic missile system. The Arrow has yet to be fully deployed, but meeting its research and development costs, estimated at $1.6 billion, would not have been possible without Washington meeting at least two-thirds of the expense incurred.[48] As such, Israel places a high premium upon maintaining the 'special relationship' with the United States. To quote Robert Bowker, 'The maintenance of a clear qualitative military edge over all potential adversaries and open guaranteed access to U.S. technology are basic elements of [Israeli] government policy'.[49]

Israel's relations with the United States

Israel has been a huge beneficiary of Washington's munificence, being the single largest recipient of United States economic and military aid, estimated to have totalled some $65 billion for the period 1948 to 1996.[50] This would suggest a dependency relationship, and one that limits severely the sovereign autonomy of the Jewish state. The fact, however, that the relationship is deemed 'special', negates dependency as the determining feature of bilateral ties. Rather the relationship has been constructed around both 'soft' and 'hard' variables. Soft variables include the identification of Israel with democratic, western values, and more tangibly, the influence that American Jewry, and in particular, powerful pro-Israel lobby groups on Capitol Hill, can and do exercise in both Houses of Congress. Hard variables centre on the shared strategic interests of the two states, a position, however, that has yet to be enshrined in a formal strategic or defence treaty between Washington and Tel Aviv. Indeed, the extent of financial assistance given to Israel has not always produced a linear subservience to Washington's foreign policy aims or aspirations. Israel's decision in April 2000 to sell advanced aircraft-mounted radar systems to China was made despite strong protests from Washington who were concerned that such technology gave Beijing a qualitative military advantage in its dispute with Taiwan.

As such, it is perhaps inaccurate to describe Israel's relationship with Washington as falling within a traditional patron–client paradigm. Despite the huge inflows of American capital the relationship between Israel and the United States has immunised the Jewish state to a very large extent from the great power leverage usually associated with core–periphery relations in international politics. Yet strong ties with the United States remain crucial to Israel's ability to make peace with the Arab world. While the Oslo Accords were negotiated without Washington's participation, the very fact they were signed on the lawn of the White House underlines the importance Tel Aviv attaches to American support for, if not outright involvement in, the peace process. Israel's conclusion of peace treaties with Egypt and Jordan were both concluded with the full support of the United States, while the Clinton administration invested a great deal of diplomatic capital in trying to facilitate a peace agreement between Syria and Israel. Moreover, Israel has come to rely heavily upon Washington to retain a qualitative edge militarily, particularly in air power. The strength derived from its alliance with Washington and its own economic, technological and military capabilities have helped sustain Israel's position as the dominant power in the region. Indeed, the shift among Arab elites towards tacit acceptance, if not formal recognition, of the Jewish state would have been impossible without the development and maintenance of a 'special relationship' in which 'soft variables' continue to transcend any overt reliance on the cold realism of shared strategic interests as the main determinant of ties between the two states.

Israel's relations with Europe

A clear paradox is discernible in Israel's approach towards the European Union (EU). While the EU provides Israel with its largest overseas market, it has remained circumspect over the political role that the EU should play in regional diplomacy. Such circumspection has its roots in the perceived bias towards the Palestinians displayed by the EU, as well as Israel's often turbulent relations with individual EU member states.

As an intergovernmental organisation, the EU has undoubtedly been critical of Israeli policies in the Occupied Territories. A growing Euro–Arab dialogue in the wake of the October 1973 war resulted in the 'Venice Declaration' of 13 June 1980. The declaration repeated calls for the implementation of UN Resolution 242 but, in addition, called for the inclusion of the PLO in future peace negotiations. It was a declaration designed to place clear water between the position of Europe and that of the United States. The declaration was met by an angry response in Tel Aviv, and with a decidedly cool reception in Washington. As Philip Gordon notes, as if to demonstrate its defiance of the Declaration, Israel almost at once announced the passing of a law through the *Knesset* which recognised *de facto* Israel's annexation of East Jerusalem in 1967.[51]

Israel in the past has, however, been helped by divisions among the Europeans themselves over how to deal with the Arab–Israeli conflict, allowing Washington's dominance as the facilitator of the peace process to continue. Berlin, for historic reasons associated with the holocaust, remains reluctant to place undue pressure upon Tel Aviv, a position supported by Holland and Denmark who have traditionally maintained close ties with the Jewish state. Britain's relations with Israel were long blighted by the legacy of the Mandate years and a perception among Israel's policy-making elite that the Foreign and Commonwealth Office was dominated by Arabists hostile to Israel. The premiership of Margaret Thatcher undoubtedly did much to thaw bilateral ties, but British commercial and strategic interests in the Arab Gulf states continue to place clear limits on London's ability to influence Israel. While sympathetic to the plight of the Palestinians in the Occupied Territories, Britain remains wary of Europe undermining Washington's predominant role, a legacy of its own special relationship with the United States and a reflection of the dilemma London now faces in either following an Atlanticist or European orientated foreign policy. The French have been the most vociferous in their criticism of Israeli policies in the Occupied Territories, its wide trading relations with its former colonies in Arab North Africa, as well as historic ties to Lebanon and Syria, resulting in Paris being particularly outspoken regarding Israel's treatment of the Palestinians.

The EU has made some progress in trying to adopt a coherent policy, rather than just a series of agreed-upon declarations, towards Israel and the Palestinans. To this end, it has appointed a European envoy to co-ordinate with both Israeli and Palestinian negotiating teams, while Israel has a fully accredited ambassador to the EU in Brusssels. The EU fully supported the Oslo Accords and has proved the biggest donor of funds to the Palestine National Authority (PNA), giving $1.5 billion between 1993 and 1998.[52] Yet lacking the unified decision-making structure of a single-nation state imposes clear limits on the political influence that the EU should be able to exercise given its economic power. It is a position that, at present, suits Israel well. Tel Aviv fully supports EU aid to the PNA, realising that economic aid to the self-rule areas remains vital to ensuring the stability of the PNA. Equally, while threatening to impose limited sanctions against Israeli products originating from the Occupied Territories, the EU remains open to Israeli goods and services without any political pre-conditions that can be readily enforced. It is a win-win situation from the Israeli perspective since the tangible economic benefits it accrues from trade with the EU cannot be tied to the very cornerstone of its foreign policy: its special relationship with Washington.

Israel's relations with the Middle East

Shimon Peres, perhaps more in hope than expectation, made much of a new order emerging in the Middle East following the signing of the 1993 Oslo Accords, a new order based on a regional mutilateralism 'in which people, goods and services can move freely from place to place'.[53] Certainly, the Oslo Accords allowed Israel to build bridges to the wider world, with Tel Aviv establishing open, albeit low-level relations with the Gulf states of Bahrain, Oman and Qatar as well as Morocco and Tunisia. Moreover, Tel Aviv rekindled old diplomatic ties with a plethora of African states that had previously been severed. For many Israelis, however, Binyamin Netanyahu's acerbic declaration that Israel lives in a 'tough neighbourhood', provides a description of the Middle East more immediately recognisable than the hubris of Peres.

Shlomo Gazit, former head of Israeli military intelligence, defined the Arab–Israeli conflict from the perspective of Tel Aviv as consisting of three concentric circles – (1) Israel/Palestine, (2) Israel/Egypt, Syria, Jordan and (3) Israel/Iran, Iraq, Saudi Arabia, Libya, Sudan – each with its own level of hostility and threat capability.[54] The great importance of the bilateral peace treaties with Cairo and Amman should not be overlooked, but equally, as Israeli strategists remain quick to point out, this does not discount recourse to the use of force by individual states, or an alliance of all or some of the above to break a perceived political deadlock in the region. Primary concern among Israeli decision-makers centres on the threat, real or otherwise, of the proliferation of weapons of mass destruction throughout the region. Iran's attempt to acquire WMD is the most apposite example, and as such is interpreted as a clear threat to Israel and all too congruent with the vitriol of its anti-Zionist propaganda. Ehud Sprinzak, however, has argued that such threat perceptions have been exaggerated. Aside from their own concerns over Israel's nuclear capability, Sprinzak places Tehran's programme within the context of its own circle of regional threats and challenges, not least the continued concerns over Afghanistan, United States forces in the Gulf, Iraq with its record of using chemical weapons, Saudi Arabia and Turkey. Accordingly, Sprinzak went on to argue that:

> If one adds to this [the perception of an Iranian threat] that psychologically, modern Israeli identity has been formed by the constant presence of an enemy at the gate and the absence of an enemy will automatically prompt an identity crisis, it becomes easy to understand why it is difficult for political figures willing to give up the terrible monster from Tehran. The threat from Iran fits so well into the speeches of the defence minister [Yitzhak Mordechai] for whom the War of Independence has not even ended.[55]

Sprinzak's keen observations aside, effective deterrence remains central to Israel's national security. This includes not just the possession of a nuclear weapons capability, but the maintenance of what has been termed an 'offensive-minded defence posture' with regard to the use of conventional forces. The result has been a tendency towards pre-emption, most visibly demonstrated in the June War of 1967 and the attack on the Iraqi nuclear reactor at Osirak in June of 1981.

This offensive mind-set has also been a feature of Israeli government policy where threats to the security of the state outside any immediate existential danger have arisen. Falling under the rubric of 'regime targeting', the bloody removal of individuals or groups has included the bombing of the headquarters of the PLO in Tunisia in 1985, the killing of Khalil Wazir (*Abu Jihad*) in April 1988, the assassination of *Hizb'allah* spiritual leader Shaykh Hussein Abbas Musawi in Febuary 1992, as well as the attempted politicide of the PLO as an effective symbol of Palestinian resistance between June and September 1982.[56]

Whether such actions can be considered 'rational' remains a moot point, but Israel's military alliance with Ankara, and allegations of developing technological and strategic links with New Dehli, fall within a classic realist paradigm of an order based on power politics and regional alliances.[57] The close military relationship with Turkey that has developed since 1995 is, according to Neill Lochery, 'as important a development in the Middle East region as any of the peace treaties that [Israel] has signed with the Arabs'.[58] Tel Aviv has stated its desire to see this axis develop into the dominant security structure for the region, though Ankara has made such development contingent on political progress with the Palestine National Authority (PNA).[59] Still, given Turkey's history of tense relations with Syria, the alliance with Ankara acts as a natural force multiplier as Israel seeks to maintain both its conventional and non-conventional military advantage over Damascus. It is an advantage that Tel Aviv will not relinquish if it is to withdraw from the Golan Heights.

Long regarded as essential for the security of northern Israel, withdrawal from the Golan Heights back to the boundaries held by Tel Aviv on 4 June 1967 was a position that Rabin was prepared to discuss, if not condone openly, provided a 'full peace' proved forthcoming from Damascus. Meaningful negotiations were held in Washington between January 1994 and April 1995 but an agreement was never finalised. Professor Itamar Rabinovich, appointed personally by Rabin as Israel's ambassador to Washington with a specific mandate to negotiate with his Syrian counterpart, has suggested that President al-Assad missed a window of opportunity to make peace, 'not under the full terms that he would have wanted but under reasonable, acceptable conditions'.[60] These 'reasonable, acceptable conditions' included demilitarisation of the Golan, early-warning stations, as well as the establishment of full diplomatic relations.[61] More recently, Ehud Barak attempted to revive the negotiations. He was the first Prime Minister to openly declare his intent to return the strategic mountains to full Syrian sovereignty, save for a small strip of land on the banks of the Kinneret that had been controlled by Damascus prior to the June 1967 war.[62] For Israelis, control of the Kinneret is an issue of national strategic importance, providing as it does nearly half of Israel's fresh water supply. Yet it remains a position at odds with the Syrian demand for Israel to comply fully with UN Resolution 242, and return all land captured during the June 1967 war.

Stalemate in negotiations between Damascus and Tel Aviv inevitably helps to focus attention on the state of relations between Israel and the Palestine National Authority. The hope that the Oslo Accords would result in final status negotiations beginning by the third anniversary of their signing proved hopelessly optimistic. By June 2000, Israel had conceded some 40 per cent of the West Bank and Gaza Strip to Palestinian self-rule, but negotiations between the parties remain mired in bitter disagreement. The terrorist atrocities committed by Islamic extremists undoubtedly did much to focus Israel's attention upon security, a fixation that allowed for the election of Binyamin Netanyahu in 1996. But equally, the glacial progress of negotiation has done much to undermine the Accords as helping to build a bridge of trust between the two parties. Since the signing of the Declaration of Principles on 13 September 1993, the tortuous path of nego-tiations has seen a whole raft of agreements signed between the two parties – the Oslo II Accords, the Hebron Agreement, the Wye Accords, and the Sharm al-Sheikh Agreement – all of which have been subject to review or renegotiation by Israel.

These agreements, mostly negotiated under the auspices of Washington, remain focused upon Israel handing over carefully delineated parcels of land to Palestinian control. The more substantive issues – the future of the settle-ments, the issue of Palestinian refugees, the future of East Jerusalem, water issues – have yet to be addressed. Whatever its conceptual flaws, the Oslo process has seen Israel recognise formally the national aspirations of the Palestinian people. There is substantial evidence to suggest that Israelis have begun to internalise the meaning of peace. Recent surveys have shown that not only do most Israelis now believe that a Palestinian state will emerge, but, more importantly, a majority, albeit small, believe that Palestinians actually deserve such a state.[63]

But equally, the Accords themselves have become hostage to those on both sides whose very identities, usually expressed in cosmic terminology, remain inextricably linked to the future of the West Bank. Particularly in Israel, such opposition, feeding directly through to Israel's political system, provides a real impediment to any Prime Minister wishing to clearly identify the physical borders of the Jewish state. Because of such bitter internal divisions, the language of national security remains dominant in Israel's approach to discusssing the future of the Occupied Territories. It is a lan-guage that presents issues in black and white, obviating the need to address other, equally pressing issues that actually determine Israel's approach to the Occupied Territories. The paradox is clear: Israel has the proven cap-ability to defend itself against any external threat. Replicating that capabil-ity to defend against threats from within, however, remains Israel's true national security challenge of the future.

Conclusion

Whatever the changes in the political landscape of the Middle East, Israel's foreign policy remains conditioned by a hierarchical foreign policy decision-making structure, biased internally towards the politics, if not the cult, of national security. Israelis argue that it is an approach that has served them well. The establishment of a strong military, including the deliberate policy of nuclear ambiguity, and its close ties with the United States, has not only ensured Israel's continued survival in the Middle East, but its acceptance by much of the Arab world, however grudging, that it is a permanent fixture in the political constellation of the Middle East.

Notes

1 Martin Sherman, 'Diversifying Strategic Reliance: Broadening the Base of Israel's Sources of Strategic Support', *JCSS Strategic Assessment*, Vol. 1, No. 4 (January 1999), p. 1.
2 Gad Barzilai, *Wars, Internal Conflicts, and Political Order: A Jewish Democracy in the Middle East* (New York: SUNY, 1996), pp. 3–24.
3 Ze'ev Schiff, 'The Spectre of Civil War in Israel', *Middle East Journal*, Vol. 39, No. 2 (Spring 1985), pp. 231–45.
4 Michael Brecher, *The Foreign Policy System of Israel: Images, Setting Processes* (Oxford: OUP, 1972), p. 229.
5 Ibid., p. 232.
6 Ian Traynor, 'Those who are called', *The Guardian Weekend*, 10 December 1994.
7 Tom Segev, *The Seventh Million: The Israelis and the Holocaust* (New York: Hill and Wang, 1994), p. 514.
8 Efraim Inbar, 'Israeli National Security, 1973–1996', *Begin-Sadat (BESA) Security and Policy Study Papers* No. 63 (Ramat Gan: Bar Ilan University, 1998), p. 63.
9 Daniel Ben Simon, 'Ministry in search of a leader – but has it found one?', *Ha'aretz*, 16 October 1998.
10 For example, Uzi Arad, foreign policy adviser in the PM's office, was charged with policy formulation towards the United States and Europe, Cabinet Secretary Danny Naveh and Yitzhak Molco with conducting negotiations with the Palestinians, Ariel Sharon (until October 1998) with relations with Jordan, and Trade Minister Natan Sharansky with relations with the states of the former Soviet Union. See Sarah Leibovich-Dar, 'Left out of the loop', *Ha'aretz*, 11 September 1998.
11 Uri Bar Joseph, 'A Bull in a China Shop: Netanyahu and Israel's Intelligence Community', *International Journal of Intelligence and Counter-Intelligence*, Vol. 11, No. 2 (1998), p. 162.
12 David Makovsky, 'Government approves national security council concept', *Ha'aretz*, 8 March 1999.
13 Clive Jones, 'Ideotheology: Dissonance and Discourse in the State of Israel', *Israel Affairs*, Vol. 3, Nos 3&4 (Spring/Summer 1997), pp. 28–46.
14 Don Peretz, *Intifada: The Palestinian Uprising* (London: Westview Press, 1990), pp. 119–62.
15 Shibley Telhami, 'Israeli Foreign Policy: A Static Strategy in a Changing World', *Middle East Journal*, Vol. 44, No. 3 (Summer 1990), p. 400.
16 Yaacov Bar-Siman-Tov, 'The United States and Israel since 1948: A Special Relationship?', *Diplomatic History*, Vol. 22, No. 2 (Spring 1998), p. 234.
17 Benny Morris, *Israel's Border Wars* (Oxford: Oxford University Press), pp. 263–91.
18 For a detailed discussion see Seymour Hersh, *The Sampson Option: Israel and the Bomb* (London: Faber & Faber, 1991).
19 Bar-Siman-Tov, op. cit., p. 235.
20 For a detailed account of the origins of the Suez Crisis see Keith Kyle, *Suez* (London: Wiedenfeld and Nicolson, 1991).
21 Andrew and Leslie Cockburn, *Dangerous Liaisons: The Inside Story of the US-Israeli Covert Relationship* (London: Bodley Head, 1992), pp. 127–30.

22 Bar-Siman-Tov, op. cit., p. 236.

23 Ibid., p. 237.

24 A detailed account of the origins of the June 1967 war can be found in Richard Parker, 'The June War: Some Mysteries Explored', *Middle East Journal*, Vol. 46, No. 2 (Spring 1992), pp. 177–97.

25 Telhami, op. cit., p. 409.

26 Ritchie Ovendale, *The Origins of the Arab-Israeli Wars* (Harlow: Longman Press, 1999 edn), pp. 199–205.

27 Ahron Bregman and Jihan El-Tahri, *The Fifty Years War: Israel and the Arabs* (Harmondsworth: Penguin/BBC Books, 1998), pp. 73–5.

28 Abba Eban, *An Autobiography* (London: Weidenfeld and Nicolson, 1977), p. 446.

29 Bar-Siman-Tov, op. cit., p. 243.

30 Ian Black and Benny Morris, *Israel's Secret Wars* (New York: Grove Wiedenfeld, 1991), pp. 282–321.

31 For a full account of the War see Edgar O'Balance, *No Victor, No Vanquished* (London: Barrie and Jenkins, 1979).

32 Bar-Siman-Tov, op. cit., p. 248.

33 Telhami, op. cit., p. 410.

34 See Ezer Weizmann, *Battling for Peace* (New York: Bantam Press, 1981).

35 See Zeev Schiff and Ehud Ya'ari, *Israel's Lebanon War* (London: Allen and Unwin, 1985).

36 Dan Horowitz, 'Israel's War in Lebanon: New Patterns of Strategic Thinking and Civilian-Military Relations', in Moshe Lissak (ed), *Israeli Society and its Defence Establishment* (London: Frank Cass, 1984), pp. 83–102.

37 Shlomo Gazit, 'Israel and the Palestinians: Fifty Years of Wars and Turning Points', *Annals* (AAPS), No. 555 (January 1998), pp. 90–1.

38 Clive Jones, *Soviet Jewish Aliyah 1989–1992: Impact and Implications for Israel and the Middle East* (London: Frank Cass, 1996), p. 93.

39 Ziva Flamhaft, *Israel on the Road to Peace: Accepting the Unacceptable* (Oxford: Westview Press, 1996), pp. 77–90.

40 Ibid., p. 85.

41 David Kimche, 'The Arab-Israeli Peace Process', *Security Dialogue*, Vol. 27, No. 2 (1996), pp. 139–40.

42 Jones, op. cit., p. 207.

43 JoAnn A. DiGeorgio-Lutz, 'The PLO and the Peace Process', in Ilan Peleg (ed), *The Middle East Peace Process* (New York: SUNY, 1998), pp. 123–40.

44 Flamhaft, op. cit., p. 95.

45 Laura Zittrain Eisenberg and Neil Caplan, 'The Israeli-Palestinian Peace Process in Historical Perspective', in Ilan Peleg (ed), *The Middle East Peace Process* (New York: SUNY, 1998), p. 11.

46 Efraim Inbar, 'Israel's Predicament in a New Strategic Environment', in Efraim Inbar and Gabriel Sheffer (eds), *The National Security of Small States in a Changing World* (London: Frank Cass, 1997), p. 156.

47 Amos Harel, 'Swimming with the Dolphin', *Ha'aretz*, 28 October 1998.

48 Amnon Barzilai, Yossi Verter and Amos Harel, 'Chetz Hits Virtual Target', *Haaretz*, 15 September 1998.

49 Robert Bowker, *Beyond Peace: The Search for Security in the Middle East* (London: Lynne Reinner, 1996), p. 114.

50 Bar-Siman-Tov, op. cit., pp. 231–62.

51 Philip H. Gordon, *The Transatlantic Allies and the Changing Middle East*, Adelphi Paper 322 (Oxford: IISS/OUP, 1998), p. 18.

52 Ibid., p. 28.

53 Shimon Peres, *Battling for Peace* (London: Wiedenfeld and Nicolson, 1995), p. 358.

54 Shlomo Gazit, 'The Quiet Option', *Ha'aretz*, 19 August 1998.

55 Ehud Sprinzak, 'Revving up an Idle Threat', *Ha'aretz*, 29 September 1998.

56 David Rodman, 'Regime-Targeting: A Strategy for Israel', *Israel Affairs*, Vol. 2, No. 1 (Autumn 1995), pp. 153–67.

57 P.R. Kumaraswamy, 'India and Israel: Evolving Strategic Partnership', *BESA Security Studies Policy Paper* No. 40 (Ramat Gan: Bar-Ilan University, 1998), pp. 3–33.

58 Neill Lochery, 'Israel and Turkey: Deepening Ties and Strategic Implications', *Israel Affairs*, Vol. 5, No. 1 (Autumn 1998), pp. 45–6.

59 David Makovsky and Daniel Sobelman, 'PM urges Turkey-Israel Defense Axis', *Ha'aretz*, 2 September 1998.

60 For the full text of Rabinovich's comments see Douglas Jehl, 'Rabin showed willingness to give Golan back to Syria', *The New York Times*, 29 August 1997.

61 Bregman and El-Tahri, op. cit., p. 267.

62 Danna Harman, 'Barak OK's Syrian '67 Lines', *The Jerusalem Post* (International Edition), 31 March 2000.

63 Ephraim Yaar and Tamar Hermann, 'The Peace Index/March 1999: After all, most believe the Palestinians deserve a state', *Ha'aretz*, 5 April 1999. According to the survey carried out among 497 Israeli adults by the Tami Steinmetz Center for Peace Research at Tel Aviv University, 69 per cent thought that a Palestinian state was inevitable while 56 per cent believe that the Palestinian demand for a state was justified.

5 Conclusion

Redefining the Jewish state

The chapters of this volume have shown that Israel is undergoing what may be termed 'normalisation'. Even as its Arab neighbours are ultimately being forced to accept the presence of the Jewish state in their midst, so Israelis have themselves been discovering the terms and requirements of their own citizenship. Neither process is complete, and both have involved conflict and compromise for Israelis and their state. Indeed, they have been inextricably linked in so far as Israeli identity for most of its incarnation has been profoundly shaped by its juxtaposition with the hostile 'other'. Thus we cannot unravel the complexities of Israeli identity without referring to the struggle for regional acceptance and the recent and ongoing peace process.

During the course of an interview that marked his first year as Prime Minister of Israel, Ehud Barak noted that:

> Achieving peace won't transform the Middle East into another Benelux. But it will bring us into another reality. And it will put us onto a path wherein there is a chance of gradually, over time, stabilizing a situation where there is acceptance and economic co-operation. The hostility won't disappear right away, but it will gradually shrink to its proper place. In the new reality that will be created, we will be able to launch Israel forward.[1]

Barak's comments were directed at Israel's external environment, an environment that he defined as 'confrontational' and 'atavistic' in nature. But equally, his comments provide an apt description of Israel's domestic political scene, where questions of identity have come to determine the scope of political discourse. Any attempt to 'stabilise' or ameliorate the tensions inherent within competing claims over land, symbols, and the institutions of the state are a recognition that defining identity remains key to recognising Israel's security dilemma. As such, Israel's foreign policy, particularly after 1967, came to be as much 'about the pursuit of domestic politics by other means', as the need to secure Israel's territorial sovereignty amid the animus of the Arab world.

Identities are evolutionary, both innate and constructed, with the balance between the two subject to a given context at any one time. Nonetheless, between 1948 and 1967 Israel's competing identities based on ethnicity, religion, as well as political affiliation remained ordered by, and largely subject to, the demands of *mamlachtiyut*. Given the demands of trying to mould disparate Jewish communities into a collective whole, any criticism of Israel's expression of statism must be tempered. Whatever the machinations of élite politics and decision-makers, the majority of Israelis believed themselves to be a nation under threat and proved willing to bear the costs – both human and economic – of a being a nation in arms. The aphorism, 'we fight therefore we are', became the motif of a generation of Israelis raised in the shadow of the Holocaust.

Yet *mamlachtiyut* held in check, rather than resolved, the issue of identity. The period from 1967 onwards not only saw demands for social emancipation from Oriental Jews, but equally, witnessed such demands become entwined in the thorny issue of the Occupied Territories. A military rationale justified Israel's occupation for over two decades. The need for strategic depth, however, masked more potent claims to the land based upon biblical and historical precedent that denied legitimacy to the national aspirations of the Palestinian people. The approbation heaped upon Jewish settlers in the West Bank and Gaza Strip, particularly under governments led by Menachem Begin and Yitzhak Shamir, was also incongruent with Israel's claims to democratic accountability. As such, Israel's invasion of Lebanon in June 1982 was an attempt to square this political circle by military means.

Eighteen years after the 'Operation Peace for Galilee', the Israel Defence Forces (IDF) withdrew finally from Lebanon. The failure to realign the constellation of Lebanese politics in favour of a pro-Israel dispensation, or to defeat the indigenous *Hizb'allah* guerrillas of south Lebanon, demonstrated the limits of using military power to solve political problems.[2] Some have claimed that the withdrawal of Israeli forces from south Lebanon without a peace agreement with either Beirut or Damascus bodes ill for Israel, not least because it undermines Israel's deterrent capability. Others lament the inability of contemporary Israeli society to tolerate battlefield casualties among its young soldiers, a symptom for some of the malaise at the heart of Zionism whose very appeal was built upon the statist demands of self-sacrifice. Such sentiment, while no doubt well intentioned, laments the passing of a golden age in Israeli society when generals were venerated like pop stars, and a sense of a coherent national identity was defined against the 'other'.

Such certainties are increasingly the legacy of the past rather than a template for the present or the future. The marked reluctance of increasing numbers of Israel's youth to serve in the IDF should perhaps be seen as a society adjusting to normalisation and where the existential threat to Israel is now low.[3] Peace treaties with Egypt and Jordan, the ongoing peace process, however flawed, with the Palestinians, a largely quiescent border with

Syria, and a host of contacts, if low level, with other Arab states have reduced threat perceptions. Even if Israel remains concerned over the development of non-conventional weapons by Tehran and Baghdad, mass conscript armies do not offer a strategic palliative. For many Israelis, the appeal of consumerism has greater meaning than styptic debates over Zionism or the future of the Occupied Territories. But for others, such consumerism denies legitimacy to their view of what it means to be Israeli. Oren Yiftachel, for example, has traced a correlation between ethnicity and support for the Oslo Accords. His research has shown that perceived failure by Oriental Jews to derive economic benefits from the Accords has resulted in a recrudescence of accusations that the peace process only serves to privilege an *Ashkenazim* élite.[4] Accordingly, this has resulted in antipathy, and in some cases outright hostility, towards further territorial concessions towards the Palestinians.

It is religious-nationalists who carry the conviction of political identity most forcefully in Israeli politics. Their identity remains indivisible from a mythic attachment to a land which regards territorial compromise as anathema to the logic of a Zionism perceived in eschatological terms. In short, whatever benefits Israel may derive from a peace process can never compensate a community whose very identity remains mortgaged to continued Jewish dominion over the West Bank and East Jerusalem. For the most part, their demonstrations against the Oslo process have remained within lawful boundaries, though the rhetoric accompanying such displays carries with it the latent threat of violence. While Israelis may like to believe that Rabin's assassination, however traumatic, remains a national aberration, threats to the well-being of Barak act as a sober reminder that national identity remains a contested issue.[5] In this respect, the Oslo Accords is not just about defining the physical borders of Israel, or indeed, seeking justice for the Palestinians. Rather, it is about defining the political balance to be struck in Israel: a state for the Jews or a Jewish state?

For Ben-Gurion, who drew his vision from the combination of political Zionist ideals developed by Herzl and his contemporaries on the one hand, and from the bitter lessons of the Holocaust on the other, the urgent need was for a distinctively and exclusively Jewish state. The doctrine of *mamlachtiyut* attempted to create an essentially new hegemonic Jewish political culture. While the state itself was secular, it nonetheless drew upon religious symbolism, myth and ritual to preserve the cohesion of the collectivity. Political concepts drawn from European philosophical traditions such as secularism, democracy, nation and state were utilised in support of this greater goal but were not allowed to define it. Expediency and compromise – learnt from the era of practical Zionism under the Mandate – were ultimately more important than ideological dogma or affiliation in determining how the state should be constructed and to what purpose. The bottom line was that it was not enough to create a state for the Jews. Given the ethnic, religious and ideological divergencies within the Jewish population, such an entity would inevitably be torn apart by division and disagreement. It would be weak and unable to defend itself, or the Jewish people, from external threat. What was needed was the manufacture of a new collective identity that would bind the diverse Jewish communities together. Establishing this political culture was the single most important task of the young state and all others were subordinated to it.

Baruch Kimmerling has described how the manufacturing of the identity drew upon the range of Jewish experience.[6] The biblical heritage provided symbolic myths: of return and redemption, of divine property rights and collective obligations. The *diaspora* experience and the holocaust in Europe added another layer, this time rejecting past lives and asserting the moral right to a new destiny. The struggle for independence and the processes of state-building (including the defence of the identity against the hostile other) provided a third tier of mythical characteristics: the barefoot pioneer turning the desert green, the purity of arms and the ingathering of exiles. Despite their previous dispersal, the Jews now had a common history, a common ideal and a common purpose to unite them. This was to be the 'Jewishness' that defined the state.

To some extent this 'covenantal world view' was ultimately to fragment. As the state grew in military and economic strength, as the holocaust generation became a minority, and as the ethnic origins of the incoming immigrants began to diversify, the external threat diminished and Jewish citizens began to question whether the prevailing political culture was after all what they wanted. Infringements on democratic practice that resulted from *mamlachtiyut* should, perhaps, have been challenged first and foremost by the left-wing parties, but the largest of these, Ben-Gurion's own *Mapai*, was too busy holding on to power to pursue its ideological commitments properly. Thus it was the Oriental *Mizrahim* who posed the first real challenges to the state in the form of protest groups like the Black Panthers in the 1970s. The victories of the 1967 war and the subsequent occupation of the West Bank (biblical Judea and Samaria) and East Jerusalem meanwhile fuelled a growing religious nationalism that questioned the secular orientation of the state, arguing for compulsory observance of some religious practices, for the absolute supremacy of orthodox Judaism over less strict denominations, and for religious determination of policy towards contested territories with religious significance. These two challenges to the prevailing definition of what it meant to be a 'Jewish' state became oddly intermingled, with ethnic affiliations to religious leaderships becoming yet another factor in domestic politics. Some groups among the *Haredim* went further still, asserting not only the incorrect interpretation of 'Jewishness' when applied to the state, but adding that the state itself was only a marginal, transient and – in some cases – illegitimate manifestation of the Jewish collective destiny.

Further destabilisation of the cultural consensus came with the invasion of Lebanon in 1982 and the Palestinian *Intifada* in 1987, both of which generated protest against and within the armed forces. Economic crisis in the mid-1980s also prompted economic reforms that reduced the interventionist role and stature of the state. By the 1990s, the hegemonic culture had all but broken down, and what Kimmerling calls four previously dormant or suppressed 'counter-cultures' had surfaced. The religious culture envisages a theocratic state and the abandonment of secular norms. Liberal secularism, on the other hand, argues for greater individualism and a better-functioning democracy (although it shies away from reforms that might transform into a state 'for the Jews'). Traditionalism attempts to keep Israel on the same path of compromise, substituting cultural hegemony with co-existence, while the final Arab culture remains as yet excluded from political empowerment. All must reconcile themselves with a deepening Israeli nationalism that has been the inevitable product of 50 years of statehood. They must also adapt to the reality that Israel has probably witnessed its last great *aliyah*. After the influx of Russian Jews in the 1990s, there remains no significant population of Jews elsewhere that seeks to immigrate to Israel. The substantial American Jewish population is not only comfortably resident on the other side of the Atlantic, but its composition is also being steadily eroded by inter-marriage with non-Jews. It is furthermore deeply fractured, with the majority Reform and Conservative communities being deeply uncomfortable with the Israeli version of orthodoxy. In sum, the ingathering of the exiles is over. Deprived of its principal mission, with the hostile 'other' fast retreating into a cold but nonetheless peaceful neighbourliness, Israeli Jews must reassess the 'Jewish' attributes of the state and re-determine the components of their own Jewishness.

Akiva Orr has gone further, arguing that for some Israelis, Jewishness is no longer a requisite of their national or 'ethnic' identity. He has argued that:

> Israeli ethnic identity is shared by people brought up in Hebrew in a secular Israeli culture, that is, rejecting religion and *mitzvot*. It differs qualitatively from Jewish cultural identity. It is unique and recognisable.[7]

That some Israelis could have so severed their cultural and national identities is as much of an anathema to the original Ben-Gurionist vision of a shared national culture as it is to religious Zionists for whom Judaism is the only morally defensible *raison d'être* for a Jewish state. The task of determining a secular definition of Jewishness, and of reconciling it to both modern Israeli nationalism on the one hand, and religious considerations on the other, remains the single greatest challenge for Israel today. Urgency is added to the problem by assertions that Israel is suffering a moral and social crisis that stems from the younger generations' inability to locate their existence within a specific identificational context. As incidents of street and domestic violence become more prolific, as political corruption and organised crime become features of everyday life, and as the political arena becomes fraught with personal attacks and incitement to racial and religious hatred, analysts comment on how Israel has become 'violent, frightening and impatient to a fatal degree'.[8] This departure from the ideals of the early pioneers has been attributed to the decline of the Jewish identity in the *sabra* generations. Being a majority in their own country and experiencing lives untarnished by immediate anti-Semitism, they have lost touch with the past sufferings that united Jewish peoples. In the 1950s the government tried to rectify this by introducing classes in state schools on 'Jewish consciousness', and in later years organised tours have taken countless schoolchildren to Nazi extermination camps in Europe to revisit their ancestors' common past and with the deliberate intention of reviving specifically Jewish identities. Yet inevitably it becomes increasingly difficult to reconstruct a Jewish identity based on past sufferings as the memory of those sufferings becomes second-hand and is displaced by other more recent experiences.

It is inaccurate, however, to portray Israel as a collapsing society, fatally fissured by tensions arising from questions of collective identity. Nor is it reasonable to imply that the failure to comfortably accommodate all the competing identities has resulted in the complete degradation of democratic credentials. All nation-states seek to project a strong external identity, one that can often appear at odds with the rights of the individuals or minorities that the self-same state professes to uphold and protect. Israel is a vibrant reminder of such juxtapositions, but equally, its claims to democratic governance remain impressive. Its judiciary is independent, the press refreshingly irreverent in its analysis of political actors, while it possesses a civil society whose scope and breadth remains unmatched throughout the Middle East and indeed much of Europe. Political debate in the *Knesset* remains passionate, sometimes vitriolic, but rarely circumscribed. In this regard, the early Zionist aim to 'normalise' the Jews by building a state as a necessary precursor to escaping the age-old racial nemesis of anti-Semitism has been an undoubted success. That having been said, the problems associated with identity-driven social division have made their way into the day-to-day political life of the country. One example, and a distinguishing feature of Israeli politics over the past decade, has been the erosion of support for the two main political groupings over successive elections to the *Knesset*. A proliferation of parties, allied to a myriad of causes and issues, now litter the political landscape. Moreover, when political parties, and the realms within which they operate, have failed to address minority interests, protest groups and extra-parliamentary pressure groups have mushroomed, indicating that the formal political system has not been sufficient an arena to contain the struggle to re-establish a consensus over national identity.

On occasion, the political debate has descended into direct action and even violence, perhaps the most traumatic illustration of which was the assassination of Yitzhak Rabin in November 1995. Yet, while this fragmentation of political representation is evidence of the decline of a unifying consensus on the nature of the Jewish state, it should also be remembered that the emergence of a multiplicity of political parties has also been, at least in part, the result of Israel's pure system of proportional representation. At the outset of statehood, proportional representation was viewed as the best means to cohere disparate Jewish communities into a collective whole and, being an inclusive political system, appeared to represent the democratic ideal. In truth, few states anywhere equate to such a standard. Democratic values rarely define the boundaries of inclusion in any society. Rather, such boundaries are determined in part or all by ethnicity, religion, ideology and history. Basing both its sovereignty and identity on its unique claim to 'Jewishness' – however that is defined – clearly demarcates limits upon the inclusion of non-Jewish individuals and organisations in Israel's political and social arena. To be sure, such exclusion is not unique in the region. Saudi Arabia imposes exacting criteria based upon religious affinity and tribal grouping upon claims to citizenship, while political participation clearly remains limited in autocracies, be they dynastic or republican, throughout the Middle East and North Africa. Yet such comparisons should not detract from the fact that Israel, which portrays itself as a democracy and which has formally aspired to democratic ideals, is perhaps ultimately better described as what Yiftachel among others has termed an 'ethnocracy'. The term refers to political entitites which maintain the veneer of popular participation but with access to real power determined by a stratified ethnic order. In the case of Israel, the implication is that Ben-Gurion's Jewish state, in which Jews – united by a common hegemonic culture – ruled themselves via democratic processes, has been steadily transformed into a two-tiered system in which conflicting 'Jewish' identities compete for dominance over the state (albeit by democratic means) while those citizens with non-Jewish identities remain excluded and marginalised.

At this point, it becomes relevant to refer to a new discourse which is gathering momentum within Israel itself, that of *post-Zionism*. Defining exactly its intellectual content remains a vexed issue, not least because its proponents range from those who see it as a reflection of Israel's present political condition, to those who view it as prescriptive. It is certainly controversial, not least because it eschews reliance upon the history and iconography of Zionism as the symbols of an Israeli identity. Such symbols are seen as exclusive in their political message, negating the inclusion, most notably, of Israeli Arabs as political and social equals. Noting the impact that so-called revisionist historians have had in questioning the received wisdom of Israel's historical past, Laurence Silberstein noted that:

[Post-Zionism] is based on the assumption that democratic processes in Israel require a new mapping of the power relations within Israeli society. As these post-Zionists realize, a process of change that builds only from the top down will not succeed . . . post-Zionism could only have emerged as the result of far-reaching changes at the grass roots level, for example the generational shift in attitude brought on by the occupation.[9]

This is in many ways the correlate of Orr's 'Israeli ethnic identity', mentioned earlier. The logic of post-Zionism mandates that national identity be defined in terms of territorial affinity, rather than through ethnic or religious ties. It suggests that ultimately Israelis must choose between democracy and the Jewish state, that the contradictions and tensions within Ben-Gurion's vision simply cannot be either ignored or resolved. If Israel is to continue its political and economic development as a nation-state within the community of such states, it must abandon its cultural exclusivity, assert the ultimate separation of religion and politics, and assume genuinely representative dimensions.

Silberstein concedes that, to date, such debates have been confined to the margins of Israeli society. Not surprisingly, they challenge the fundamental 'sacred cows' of Zionism, not to mention those of religious nationalism. Yet if, as Silberstein argues, post-Zionism comes to inform mainstream political discourse in Israel, the consequences will be profound. Some would argue that even the name 'Israel' would become dispensable as the definition of that small geographical space on the edge of the Mediterranean. This remains an unthinkable prospect for most Israelis, but the need to address the logic of the discourse is ultimately undeniable.

For now, the intricacies of making peace with Palestinians continue to dominate Israel's political horizons. Indeed, in the immediate term Israelis can take comfort from their status as a regional superpower, possessing a powerful military and an economic base unmatched throughout the region. In those regards, Zionism has proved an undoubted success. Nonetheless, Israelis cannot defer indefinitely the task of redefining an internal identity. How the body-politic meets this challenge will determine not only Israel's future, but also that of the wider Middle East.

Notes

1 Ari Shavit, 'Deconstructing Ehud', *Ha'aretz* (English Edition), 19 May 2000.
2 For a detailed discussion of the war in south Lebanon see Clive Jones, 'Israeli Counter-Insurgency Strategy and the War in South Lebanon', *Small Wars and Insurgencies*, Vol. 8, No. 3 (Winter 1997), pp. 82–108.
3 Uriya Shavit, 'To Serve or not to Serve', *Ha'aretz* (English Edition), 26 May 2000.
4 Oren Yiftachel, 'Israeli Society and Jewish-Palestinian Reconciliation: Ethnocracy and its Territorial Contradictions', *Middle East Journal*, Vol. 51, No. 4 (1997).
5 Yossi Melman, 'After Threats, Security for PM Tightened', *Ha'aretz* (English Edition), 4 June 2000.
6 Baruch Kimmerling, 'Between Hegemony and Dormant Kulturkampf in Israel', in Dan Urian and Efraim Karsh (eds), *In Search of Identity: Jewish Aspects in Israeli Culture* (London: Frank Cass, 1999), pp. 49–72.
7 Akiva Orr, *Israel: Politics, Myths and Identity Crises* (London: Pluto Press, 1994), p. 22.

8 *Independent*, 21 June 2000.
9 Laurence J. Silberstein, *The Postzionism Debates: Knowledge and Power in Israeli Culture* (London: Routledge, 1999), p. 208.

6 Epilogue

One step forward, two steps back

On 6 February 2001, Israelis elected Ariel Sharon to be their new Prime Minister by an overwhelming margin.[1] Sharon's election clearly reflected deep unease among many Israelis over the failure of Barak, despite his impeccable security credentials, to bring about an end to the Al Aqsa *Intifada* or uprising, the outbreak of which on 29 September 2000 was occasioned by the visit of one Ariel Sharon to the *Haram al-Sharif* or Temple Mount. Indeed, the hubris of Barak's self-declared aim of bringing down the final curtain on the Israel–Palestine conflict was exposed by a level of violence that had, by the end of February 2001, claimed the lives of over 400 Palestinians and 60 Israelis. For some observers, the promise of future reconciliation between the two competing national movements was dealt a shattering blow with the election of a man widely reviled in the Arab world as a war criminal for his role in the massacre of Palestinian refugees at the Sabra and Chatilla camps in 1982.[2]

In offering an explanation for the election of Sharon, one is tempted to quote the Israeli strategist Martin Van Crevald who, in a different context, noted that 'We have seen the future and it does not work'.[3] Despite the clear disparity in casualties between the protagonists, the term 'betrayal' marked popular Israeli discourse regarding relations with the Palestinians. Did not, for example, Barak offer the most far-reaching concessions to Palestinian leader Yasser Arafat during the course of the ill-fated Camp David Summit hosted by President Clinton in July 2000? Was Barak not reputed to have offered the *de facto* re-division of Jerusalem that handed practical sovereignty to the Palestinian National Authority? Moreover, Israel had conceded ground over the issue of Palestinian refugees, acknowledging the 'right of return' in Palestinian-controlled areas as well as admitting several thousand refugees into Israel proper under a family reunification scheme.[4]

The rejection of such far-reaching proposals, including putting the vexed issue of Jerusalem up for negotiation, was proof to many Israelis that such concessions would never be enough to satisfy a leadership that now demanded full Palestinian sovereignty over East Jerusalem, including the holy sites, and the full right of return of Palestinian refugees to Israel proper, a demand seemingly at odds with Palestinian recognition of Israel's right to exist as a Jewish state. In short, the Al-Aqsa *Intifada* was a violent reminder that, despite peace treaties and other such diplomatic niceties, Israel still faces the animus of the Arab world. As Linda Grant observed in her treatment of the Israeli psyche:

> Like fairground distorting mirrors, the world looks at the Israelis and sees a giant, a monster, but the Israeli looks and sees a tiny cowering figure, a puny kid walking to school, tormented by bullies. He needs a Charles Atlas course. He needs to make himself stronger, not weaker. When the cameras report from Gaza and we see a boy, not unlike a boy we have at home ourselves perhaps, but with a stone in his hands, we are looking at an angry child. That's not what the Israeli sees. The boy is a hazy presence, ill-defined. They are peering past him to glimpse the shadowy figures in the windows of the apartment building, the *Tanzim*, the armed civilian militias, and beyond them Hamas. . . . And beyond Hamas is the figure of Saddam Hussein surrounded by four million Iraqis who have volunteered to destroy Israel.[5]

For those Israelis who cast their vote, electing Sharon was recognition that Israel needed a 'Charles Atlas course', a course that would re-establish Israel's deterrent capability and military authority. Indeed, despite his military record, Barak was accused of vacillation in the face of Palestinian violence, a position summed up in the proliferation of car bumper stickers that demanded that he 'Let the IDF win'. This primordial resort to violence as the panacea to what in essence remains a political problem was evidence of the fact that recourse to the language of 'national security' could still act as a powerful discourse, if not organising programme, around which Israelis could coalesce.

Such sentiment, however profound, tends to negate any meaningful critique of Israel's contribution to the current impasse in relations with the Palestinians. While Sharon's ill-timed, and some would add insensitive, visit to the Temple Mount was an act that *occasioned* the violence, it was not an act that by itself *caused* such violence or explains its intensity. It should be stated quite openly that the failure of the Palestinian National Authority to provide efficient, accountable government to those areas under its control has led to a system of rule where nepotism and corruption have become the leitmotiv. But equally, Israeli negotiating strategies under the Oslo process have created a situation in which tremendous investment in diplomatic wrangling by the Palestinians has yielded few sovereign gains. Indeed, Barak failed to honour an agreement with Arafat reached at the Sharm al-Sheikh summit on 4 September 1999 that reaffirmed Israel's commitment to further troop re-deployments away from Palestinian areas by January 2000. Such events, coupled with the continued expansion of settlements in the West Bank at a rate not even seen under the Netanyahu administration, appeared incongruous with Barak's claim to be the true inheritor of Rabin's legacy. Thus, when Barak claimed to be closer emotionally to the settlers of Beit El than to the position of *Meretz* leader Yossi Sarid, it appeared to cancel the very premise on which the Oslo process was based: land for peace.

This analysis of Ehud Barak's time in office, however, fails to grasp the complexity of domestic constraint under which he had to operate. On assuming office, Barak made it clear that he intended to work towards healing the divisions in Israeli society, divisions that had been violently expressed in the assassination of his mentor. This explains his decision to assemble a coalition government that comprised such uneasy bedfellows as *Shas, Meretz, Yisrael be'Aliyah,* United Torah Judaism, the *Mafdal,* the Centre Party as well as his own *Yisrael Ahad.* While his sentiments towards the settlers may have been deep-felt, allowing the expansion of the settlements in the West Bank was a calculated risk designed to tie the religious parties into supporting his coalition while he negotiated an agreement with Syria over the Golan Heights, so that, once concluded, he could deal with the Palestine National Authority from a position of regional strength. Yet the vicissitudes of coalition politics in Israel, ranging from tension between Eli Yishai and Yossi Sarid over the latter's refusal to increase state subsidies for the *Shas* schools system, to the resignation of *Yisrael be'Aliyah,* the *Mafdal* and *Shas* over the proposals Israel intended to place on the negotiating table at Camp David, clearly limited Barak's room for manoeuvre. Before he even left for the summit in July 2000, Barak was already heading a minority government.

Yet, despite the present level of violence, Israel as a society has moved beyond the historical projection of 'the other' around which politics and society came to be ordered. Despite strong pleas from Arafat to adopt more proactive measures against Israel, the special meeting of the Arab League held in Cairo in November 2000 was notable for the absence of any agreement over punitive measures, economic or otherwise, to be adopted against the Jewish state. While no one would deny that widespread popular antipathy still informs discussion of Israel throughout the Middle East, the efficacy of a siege mentality no longer corresponds with a regional reality in which the present level of violence, despite the often appalling images, has proved insufficient to mobilise a more belligerent response on the part of the wider Arab world.

It would be foolish to deny that Israel no longer faces any external threat. But equally, the extent to which it relates to its immediate environment remains a function of competition between identities that often deny each other legitimacy. It is an issue that directly links Israel's domestic milieu to the future map of the Middle East. As the authors have suggested throughout this book, identity remains Israel's most pressing security dilemma. Only with a solution to this issue will Israelis ever be able to finally claim the physical boundaries of their state.

Notes

1 Sharon won 62.5 per cent of votes cast against 37.5 per cent for Barak. It was the first direct election in Israel's history for the office of Prime Minister only. The results are less impressive than they would appear at first sight. The turnout was the lowest in Israel's political history, with popular participation registered at only 59 per cent of those eligible to vote. In short, Sharon received an endorsement from only 36 per cent of the Israeli electorate.
2 See for example the commentary of Robert Fisk, 'This is a Place of Filth and Blood', *The Independent*, 6 February 2001.
3 M. Van Crevald, *Command in War* (Cambridge, MA: Harvard University Press, 1985).
4 For a detailed discussion of the proposals, as well as Clinton's subsequent bridging ideas, see Uri Horowitz, 'Camp David 2 and President Clinton's Bridging Proposals – The Palestinian View', *Strategic Assessment*, Jaffee Centre for Strategic Studies, Tel Aviv University, Vol. 3, No. 4 (January 2001).
5 Linda Grant, 'What Lies Beneath', *The Guardian G2 Magazine*, 24 October 2000, p. 3.

Select bibliography

Books

Aharoni, Yair. *The Israeli Economy: Dreams and Realities* (London: Routledge, 1991).

Arian, Asher. *Politics in Israel: The Second Republic* (New Jersey: Chatham House Publishers, 1998).

Barnett, Michael (ed). *Israel in Comparative Perspective: Challenging the Conventional Wisdom* (New York: State University of New York Press, 1996).

Bar-On, Mordechai. *In Pursuit of Peace: A History of the Israeli Peace Movement* (Washington, D.C.: United States Institute of Peace, 1996).

Barzilai, Gad. *Wars, Internal Conflicts, and Political Order: A Jewish Democracy in the Middle East* (New York: SUNY, 1996).

Beilin, Yossi. *Israel: A Concise Political History* (London: Weidenfeld and Nicolson, 1992).

Bowker, Robert. *Beyond Peace: The Search for Security in the Middle East* (London: Lynne Reinner, 1996).

Brecher, Michael. *The Foreign Policy System of Israel: Images, Setting Processes* (Oxford: OUP, 1972).

Bregman, Aharon and Jihan El-Tahri. *The Fifty Years War: Israel and the Arabs* (Harmondsworth: Penguin/BBC Books, 1998).

Chamish, Barry. *The Fall of Israel* (Edinburgh: Canongate Publishers, 1992)

Cockburn, Andrew and Leslie. *Dangerous Liaisons:The Inside Story of the US–Israeli Covert Relationship* (London: Bodley Head, 1992).

Cohen, Mitchell. *Zion and State: Nation, Class and the Shaping of Modern Israel* (Oxford: Basil Blackwell, 1987).

Cohen, Stuart. *The Scroll or the Sword? Dilemmas of Military Service in Israel* (Amsterdam: Harwood Academic Publishers, 1997).

Diamond, Larry and Ehud Sprinzak. *Israeli Democracy under Stress* (London: Lynne Reinner, 1993).

Eban, Abba. *An Autobiography* (London: Weidenfeld and Nicolson, 1977).

Evron, Boas. *Jewish State or Israeli Nation?* (Indiana: Indiana University Press, 1995).

Flamhaft, Zivah. *Israel on the Road to Peace: Accepting the Unacceptable* (Oxford: Westview Press, 1996).

Freedman, Robert O. (ed). *Israel Under Rabin* (Boulder, Co.: Westview Press, 1995).

Giladi, G. N. *Discord in Zion* (London: Scorpion Publishing, 1990).

Goldberg, David J. *To the Promised Land: A History of Zionist Thought* (Harmondsworth: Penguin, 1996).

Haidar, Aziz. *On the Margins: The Arab Population in the Israeli Economy* (London: Hurst, 1995).

Halevi, Nadav and Ruth Klinov-Malul. *The Economic Development of Israel* (New York: Praeger, 1968).

Hall-Cathala, David. *The Peace Movement in Israel 1967–87* (London: Macmillan, 1990).

Hersh, Seymour. *The Sampson Option: Israel and the Bomb* (London: Faber & Faber, 1991).

Ilan Troen, S and Noah Lucas (eds). *Israel: The First Decade of Independence* (Albany: State University of New York, 1995).

Inbar, Efraim and Gabriel Sheffer (eds). *The National Security of Small States in a Changing World* (London: Frank Cass, 1997).

Jones, Clive. *Soviet Jewish Aliyah 1989–92: Impact and Implications for Israel and the Middle East* (London: Frank Cass, 1996).

Karsh, Efraim (ed). *From Rabin to Netanyahu: Israel's Troubled Agenda* (London: Frank Cass, 1997).

Karsh, Efraim. *Fabricating Israeli History: The New Historians* (2nd edition) (London: Frank Cass, 2000).

Karsh, Efraim and Gregory Mahler (eds). *Israel at the Crossroads: The Challenge of Peace* (London: British Academic Press, 1994).

Keller, Adam. *Terrible Days: Social Divisions and Political Paradoxes in Israel* (Amstelveen: Cypes, 1987).

Khalidi, Raja. *The Arab Economy in Israel* (London: Croom Helm, 1988).

Kyle, Keith. *Suez* (London: Weidenfeld and Nicolson, 1995).

Kyle, Keith and Joel Peters. *Whither Israel: The Domestic Challenges* (London: I.B. Tauris, 1993).

Landau, David. *Piety and Power* (London: Secker and Warburg, 1993).

Landau, Jacob M. *The Arab Minority in Israel 1967–1991* (Oxford: Clarendon Press, 1993).

Laquer, Walter and Barry Rubin (eds). *The Israel-Arab Reader* (Harmondsworth: Penguin, 1984).

Levi-Faur, David, Gabriel Sheffer and David Vogel. *Israel: The Dynamics of Change and Continuity* (London: Frank Cass, 1999).

Lewin-Epstein, Noah and Moshe Semyonov. *The Arab Minority in Israel's Economy* (Boulder, Co.: Westview Press, 1993).

Lissak, Moshe (ed). *Israeli Society and its Defence Establishment* (London: Frank Cass, 1984).

Lustick, Ian. *For the Land and the Lord* (New York: Council on Foreign Relations, 1988).

Mergui, Raphael and Philippe Simonnot. *Israel's Ayatollahs: Meir Kahane and the Far Right in Israel* (London: Saqi Books, 1987).

Morris, Benny. *The Birth of the Palestinian Refugee Problem* (Cambridge: Cambridge University Press, 1987).

Morris, Benny. *Israel's Border Wars* (Oxford: Oxford University Press, 1995)

Newman, David (ed), *The Impact of Gush Emunim: Politics and Settlement on the West Bank* (London: Croom Helm, 1985).

Orr, Akiva. *Israel: Politics, Myths and Identity Crises* (London: Pluto Press, 1994).

Ovendale, Ritchie. *The Origins of the Arab–Israeli Wars* (3rd edition) (Harlow: Longman Press, 1999).

Ovendale, Ritchie. *Britain, the United States and the Transfer of Power in the Middle East* (Leicester: Leicester University Press, 1996).

Peres, Shimon. *Battling for Peace* (London: Wiedenfeld and Nicolson, 1995).

Peretz, Don. *Intifada: The Palestinian Uprising* (London: Westview Press, 1992).

Peretz, Don and Gideon Doron. *The Government and Politics of Israel* (3rd edition) (Oxford: Westview Press, 1997).

Peri, Yoram. *Between Battles and Ballots: The Israeli Military Politics* (Cambridge: Cambridge University Press, 1983).

Peleg, Ilan (ed). *The Middle East Peace Process: Interdisciplinary Perspectives* (New York: State University of New York Press, 1998).

Razin, Assaf and Efraim Sadka. *The Economy of Modern Israel* (Chicago: University of Chicago Press, 1993).

Rivlin, Paul. *The Israeli Economy* (Boulder, Co.: Westview Press, 1992).

Rouhana, Nadim. *Palestinian Citizens in an Ethnic Jewish State* (New Haven: Yale University, 1997).

Sachar, Howard M. *A History of Israel: From the Rise of Zionism to Our Time* (Oxford: Basil Blackwell, 1976).

Schiff, Ze'ev, and Ehud Ya'ari. *Israel's Lebanon War* (London: Unwin and Allen, 1986).

Schoenbaum, David. *The United States and the State of Israel* (Oxford: Oxford University Press, 1993).

Segev, Tom. *The First Israelis* (New York: Free Press, 1986).

Segev, Tom. *The Seventh Million: The Israelis and the Holocaust* (New York: Hill and Wang, 1994).

Shalev, Michael. *Labour and the Political Economy in Israel* (Oxford: Oxford University Press, 1992).

Shepherd, Naomi. *Ploughing Sand: British Rule in Palestine 1917–1948* (London: John Murray, 1999).

Shindler, Colin. *Israel, Likud and the Zionist Dream* (London: I.B. Tauris, 1995).

Silberstein, Laurence J. (ed). *Jewish Fundamentalism in Comparative Perspective* (New York: New York University Press, 1993).

Silberstein, Laurence J. *The Postzionism Debates: Knowledge and Power in Israeli Culture* (New York: Routledge, 1999).

Sohar, Ezra. *Israel's Dilemma: Why Israel is Falling Apart and How to Put it Back Together* (New York: Shapolsky, 1989).

Sprinzak, Ehud. *The Ascendance of Israel's Radical Right* (Oxford: Oxford University Press, 1991).

Sprinzak, Ehud. *Brother Against Brother: Violence and Extremism in Israeli Politics* (New York: Free Press, 1999).

Swirski, Shlomo. *Israel: The Oriental Majority* (London: Zed Books, 1989).

Tessler, Mark. *The Israeli–Palestinian Conflict* (Indiana: Indiana University Press, 1994).

Urian, Dan and Efraim Karsh. *In Search of Identity: Jewish Aspects in Israeli Culture* (London: Frank Cass, 1999).

Wheatcroft, Geoffrey. *The Controversy of Zion* (London: Sinclair-Stevenson, 1996).

Whitelam, Keith W. *The Invention of Ancient Israel* (London: Routledge, 1996).

Wolffsohn, Michael. *Israel, Polity, Society and Economy 1882–1986* (New Jersey: Humanities Press International, 1987).

Yaniv, Avner (ed). *National Security and Democracy in Israel* (London: Lynne Reinner, 1993).

Zeubavel, Yael. *Recovered Roots: Collective Memory and the Making of Israeli National Tradition* (Chicago: University of Chicago Press, 1995).

Journal articles and working papers

Bar Joseph, Uri. 'A Bull in a China Shop: Netanyahu and Israel's Intelligence Community', *International Journal of Intelligence and Counter-Intelligence*, Vol. 11, No. 2 (1998).

Bar-Siman-Tov, Ya'acov. 'The United States and Israel since 1948: A Special Relationship?', *Diplomatic History*, Vol. 22, No. 2 (Spring 1998).

Bartlett, Bruce. 'The Crisis of Socialism in Israel', *Orbis* (Fall 1989), pp. 53–68.

Beitler, Ruth Margolies. 'The Intifada: Palestinian Adaptation to Israeli Counterinsurgency Tactics', *Terrorism and Political Violence*, Vol. 7, No. 2 (Summer 1995), pp. 55–6.

Ben-Eliezer, Uri. 'Rethinking the Civil-Military Relations Paradigm', *Political Studies*, Vol. 30, No. 3 (June 1997).

Brichta, Avraham. 'The New Premier-Parliamentary System in Israel', *The Annals* (AAPSS), No. 555 (January 1998).

Bruno, M. 'From Sharp Stabilization to Growth: On the Political Economy of Israel's Transition', *European Economic Review*, No. 36 (1992).

Chartouni-Dubarry, May (ed). *Armée et Nation en Israel: Pouvoir Civil, Pouvoir Militaire* (Paris: Institut Français des Relations Internationales, 1999).

Dutter, Lee E. 'Eastern and Western Jews: Ethnic Divisions in Israeli Society', *Middle East Journal*, Vol. 31, No. 4 (Autumn 1977).

Gazit, Shlomo. 'Israel and the Palestinians: Fifty Years of Wars and Turning Points', *The Annals* (AAPSS), No. 555 (January 1998).

Gordon, Philip H. 'The Transatlantic Allies and the Changing Middle East', *Adelphi Paper 322* (Oxford: IISS/OUP, 1998).

Halevi, Yossi Klein. 'Democracy or Theocracy?', *The Jerusalem Report*, Vol. VIII, No. 23 (19 March 1998).

Inbar, Efraim. 'Israeli National Security, 1973–1996', *Begin-Sadat (BESA) Security and Policy Study Papers* No. 63 (Ramat Gan: Bar Ilan University, 1998).

Israeli, Raphael. 'Muslim Fundamentalists as Social Revolutionaries: The Case of Israel', *Terrorism and Political Violence*, Vol. 6, No. 4 (Winter 1994), pp. 417–43.

Jones, Clive. 'Ideotheology: Dissonance and Discourse in the State of Israel', *Israel Affairs*, Vol. 3, Nos 3&4 (Spring/Summer 1997), pp. 28–46.

Kimche, David. 'The Arab-Israeli Peace Process', *Security Dialogue*, Vol. 27, No. 2 (1996).

Kleiman, Ephraim. 'The Waning of Israeli Etatism', *Israel Studies*, Vol. 2, No. 2 (1998)

Kumaraswamy, P.R. 'India and Israel: Evolving Strategic Partnership', *BESA Security Studies Policy Paper* No. 40 (Ramat Gan: Bar-Ilan University, 1998), pp. 3–33.

Levy-Faur, David. 'State and Nationalism in Israel's Political Economy', *Israel Affairs*, Vol. 3, No. 1 (Autumn 1996).

Liebman, Charles, 'Judaism and Jewishness in the Jewish State', *The Annals* (AAPSS), No. 555 (January 1998).

Lissak, Moshe. 'The Unique Approach to Military Societal Relations in Israel and its Impact on Foreign and Security Policy', *Davis Occasional Papers No. 62*, The Leonard Davis Institute for International Relations, Hebrew University of Jerusalem, Israel (September 1998).

Lochery, Neill. 'Israel and Turkey: Deepening Ties and Strategic Implications', *Israel Affairs*, Vol. 5, No. 1 (Autumn 1998).

Murphy, Emma C. 'Structural Inhibitions to Economic Liberalization in Israel', *Middle East Journal*, Vol. 48, No. 1 (Winter 1994).

Norton, Augustus Richard. 'The Future of Civil Society in the Middle East', *Middle East Journal*, Vol. 47, No. 2 (1993).

Rodan, Steve and Jacob Dallal. 'A Fundamental Gamble', *The Jerusalem Post Magazine*, 19 August 1994.

Rodman, David. 'Regime-Targeting: A Strategy for Israel', *Israel Affairs*, Vol. 2, No. 1 (Autumn 1995).

Schiff, Ze'ev. 'The Spectre of Civil War in Israel', *Middle East Journal*, Vol. 39, No. 2 (Spring 1985).

Sherman, Martin. 'Diversifying Strategic Reliance: Broadening the Base of Israel's Sources of Strategic Support', *JCSS Strategic Assessment*, Vol. 1, No. 4 (January 1999).

Telhami, Shibley. 'Israeli Foreign Policy: A Static Strategy in a Changing World', *Middle East Journal*, Vol. 44, No. 3 (Summer 1990).

Tessler, Mark and Audra E. Grant. 'Israel's Arab Citizens: The Continuing Struggle', *The Annals* (AAPSS), No. 555 (January 1998).

Yiftachel, Oren. 'Israeli Society and Jewish–Palestinian Reconciliation: "Ethocracy" and its Territorial Contradictions', *Middle East Journal*, Vol. 51, No. 4 (Autumn 1997).

Yishai, Yael. 'Civil Society in Transition: Interest Politics in Israel', *The Annals* (AAPSS), No. 555 (January 1998).

Index